HISTORICISM

GUIDES TO THEOLOGICAL INQUIRY

Edited by Kathryn Tanner of the University of Chicago and Paul Lakeland of Fairfield University, Guides to Theological Inquiry are intended to introduce students, scholars, clergy, and theologians to those academic methods, disciplines, and movements that are most germane to contemporary theology. Neither simple surveys nor exhaustive monographs, these short books provide solid, reliable, programmatic statements of the main lines or workings of their topics and assessments of their theological importance.

Already available are *Nonfoundationalism* by John E. Thiel, *Literary Theory* by David Dawson, *Postmodernity* by Paul Lakeland, *Theories of Culture* by Kathryn Tanner, *Feminist Theory and Christian Theology* by Serene Jones, and *Critical Social Theory* by Gary M. Simpson. Forthcoming titles in the series include *Hermeneutics* by Francis Schüssler Fiorenza, *African American Critical Thought* by Shawn Copeland, and *Postcolonial Theory and Theology* by Jan Pranger.

HISTORICISM

THE ONCE AND FUTURE CHALLENGE FOR THEOLOGY

SHEILA GREEVE DAVANEY

GUIDES TO THEOLOGICAL INQUIRY

FORTRESS PRESS / MINNEAPOLIS

For
Gordon D. Kaufman,
who first introduced me to historicism

HISTORICISM
The Once and Future Challenge for Theology
Guides to Theological Inquiries series

Copyright © 2006 Augsburg Fortress. All rights reserved. Except for brief quotations in critical articles or reviews, no part of this book may be reproduced in any manner without prior written permission from the publisher. Write: Permissions, Augsburg Fortress, Box 1209, Minneapolis, MN 55440.

This volume includes material I have formulated for prior publications: "Response to My Interlocutors," in *Journal of Religion and Society* 4 (2002); "The Outsideless Life: Historicism, Theology, and the Quest for Jesus," in *Sourcing the Quests: The Roots and Branches of the Quest for the Historical Jesus,* ed. Peter De Mey (Louvain: Peeters, 2006).

Cover design: Craig Claeys
Cover photo: © Tony Stone/Getty Images. Used by permission.

Library of Congress Cataloging-in-Publication Data
Davaney, Sheila Greeve.
    Historicism : the once and future challenge for theology / Sheila Greeve Davaney.
        p. cm.
    Includes bibliographical references.
    ISBN 0-8006-3219-2 (alk. paper)
    1. History—Religious aspects—Christianity. 2. Historicism. 3. Theology—Methodology. 4. Pragmatism. I. Title.

BR115.H5D27 2006
230'.046—dc22

                                                                        2005036146

The paper used in this publication meets the minimum requirements of American National Standard for Information Sciences — Permanence of Paper for Printed Library Materials, ANSI Z329.48-1984.

Manufactured in the U.S.A.   AF 1–2916

05   04   03   02   1   2   3   4   5   6   7   8   9   10

Contents

Foreword

The Guides to Theological Inquiry series aims to familiarize people with major trends and movements across a variety of academic disciplines and to suggest their importance for the way theology is done today. No such movement is more important, or more widely felt across the disciplines, than historicism, the recognition of the conditioned, located, particular, and relative character of all human thought and experience, including the religious. Taking a historicist approach, appropriately enough, to the exposition of historicism, Sheila Davaney very helpfully situates the development of historicism—in all its promise and problems—within the broader intellectual and socio-cultural trajectories of both modern Europe and the United States. She lays out, with all the clarity, cogency, and thoroughgoing intellectual honesty she is so well known for, the challenges that historicism poses to theology—challenges, for example, to the normativity of the Christian past, to the uniqueness and absoluteness of Christian claims to truth, and to Christianity's commonly supernatural understanding of God. Undaunted by these challenges, Davaney offers a powerful account of how theology can meet them and in the process brings together, in a marvelously irenic spirit, some of the best insights of contemporary theological trends in the United States—be they liberal, postliberal, or liberationist. No intellectually responsible Christian can avoid the challenges of historicism, nor afford to overlook, therefore, the help that Davaney's important new book offers in these trying times.

—*Kathryn Tanner*

Preface

This book explores historicism, that intellectual movement that took shape in the late eighteenth century and flourished especially in the nineteenth and early twentieth centuries. This movement has had numerous forms and has influenced a wide variety of topics and issues ranging from epistemological concerns to the nature of tradition to the character of the universe. Importantly, historicism both challenged traditional theology and engendered historicist modes of theological reflection. This volume will explicate a variety of the most important forms of earlier historicisms in Germany and in the United States and will especially detail their impact upon theological reflection during that era. Thus a central task of the book is to set forth a short and, admittedly, selective history of historicism, to contextualize its emergence and elaborate its implications.

While historicism was especially important in the nineteenth and early twentieth centuries, its implications have continued to reverberate in our contemporary period. Significant theological perspectives today reflect the influences of the historicist recognition that humans live in and out of history and are dependent upon the resources of place and time to gain meaning and direction in life. Revisionist theologies, a variety of liberationist perspectives, postliberalism, and pragmatic historicism all have been shaped by the moves to particularity, historical specificity, and cultural locatedness that emerged two centuries ago. Moreover, they are further marked by the repudiation of universalism and claims to absoluteness that were first articulated by the historicists of that earlier period. Often, however, contemporary thinkers, including theologians, do not recognize or acknowledge these historical predecessors; such amnesia results in failing to identify both the resources our forebears offer the current scene as well as the dangers and crises these developments have bequeathed us. Hence, an important assertion of this volume is that it is imperative that contemporary thinkers have a clearer understanding of their historicist predecessors so that we may see how we continue that heritage, how far we have distanced ourselves from it, and why we have done so.

Historicism is not only an artifact from an earlier period. Contemporary forms of historicist thought are evident in every field from philosophy to anthropology to literary theory and theology. But these perspectives not only continue earlier historicist insights. They, like earlier forms, have emerged at a specific historical moment and reflect and contribute to this present situation. In particular, contemporary historicisms have distanced themselves from the metaphysical assumptions of their precursors and have refracted their positions through a profound sense of power, fragmentation, and multiplicity. Hence, contemporary historicisms, including theological ones, both continue and depart from the historicisms of the past. Chapter 4 of this volume has as its central task the exploration of several forms of contemporary theological historicism with the aim of challenging present-day theologians to confront historicist challenges more fully. This volume thus engages both the genealogical task of exploring the varied forms of earlier historicisms and the constructive task of proposing a direction for historicist-informed theology today.

This book represents, in good historicist fashion, the input and influences of many friends and colleagues. I am especially grateful to Kathryn Tanner and Paul Lakeland, the co-editors of this series, and J. Michael West of Fortress Press for inviting me to write this volume. Their invitation allowed me to revisit important material that has shaped my work thus far as well as to explore gaps in my own intellectual heritage. I know far more now than when I began the project, to say nothing of all the future projects this work has suggested to me. I am grateful as well to my administrative assistant, Maggi Mahan, for all of the extraordinary effort she has put into this volume and to my student assistants, Anne Williams and Marc-Paul Johnsen, for their bibliographic efforts, proofreading, and editing assistance. As always, I am grateful to my family, especially my husband, Larry Kent Graham, and children, Peter Davaney-Graham and Emily Davaney-Graham, for their patience and support. They are, I know, more than pleased that this phase of my scholarly endeavors has come to a conclusion.

1

Modernity and the Emergence of Historicism

The Emergence of Modernity: The Western Enlightenment

History has long been a concern of Western thinkers. From the Greeks Herodotus and Thucydides, to Hebrew and Christian scriptural writers, to medieval chroniclers and Renaissance antiquarians, history has been a vexing concern for many humans, especially in the West. However, it was only in the later modern period, from the late eighteenth century onward, that thinking about history was itself historicized; only in this era did historicism develop as a worldview, the critical historical method take determinative shape, and epistemological questions concerning the historical character of human thought itself come to the fore.

Historicism is a perspective or set of convictions that provides categories and ways of thinking about human existence. But it is also a movement that came into being at a particular time in human history, in response to a specific set of problems and circumstances. In order to understand historicism we must situate it more fully within the historical context within which it emerged and took shape. Historicism itself asserts that such contextualization both illuminates and is indispensable for understanding its viability and uses.

The rise of historicism is part of the story of modern thought in the West. In particular, it is both an outcome and a rejection of the developments that commenced in Europe with the Protestant Reformation. The Reformation, with its repudiation of the ecclesial authority of the Catholic Church and its assertion of the primacy of Scripture, sought to offer a new basis for religious belief and practice. Over against the often conflicting voices of church traditions and ecclesial proclamations, the Bible was to be the mediating authority for Christians, providing a way out of the morass of church hierarchies and a means beyond what for many had become the corrupting practices of a too powerful religious institution. In matters of Christian belief and practice Scripture alone would inform and determine what was correct. But, as religion and ethics scholar Jeffrey Stout has pointed out, the turn to Scripture did not solve the problem of religious authority; the ecclesial authority of the clergy and the weight of church traditions were replaced not by a singular transparent Scripture but by multiple communal and individual voices all claiming the correct interpretation of the Bible. The appeal to *sola scriptura* resulted in the multiplication of authorities, not their contraction or simplification. Stout refers to this situation as the "problem of many authorities" and asserts that, to a significant degree, it precipitated the "crisis of authority" that gave birth to the modern world.[1]

Many other factors also contributed to the creation of this crisis. The medieval world had long been in the process of disintegration as philosophical assumptions, political organization, scientific convictions, and economic systems underwent profound changes. The Renaissance, viewed by some as the last moments of the medieval world and by others as the beginnings of the modern world, had already created a "new lay culture" in which ancient literature reached more and more people, dogmatism was beginning to be questioned, and there took place a revival of ancient skeptical writings that contributed both to a certain modesty and a burgeoning undermining of earlier claims to certainty and truth.[2] For complex historical reasons, the irenic dimensions of Renaissance humanism did not prevail for long. The Reformation and its aftermath both expressed and intensified the growing movement away from the medieval period without maintaining the Renaissance's tolerant skepticism. The proliferation of religious voices issued forth in religious renewal but also catapulted Europe into widespread and disastrous religious warfare. From the mid-sixteenth century until the Peace of Westphalia in the middle of the seventeenth century, religious conflicts raged across Europe, engulfing much of Western Europe and the German states. The religious disputes were not just between Catholics and Protestants. Conflicts also raged across and within Protestant groups, such as the strife between Lutherans and Calvinists. Religiously driven hostilities were especially destructive in the German lands where the Catholic emperor and bishops opposed Protestant princes in the Thirty Years War (1618–1648). Much of the population of the German-speaking lands was decimated as millions died in the conflicts from battle or disease and malnutrition.

Other elements contributed to the growing crisis. Economic growth, fueled especially by Spanish colonial expansion in the sixteenth century, was replaced by economic depression. Such depression in turn spawned changes in Europe's population distribution and created a ready pool of available fighters for the religious wars.[3] The plague broke out in numerous places, and the witch craze reached its height in the seventeenth century. The tolerance that had characterized some forms of religious thought in the Renaissance gave way to new forms of dogmatism and demands for religious orthodoxy by both Catholics and Protestants. Little in either Reformation-born Protestantism or the Counter-Reformation of Catholicism offered a way to reestablish political and social peace. Europe in many ways faced destruction or radical change. Those changes would alter virtually every area of Western life and thought.

The Peace of Westphalia, concluded in 1648, ushered in the end of the religious wars that had engulfed Europe but also signaled a profound change of political realities. The Holy Roman Empire continued to exist only in a greatly weakened manner, and the modern European state was inaugurated. Political loyalty would come to be identified with particular nations, and less and less with transnational religious institutions or smaller political configurations.

Galileo and Descartes

For our purposes, twin developments in the sciences and philosophy that decisively marked the shifts to what we now term Enlightenment modernity must be noted. Galileo Galilei (1564–1642) and René Descartes (1596–1650) ushered in new eras in Western thought, not the least by their repudiation of authority. Galileo's defense of the freedom of inquiry in scientific matters, his assertion of the centrality of mathematics for science, and his methodological preoccupations, though challenged especially by religious authorities, contributed greatly to the growing power of science. Descartes, whose *Discourse on Method* (1637) was published in the same decade as Galileo's *Dialogues Concerning the Two Principal World Systems* (1632), is widely considered the founding figure of the Enlightenment. Faced with the disintegration of earlier forms of authority and with them a loss of certainty about claims to truth, Descartes sought to find a way beyond the impasse of conflicting voices. As Stout states, in the aftermath of the Reformation and nearly one hundred years of religious wars "theism ceased to provide a vocabulary in terms of which matters of public importance could be debated and decided by Christians of various persuasions without resort to violence."[4]

With the demise of the medieval world, the failure of the Renaissance to prevail, and the conflicts engendered by religious change, Descartes and his fellow seventeenth-century denizens faced significant political, philosophical, and religious crises. Descartes' response was to attempt to articulate a new philosophical method and with it new foundations for certitude no longer predicated upon appeals to religious authority or to the traditions of any particular community but to reason above all else.

While many of Descartes' specific proposals would be quickly challenged, in numerous ways Descartes set much of the agenda for the Enlightenment modernity, at least in its Franco-British or Western European mode. In contrast to the ever-shifting sands of tradition and the conflicting claims of external authorities, Descartes set out, through his process of methodical doubt, to ascertain sure foundations upon which humans might build their positions. He sought, as he proclaimed in his great treatise *Meditations*, to be like Archimedes, the Greek mathematician and physicist, who sought one still place to stand.[5] For those who would follow Descartes, the task was not to accept claims on authority but to seek indubitable truths predicated upon unassailable foundations. Reason was to be humanity's only authority, and upon reason alone human beings would establish a "firm and permanent structure."[6] For Descartes and many others in the Enlightenment the clearest places such methodical displacing of prejudice and superstition, tradition and authority occurred were in the sciences, especially arithmetic and geometry. Science hence became the model for certain truth and mathematics was the prototype for all science.

Philosopher Richard J. Bernstein reminds contemporary thinkers that Descartes' reflections were not just the abstract musings of an intellectual. They were born, as was modernity itself, out of a moment of historical crisis—political, epistemological, moral, and religious. Descartes and his fellow Enlightenment thinkers sought new ways to adjudicate disputes and to ground the most basic claims to truth; they sought ways beyond the bloody impasses of religious warfare, political intrigue, and personal skepticism. Bernstein reads Descartes' *Meditations* not merely as ruminations on epistemological and metaphysical problems but as the journey of a soul engaged in a quest "for some fixed point, some stable rock upon which we can secure our lives against the vicissitudes that constantly threaten us."[7]

The Elevation of Reason

The Western Enlightenment developed in many different directions, including rationalism and empiricism. But in almost all its manifestations, from Descartes to John Locke to Immanuel Kant, reason and the commitment to critical inquiry unencumbered by tradition and external authorities were the ideals. For Enlightenment thinkers, such elevated reason was assumed to be essentially the same in all human beings and hence to provide a means for ascertaining truths acceptable for all capable of rational reflection. Reason, though variously described, was thus to govern all areas of human life from the scientific to the political to the aesthetic. It was to be the basis for scientific advances, philosophical truth, and that upon which the newly emergent nation-states were to develop governments that guaranteed freedom and the rights of modern humanity. It was envisioned as the means to progress, peace, tolerance, and human freedom. Reason was to be autonomous, serving no master but reason alone, pursuing no goals but those dictated by rationality itself.

For purposes of this study, what is perhaps most important to note in the Enlightenment turn to an autonomous rationality is how it was vehemently contrasted with tradition, with community, with inherited ideas and judgments. Reason was taken to be ahistorical or transhistorical, yielding universal, absolute, and timeless truths. According to philosopher Stephen Toulmin, the three dreams of rationalism—dreams of a rational method, a unified science, and an exact language to express unchanging truth—were all assumed "to 'purify' the operations of human reason, by decontextualizing them, i.e., by divorcing them from the details of particular historical and cultural situations."[8] Everything associated with history, with tradition, with inherited opinion was seen as tainted, uncertain, merely the product of uninformed and less than fully rational prejudices. As Stout states, "What was for Aquinas the virtue of faith became for the Enlightenment the vice of gullibility, soft-mindedness, and superstition. What Aquinas found authoritative the *philosophes* came to denounce as merely authoritarian."[9]

For religion, these developments had widespread and enormous repercussions. The irenic impulses of the Enlightenment found numerous expressions in calls for religious freedom and tolerance. The recognition of the plurality of religious communities and commitments, the inability of religions to provide nontradition-bound criteria for adjudicating among their conflicting claims, the emphasis upon the individual and his (not yet her) freedom all pushed Enlightenment thinkers toward the creation of new public policies that sought to guarantee religious liberty and choice. Modern religious freedom thus became one of the defining marks of the modern liberal Western state. This commitment to religious freedom found expression in the eventual disestablishment of particular religious groups in many countries and the gradual separation of church and state. The free practice of religion was codified in law in England as early as the Toleration Act of 1689 and celebrated by such thinkers as Locke. Commitment to such freedom found vigorous expression in the rhetoric of the American Revolution and the American Constitution and in postrevolutionary France.[10] The results, as my analysis will indicate, have been ironic; while religion has been given relative protection it has been at the cost of increasing marginalization and privatization as the state and all areas of public life have become seemingly more and more secularized.[11] Moreover, despite the rhetoric of freedom, the reality was often far more constrained. Locke praised religious liberty except for Catholics and atheists, British dissenters and nonconformists sought greater freedom in America though they did not necessarily extend that freedom to others, and Jews continued to struggle with their status as those "set apart."

If the rhetoric and practice of religious tolerance and freedom were more constrained in Europe than the narratives of liberal modernity admit, they were often nonexistent in relation to the colonized persons of the rest of the world. As professor of comparative religion David Chidester, in *Savage Systems: Colonialism and Comparative Religion in Southern Africa*, has strongly argued, the extension of the colonial project in Africa relied heavily upon the dehumanization of the African population through many mechanisms, including prominently the denial that Africans had any religion at all.[12] The linking of rationality, Christianity, and assumptions of European superiority in a normative view of the human contributed to the strong Enlightenment sentiment that in Europe humanity had come to its fullest flourishing and simultaneously led to the undermining of the humanity of others both in Europe and certainly in the far-flung regions of the colonial world. Indeed, not only the developments of early modernity but also those throughout the later modern period went hand in hand with the global expansion of European military, political, and social power over other cultures and regions of the world. The recognition of the relation between European modernity and colonialism has led, in the contemporary period, to profound questioning of modernity and especially of its Enlightenment form. Thus, there occurred in modernity calls for greater religious tolerance for certain forms of Christianity and for religious and political freedom for particular groups of Europeans while simultaneously indigenous cultures were destroyed and non-European cultures and religious traditions were subjected to profound damage.[13]

Redefining Religion

While much of the world under the spreading reach of colonialism was denied both the status of being "rational" and "religious," there were movements within Europe and eventually America to redefine the meaning of religion, at least for those Europeans and Americans included in the category of rational humans, so that their religion might be interpreted as both more rational and less pone to divisiveness. In the seventeenth century Lord Herbert of Cherbury articulated his notion of a natural religion shared by all humans. Such a natural religious orientation both predated more parochial religious traditions and surpassed them in its capacity to unite humanity in a harmonious society. Deism, as many came to term this approach, sought a way to be religious but not entrenched in sectarian beliefs, practices, and conflict. Such names as John Toland, Matthew Tindale, Thomas Jefferson, Benjamin Franklin, and Voltaire have all been associated with some form or other of Deism. And often it was the preferred position of diplomats, lawyers, and government functionaries who sought ways to keep the peace. Deism, while it purportedly kept religion alive, removed its more divisive aspects, jettisoning such things as revelation, miracles, and parochial dogmas. God remained, but only as a deity who acted through natural causes and laws, a God now removed from direct intervention in history. Many modern defenders of religion would argue for its "reasonableness," its rational character, and hence contend that religion was not in opposition to the ideals of reason articulated by the Enlightenment. By the time of Immanuel Kant (1724–1804) in the late eighteenth century, religion, or at least Christianity, would be thoroughly transformed into a form of rationally defined morality, no longer a threat to the modern order but an important component of it.[14]

Two other developments should also be noted. The first is what religious studies scholar J. Samuel Preus calls the naturalizing of religion. Preus argues, in *Explaining Religion: Criticism and Theory from Bodin to Freud*, that from the sixteenth century onward religion was progressively treated as a human phenomena to be understood and explained in the same way as were other human realities.[15] Preus traces this trajectory to Jean Bodin, a Frenchman writing in the midst of the religious upheavals of the sixteenth century. Already at this juncture religious conflicts and the growing awareness of non-Christian traditions had begun to raise questions for Bodin and others. Preus quotes an exchange in Bodin's legendary dialogue *Colloquium of the Seven about Secrets of the Sublime,* in which one participant queries how anyone can doubt that Christianity is the true religion and another participant responds, "Almost all the world."[16]

Preus argues that from this point on, in the name of modern rationality and critical inquiry, supernatural and religious explanations for religion are slowly replaced by naturalistic and sociohistorical ones. He readily admits that alternative, more religiously located proposals continued to have influence. One strategy was to exempt Christianity and Judaism from the claims about other religions. Thus, Bernard Fontenelle, an eighteenth-century writer on the origins of myths, offered decidedly nonsupernatural-istic explanations for religion but asserted that the Hebrew and Christian traditions have their source in God. Giambattista Vico followed a similar path. But once the door was open to naturalistic and historical explanations for religion, Preus contends, such maneuvers became increasingly problem-atic. By the time of David Hume, writing in the late eighteenth century, such a move from a religious to a "scientific paradigm" for the study of reli-gions was complete. Hume, for Preus, is the pivotal figure in the develop-ment of the modern study of religion, as he firmly placed the examination of religion within the context of the "science of man" and offered explana-tions for its appearance not by reference to God or the supernatural but in terms of human fears of the unknown.[17]

A parallel path can be traced in the study of the Bible. Increasingly the Hebrew and Christian Scriptures were taken to be works that should be studied like other human documents. Already in the seventeenth century Spinoza, having studied Descartes among others, insisted that the Bible be treated like any other text. Following Spinoza there were numerous attempts to reconcile the growing influence of the critical study of the Bible and religious convictions. Critics such as Thomas Hobbes, Richard Simon, and John Locke, while trying to link devotion and criticism, all moved toward that point where critical historical examination of the Bible would come in conflict with Christian faith. By the late seventeenth century, and with ever-greater force in the eighteenth, the critical methods of modernity gained unstoppable force as biblical authority diminished.

Throughout the Western Enlightenment there also grew a decidedly anti-religious, or at least anti-Christian, strand of thought. While Voltaire thought Christianity might suffice for the less well educated of his time, he espoused Deism for the elites. By the time of the French Revolution, anticlericalism was widespread. On August 4, 1789, the clergy and nobles of the French National Assembly relinquished their privileges, effectively collapsing the remnants of feudalism in France. Numerous antireligious measures were adopted throughout the Revolution, including the nationalization of church lands (1789), suppression of religious orders (1790), and the insistence that clergy take an oath of loyalty to the state-run Civil Constitution on Clergy (1790). Increasingly in France a "religion of man" replaced devotion to the church and with it an insistence that freedom and autonomy come from humanity, not from some external religious authority.

Other developments pushed the gradual secularization of modernity as well. Science began to undermine religious beliefs, starting with the biblical time scale. Moreover, for many Enlightenment thinkers, including Voltaire, the advance of science went hand in hand with the overthrow of narrow parochial religious thought, superstition, and fanaticism. Thinkers such as Joseph Priestly and Adam Smith saw scientific progress as a protection against nonrational religion and as one of the means of safeguarding tolerance. In Smith's words, "Science is the great antidote to the poison of enthusiasm and superstition. . . ."[18] By the end of the eighteenth century the term *atheist* may still have been an epithet, but one that had now firmly entered the vocabulary of modernity.

The modern era, especially in its Western Enlightenment form, emerged out of times of tremendous transition and chaos. Out of conflict and out of the developing scientific alternatives to philosophical and religious conceptions of true and false, right and wrong, thinkers of the seventeenth and eighteenth centuries crafted new notions of human freedom and reason, of a natural world governed by natural law and human society directed by the dictates of rationality, of universal truths discovered by science, and of universal religion shorn of its divisive particularities. External authority yielded to the autonomy of the individual, tradition to an ahistorical cosmopolitanism, inheritance to a "complete transcendence of situation."[19] The Western Enlightenment, from Descartes on, sought, in the words of Jeffrey Stout, "to escape history."[20]

Transition to Historicism: The German Enlightenment

The effects of the Western Enlightenment have been immense in scope, influencing virtually every corner of the globe and every aspect of modern life. But other developments have also shaped the modern world, central among them the topic of this volume—historicism. Historicism came to full fruition in the nineteenth century, especially in Germany, and many of its own proponents interpreted it as a reaction against the Franco-British Enlightenment of the seventeenth and eighteenth centuries. Later opponents of historicism saw it as a betrayal of the Enlightenment, though some—especially contemporary—critics have interpreted historicism as a failure to challenge fully the Enlightenment and thus as the continuation of Enlightenment commitments and values in other forms. This volume will suggest that all these judgments are partially, though *only* partially, correct. The remainder of this chapter and the following chapter will sketch out the ways in which especially nineteenth-century German historicism embraced certain Enlightenment tenets while vigorously rejecting much that gave Enlightenment modernity its special character. In particular, while European historicism embraced the critical orientation of the Enlightenment, it simultaneously historicized reason itself, rejected the universalizing tendencies of the Enlightenment, and replaced Western European cosmopolitanism with a "localism," especially in the form of German nationalism. As such, historicism, particularly in its early Germanic form, represents a distinctive strand of modernity that cannot be simply equated with the increasingly discredited Enlightenment modernity though it can be seen to pose significant problems of its own.

As the opening section of this book indicated, historicism is a designation for a theoretical perspective that characterizes human life and thought utilizing historicist categories and assumptions. But it also names the age and place where this perspective first came to significant expression—nineteenth-century Germany. German historicism did not just emerge full-blown in the nineteenth century, however; nor can it be interpreted, as is often the case, as only a Germanic reaction against Franco-British Enlightenment ideas. While such opposition, especially to the French, will be seen to have played a major part in the development of German historicism, the story of its emergence entails a more complex relationship to the Enlightenment than these common characterizations suggest. It is to a version of that story we now turn.

Nineteenth-Century Germany

The Germans, like their Western European counterparts, had to recover from the religious and political wars that had torn Europe apart. The Germanic lands were devastated to an incredible extent, with a large portion of the population perishing in the conflicts, the economy in ruins, and agriculture destroyed. Other factors beyond the extensiveness of the destruction also contributed to blocking the development of a Franco-British-style Enlightenment in Germany. These factors included the lack of political unity within German-speaking lands, the failure to develop the strong traditions of science and political philosophy that emerged in France and Britain, and the ongoing presence of both Protestants and Catholics in Germanic locales. The result was a different environment than that which fostered the emergence of the Enlightenment in Western Europe. Along with these, several other elements within the German context contributed to the emergence of a different form of modernity in Germany, a form that would eventually be identified significantly with historicism.

One such development was pietism.[21] Pietism was a movement in the Lutheran, and to a lesser extent Calvinist, churches that emerged in the latter part of the seventeenth century in reaction to Protestant scholasticism and a growing rationalism that placed emphasis upon right belief at the expense of lived religion. In the aftermath of the religious wars, religious life in Germany had lost much of its vigor, civil government controlled the church in many areas, and a rigid orthodoxy focused on intellectual assent had come to prominence. Over against what appeared to pietists to be the emptying of Christianity of its experiential vitality in favor of an overly intellectual and dogmatic religion, pietists argued for a return to the experiential dimensions of Christianity and a diminution of the importance of doctrine. While many German thinkers of the eighteenth and nineteenth centuries did not become pietists themselves, pietism nonetheless had wide effects, influencing such eighteenth-century figures as Immanuel Kant and the proto-historicist Johann Gottfried Herder and contributing to the emergence of Romanticism in the nineteenth century. For our purposes, pietism turned both its adherents and those who to some degree or another were shaped by it away from abstractions and what was seen as cold reason to the liveliness of experience and to the particularities of historical existence. And importantly, in Germany pietism's religious revival contributed greatly to minimizing the antireligious fervor that was found in so many countries of Western Europe. Secularization, while it too came to Germany, came later and was accompanied with a less negative evaluation of religion.

The second development that set the stage for the growth of historicism[22] was the *Aufklärung*, or Enlightenment, which came to German-speaking lands many decades after it flourished in Western Europe and had a somewhat different, peculiarly German, character than did the Franco-British version. While it embraced certain Enlightenment convictions about reason, the *Aufklärung* was far less tied to the vision of science and scientific truth that characterized the work of many Western thinkers. *Aufklärer*, influenced by pietism, also maintained a much greater respect for history and tradition, a less hostile attitude toward religion, and a keener appreciation of the particular and the local over against the universal and cosmopolitan.

The beginnings of the *Aufklärung* are variously dated anywhere from 1700 to 1740. Its proponents were drawn mostly from the professional, legal, academic, and business classes, and it flourished most fully in university towns in association with the emergence of the modern German university. Its leaders were often influenced by pietism, even if they rejected its anti-intellectualism, and it had a decidedly reformist, rather than revolutionary, tone as it sought political, religious, and educational advance. According to historian Peter Hanns Reill, the *Aufklärung* was "bourgeois in spirit, critical of absolutism, opposed to attitudes associated with the court but not revolutionary in nature. Its intellectual center was the university and its leading proponents were drawn primarily from the professional classes."[23] Reill goes on in his work *The German Enlightenment and the Rise of Historicism* to argue that the *Aufklärung* was distinguished from the Western Enlightenment by three tendencies: its respect for tradition; its reluctance to jettison long-established institutions both political and religious; and its rejection of radical revolution in favor of reform.[24] This last point would prove to be extremely important for Germans in light of the French Revolution and the subsequent invasion of German lands by Napoleon. In the minds of many Germans, the ideals of the Enlightenment and the excesses of the French Revolution were deeply connected. Hence, there developed, after initial support for the Revolution, a strongly negative reaction against both the Revolution and the ideals of the Western Enlightenment that were thought to have fostered the lack of moderation and violence that marked the latter stages of the French upheavals.

Many names are associated with the German Enlightenment, from Gottfried Wilhelm Leibniz (generally seen as its precursor) to Frederick the Great, Christian Thomasius, Christian Wolff, Moses Mendelssohn, Gotthold Ephraim Lessing, Justus J. Moser, Johann Stephan Pulter, Hermann Samuel Reimarus, Johann Salomo Semler, and, depending on one's perspective, Immanuel Kant. It was during this period and in the thought of many of these thinkers that history began to come to prominence, that the historical-critical method of inquiry gained clarity and definition and that historicist themes began to be enunciated with ever-greater force. In contrast to the Western Enlightenment's appeals to a more abstract reason and universal values as the means to avoid the pitfalls of particularism, in the German lands it was the recognition of historical particularities that was interpreted as challenging parochialism and sectarianism, undermining the imposition on others of what were really local values and commitments.[25] Politically, knowledge of the past was interpreted as contributing to a critique of the present and to a vision of the future. Rather than the past being that which needed to be left behind in order to create a new order, the past, for Germans, provided insight and possibilities for what the future should be like. Historians began to place events within contexts and to seek to delineate networks of relations as a way to understand history. There were developments in philology, the collection and analysis of documents and archival materials, and a growing consolidation of scholarly standards. National literature, over against more cosmopolitan literary works, regained favor, and a growing interest in language as the embodiment of national identity took place.

The Study of the Bible

The study of the Bible in Germany demonstrated both the growing interest in the past and also the steady evolution of historicist attitudes toward that past. As noted above, critical biblical scholarship was on the increase throughout all of Europe during this period. But the eighteenth century witnessed, in the work of such figures as Johann Gottfried Eichhorn, Johann David Michaelis, and especially Johann Salomo Semler, a great advance that resulted in the German dominance of biblical scholarship from the mid-century onward. The Bible became increasingly viewed as a human work that emerged in a particular time and place. While few doubted its revelatory importance, scholars such as Semler began to write of the Bible as expressing God's commandments in local dialect and to emphasize the contextual conditions that gave rise to individual books in the Bible.[26] Increasingly scholars such as Semler argued for a uniform hermeneutic principle to be applied to biblical and nonbiblical material alike and by so doing laid the foundation for the hermeneutical developments of the nineteenth century by persons such as Schleiermacher and Ferdinand Baur. Others questioned the chronology of the Bible, the authorship of various books was debated, and for some the Bible now was a form of poetry. Efforts to distinguish the real message and person of Jesus apart from church tradition and doctrine began in earnest.

For many scholars and Christian thinkers the original impulse for historical study was not to undermine religion, or at least Christianity, but to provide historical grounding for the faith. However, as the eighteenth century unfolded and commitment to critical and free inquiry gained strength, the commitments of historical criticism and theological concerns began to deviate. While for many Christian scholars the Bible remained central, increasingly there were demands that both its study and its content had to conform to the dictates of reason. Thus, in Germany, like elsewhere, there were efforts to declare that both the Scriptures and Christianity were rational. By the end of the century, Jesus had emerged as an ethical ideal, a model for modern rational and moral humanity.[27]

Tensions thus began to develop for many scholars between commitments to growing historicist assumptions and historical-critical methods and to religious commitments and theological concerns that continued to assume the unique character of Christianity. For some thinkers these conflicts led to explicit criticisms of the Bible and of Christianity. Hermann Samuel Reimarus (1694–1768) represented in the eighteenth century what would become far more commonplace in the nineteenth century. While publicly supporting the church, he privately wrote a work that he, perhaps judiciously, did not publish. After his death the philosopher Gotthold Ephraim Lessing (1729–1781) published fragments of Reimarus's "Apology or Defence of the Rational Worshippers of God," unleashing both controversy and the quest for the historical Jesus that would consume so much effort in the nineteenth century. Later in the nineteenth century, the renegade thinker David Frederick Strauss published a fuller version of Reimarus's work. In this originally unpublished work Reimarus argued for the contextualizing of biblical texts, explored the relationship of Jesus and his Jewish context, rejected miracles, argued for Deism, and asserted that much of the Bible was contrary to natural religion. In Reimarus's work the growing disconnection between historical approaches to religion and the long-held assumptions about Scripture and historical Christianity became increasingly and controversially clear even while he simultaneously adhered to Enlightenment-inspired notions of natural religion.[28]

Whether in the more religiously conventional mode of Semler or the more challenging form of Reimarus, by the end of the eighteenth century and certainly within the nineteenth century, the critical study of biblical materials led to major changes in the status and interpretation of the Bible. In his classic work *The Eclipse of Biblical Narrative* Hans Frei argues that three major shifts had occurred by this point that marked the end to precritical readings of the Bible.[29] The first move was a growing questioning of the historical veracity of biblical stories. In earlier readings biblical stories were assumed to refer to events that had actually occurred. Many of those claims were now put in doubt.[30] Second, the assumption that the Bible was one narrative, that it told one comprehensive story of God's interaction with the world, also came to be questioned as scholars increasingly focused instead on individual segments and texts and gave up interest in a cumulative story.[31] Third, Frei argues that in precritical readings the Bible was assumed to embrace or take into itself the world. Every present age was to be interpreted in light of the Bible. By the late eighteenth century, this had been reversed. Now the tenets of the modern world dictated whether the biblical texts were to be considered reliable and viable. The norms of the modern world were thus coming to dominate those of the Bible.[32] The Bible was like other literature; it was to be studied as a historical artifact utilizing the tools and criteria of an ever-increasingly autonomous historical discipline. Thus, while the full development of history as a modern discipline would await the nineteenth century, the separation of historical analysis and faith was well under way within the German Enlightenment.

The German dominance of critical biblical scholarship both embodied and contributed to the emergence of historicism. It accompanied the developments noted above that, in combination, gave the German Enlightenment its distinctive character over against the Western Enlightenment. Still, reason was not dismissed; it provided the critical tools for many of these thinkers to explore the past, and often reason was assumed, as elsewhere in the Enlightenment, to be ahistorical itself, essentially the same everywhere. The full historicizing of reason was still to take place, and reason and history were not yet opposed to one another. It would take several other factors to intensify and consolidate these incipient historicist insights and push German thought toward the fuller historicism of the nineteenth century.

Kant, Hamann, Herder

The work of Immanuel Kant played an important role here. Many contemporary thinkers, especially postmodernists, have portrayed Kant as the epitome of Enlightenment sensibilities. And certainly Kant, though interested in the idea of history, did not evidence the historicist concerns that marked the thought of some of his contemporaries or those that came after him in the next century. Yet it is Kant who was, according to his contemporaries, including Moses Mendelssohn, "the all-destroyer."[33] In his rejection of speculative metaphysics and traditional theology, his delineation of the limits of reason, his turn to the human knower as active, and his rejection of inevitable progress in history, Kant challenged many of the terms by which earlier Enlightenment thinkers had made their arguments.

Kant's legacy has been a conflicted one, as contemporary debate about him continues to confirm. During his own time he was attacked both by those who thought he had betrayed the Enlightenment but also by those who were convinced that Kant continued forms of rationalism that were increasingly problematic in the late eighteenth century. Among the latter of

Kant's critics was Johann Gottfried von Herder (1744–1803), philosopher of history and language, exegete, scholar of myth and folklore, theologian, and pastor, who would provide a pivotal bridge to the historicism of the nineteenth century.

Herder was a student of Kant's in Köningsberg but rejected much of his thought in favor of that of one of his other teachers, the pietist Johann Georg Hamann (1730–1788). Hamann was a great opponent of the Enlightenment, especially in its French form, a precursor of romanticism, and a linguist of great skill who also was a proponent of the German language. Over against notions of abstract and universal reason, he espoused local and national identities shaped by distinctive languages, literatures, and myths. Where many of his predecessors eschewed the past and saw a steady movement away from the past as the route to progress and development, Hamann celebrated ancient poetry, song, and story and proposed these hoary traditions as the foundations for true identity. In each of his claims, Hamann moved German thought away from the universalism of the Western Enlightenment and toward the specifics of culture and history. Apropos of these moves, Bruce Lincoln states in *Theorizing Myth: Narrative, Ideology, and Scholarship* that "Hamann put language at the center of his reflection—simultaneously theological, philosophical, literary, and cultural-historical—such that the linguistic exerted maximal pressure against the Enlightenment model of the rational. Thus, he argued that language encompasses reason, since reason is conducted in language. . . . Where Enlightenment philosophers construed reason as abstract and universal, he insisted that language was concrete, specific, and particular: there could no more be a universal reason than there could be a universal language."[34]

Johann Gottfried von Herder followed Hamann not only in his sometimes-unfair criticisms of Kant but more importantly in his adoption of a more historicist outlook. In 1774 Herder published *Yet Another Philosophy of History*, the work that many take to be the first real articulation of historicist thought.[35] In this work Herder continued the historicizing of reason and the foregrounding of language and culture found in Hamann. He asserted that all values were historical, emerging in different locales and times, and hence were both always local and multiple. Rejected here were the universalisms and abstract ideals of the Enlightenment, including its notions of a common human nature and unified natural law. Over against these a new emphasis on individuality and a new particularism emerged containing elements that would be central to historicism and raising questions that would bedevil historicist thought till our present day.

First, Herder stressed both the uniqueness of individual men and women but also asserted that the particularity of human selfhood is the result of the contributions of environment and history. Human historical existence is marked by profound individuality, but human distinctiveness comes about by virtue of the contributions of time and place, history, and the vicissitudes of fate. Humans are malleable clay, shaped by their context and by all that has preceded them, assuming "different shape under different circumstances, needs, and burdens."[36] It is precisely out of this network of interconnecting influences that individuals emerge.

Second, and of extreme importance for Herder and for the kind of historicism that followed him in the nineteenth century, the locus of historical development is not only in the individual person but especially in the nation, and it expresses itself in the nation's unique spirit. Individuals, for their part, are primarily located within the context of some national formation; there are no longer generic human beings with a common, unvarying humanity but persons with national identities. And nations, or *Volken*, are unique, like individuals, and develop according to their own inner dynamics and principles. Thus, Herder claimed that "each form of human perfection is, in a certain sense, national, time-bound, and most specifically, individual."[37] With Herder, the Germans' shift from the cosmopolitanism of the West to a narrower nationalism began in full earnest.[38]

Third, for Herder these national formulations are always multiple and diverse, yielding distinctive values and unique characteristics. One ramification of this view is that, according to Herder, both the efforts to compare cultures and nations and to distinguish an unchanging set of criteria to judge better or worse are misguided. For Herder, "all comparison is disastrous."[39] While humans could enter the "spirit of a nation" other than their own, it should not be for the purpose of making judgments.[40] Over against many Enlightenment thinkers who viewed diversity as an indication that not all peoples or nations had attained the high level of development evident in Europeans, Herder saw in diversity a plethora of values that could not be differentiated into clearly defined levels of the good. Herder eloquently declared that

> The universal, philosophical, philanthropic tone of our century readily applies "our own ideal" of virtue and happiness to each distant nation, to each remote period in history. But can one such single ideal be the sole standard for judging, condemning, or praising the customs of other nations or periods? Is not the good scattered throughout the earth? Since one form of humanity and one region cannot encompass the good, it has been distributed

in a thousand forms, continually changing shape like a Proteus
throughout all continents and centuries.[41]

This celebration of diversity had several repercussions for Herder. He let
go of any easy notion of progress, differentiating himself from much Western Enlightenment thought. Progress, especially by the Western Enlightenment, was commonly interpreted as a movement away from the past,
viewed negatively, toward a self-evidently better present culminating in
modern European experience and thought. Moreover, despite Enlightenment notions of a common human nature, often peoples and cultures
judged different from the European ideal were evaluated as at best less
developed and at worse less than human. So ran much of the rationale of
colonialism. For Herder, history was neither a tale of progress nor a story of
loss and decline.[42] All that appeared in history had its own value, and there
were no universal or abstract norms to judge one historical moment as
superior to another. Herder thus sounded early criticisms of the elevation
of the present and the denigration of the past and, especially, of the Euro-
pocentric postures of most of modern Western thought that utilized the
norms of modern European thought and life to declare Western superiority
and the inferiority of all others.[43]

But there were other implications of Herder's position as well. Herder
also declared, in the 1774 work, that values were always local and hence
there were no transnational or transtemporal norms by which to make
judgments; neither reason nor history yielded a self-evident scale of judgment by which to make decisions beyond the borders of specific contexts.
Judgment was always local. Thus it is with Herder that the issue of historical relativism, of whether any judgments can be made when all values are
situated and indeed parochial and all historical developments are presumed
to be positive, entered the modern scene with real force.

Both in the 1774 work and in later works Herder found ways to stress
that humanity was one in its origins and that differentiation emerged in
the course of history. He continued to have throughout his life a Lutheran-
fed conviction of divine Providence in which human historical diversity
formed a "magnificent whole."[44] Still, despite this appeal to the unity
of humanity, it was diversity and multiplicity that fascinated him as he
argued that climate, language, and national character interacted to create
distinctive collective identities, unique nations, or ethnic formations. It is
through humans' situatedness and through the process of inheriting traditions that a people are formed. As did Schleiermacher in the nineteenth

century, Herder regarded such diversity not as a problem but as something positive; each *Volk* had its own contribution to make to the world. At least for Herder, if not for later nationalists, a different cosmopolitanism was envisioned than one based on the unity and sameness of humanity; in this vision the different nations would live in peace and mutual admiration precisely because of the different contributions each had to make.[45]

Herder was a very influential thinker, translated into many languages and especially admired by later nineteenth-century thinkers. Importantly, however, we must keep in mind that he not only moved German thought away from notions of abstract and universal reason and toward the particular, contextual, and conditioned, but also that he interpreted the latter in terms of collective and especially national identity. Historicism, therefore, would for many thinkers be linked, in the nineteenth and early twentieth centuries, with forms of nationalism. Thus, as historian Georg Iggers states, for Herder, "Truth, value and beauty are not one, but many. They are found only in history and manifest themselves only in the national spirit."[46]

The French Revolution and Napoleonic Wars

As was indicated earlier, another factor that must be noted in the unfolding of historicist sentiments in Germany in the late eighteenth century is the French Revolution (1789–1799) and the Napoleonic Wars that followed. Many thinkers of the German Enlightenment, including Kant, welcomed the Revolution. However, as the Revolution devolved into various forms of ongoing violence, and the French invaded, for a variety of conflicting reasons internal to French politics, bordering lands including Germany, support for the Revolution and its Enlightenment-inspired ideals diminished. Increasingly Germans identified the Enlightenment's notions of natural law, the unity of humanity, and universal truths with the French political, cultural, and military adventurism of the revolutionary period. After Napoleon came to power in 1799 and subsequently invaded Prussia in 1806, anti-French and anti-Enlightenment sentiments increased in fervor. Over against French political domination, German nationalist tendencies intensified, accompanied by a revival of national literature and myths and, importantly, the beginnings of what would come to be known as the German idea of history and the German national tradition of historiography. The turn away from Enlightenment ideals was thus not only intellectual but also political, fueled by resistance to French attempts at cultural and military control. Hence, the historicism of the nineteenth century would unfold alongside of and in the context of the German move to a new national identity, culminating in the emergence of the modern German nation-state under Bismarck in the latter part of the nineteenth century.

One of historicism's major claims is that ideas are not just abstractions. They do not just emerge out of thin air but are deeply intertwined with the contexts within which they take shape; they are responses to, reflections of, and, in turn, conditioners of those contexts. Historicism's own emergence and formation testify to the conditioned and contextualized character of human claims. By the end of the eighteenth century an interest in history and the beginnings of historicist sensibilities could be found in many places in Europe as historical topics were increasingly the subject of art, literature, and scholarly exploration. But it was in German lands, with the presence of pietism and a modified Enlightenment tradition, out of a resistance to cultural and political invasion, that historicism took one of its most distinctive forms. Thus, by the beginnings of the nineteenth century, in a way not true of other places, Iggers states that "German educated opinion now agreed that all values and rights were of historic and national origin and that alien institutions could not be transplanted to German soil."[47] It is to how these ideas developed in the nineteenth century that we now turn.

2

Nineteenth-Century German Historicism

The Rise of Historicism

As the previous chapter indicates, a sense of human historicity was well under way in the eighteenth century. Historical consciousness in its myriad forms was, however, to develop most fully in the nineteenth century affecting virtually all aspects of intellectual, artistic, political, and cultural life. Across the Western world an interest in the past and a growing awareness of both its value and its distance from the present intensified as the century unfolded. History became the touchstone for human understanding of self and world. As historian James J. Sheehan notes, "It provided the subjects for art, literature, the foundations for humanistic scholarship, even the categories of scientific analysis."[1] In scholarship, the nineteenth century was the period in which the academic discipline of history, with its professional identity, location in the modern university, and distinctive methods and theoretical juxtapositioning of itself over against the natural sciences, took definitive shape. Aesthetically, novelists, poets, and artists not only utilized historical subject matter but also self-consciously located their work within artistic and literary history. Collecting and preservation became not just the province of professionals as museums, historical journals, and historical societies flourished. They also became the obsession of broad segments of the nineteenth-century populace as individuals and groups engaged in a new interest in artifacts, architecture, ruins, and literary and cultural remains.[2] While the methods of the natural and the humanistic and social sciences were distinguished, there was, nonetheless, a mutual borrowing of categories as notions of organic growth and evolutionary development appeared widely. Speculative philosophies now focused on history, not unchanging truth. The towering philosophers of the century, most especially Hegel, sought to reunite reason and history. Theologians and biblical scholars sought as well to grapple with the implications of their historicist-oriented research and reflection as ancient texts became unstable, dogma appeared bound to time and place, and the immense diversity of human religiosity both in the ancient and contemporary worlds became ever clearer. In all these areas—empirical research, aesthetic productions, philosophy, and theology—a sense of historicity provided the framework for many nineteenth-century developments.[3]

It was not, however, merely that history became so central or that the past so thoroughly captured the attention of the nineteenth century. The recognition of historicity also raised profound questions for the period as historians, artists, theologians, and philosophers all struggled with their own historicity and the implications of that historicity for what could be known and claimed with any degree of certitude. How is the past different from the present and how can it be known? What methods are appropriate for the study of the human realm? What is the importance of origins, and can they be recovered through empirical history, geological research, or the reconstruction of a mythological past? What happens when all that remains of the past are fragments and ruins? What is the status of the knower or scholar or believer who has discovered his or her own location in history? Could the Enlightenment dream of objective knowledge be wedded to the reality of historical existence and still survive? What happens to the most revered texts of Western history—especially the Bible—when they are treated like all other human literature? What is the importance of language? What is the relation of human identity to land, national narratives, and to the emergent nation-state? Does history support or destroy religious faith? What is the relation between the universal and the historical, the divine and the finite? All these questions shaped the debates of the nineteenth century, as both intellectuals and ordinary persons participated in the revolution in historicist consciousness.

This dominance of the historical was widespread in Europe throughout the nineteenth century. But the historicist shift in consciousness had its most profound effects in Germany; it was here that historical consciousness and historicism as a general outlook came to fullest expression and had its most distinctive form as German thought came to intellectual and cultural prominence. This chapter will explore several of the most important of these developments with special attention to those that have had significant import for theological attempts to come to terms with human historicity. We turn first to the emergence of what has been termed the German tradition of historiography.

The German Historiographic Tradition

Perhaps nowhere did historicism develop more self-consciously than in the emerging scholarly discipline of history, what Van A. Harvey describes as the "formal expression" of this revolution in consciousness.[4] As with other modern disciplines of the university that were taking shape during this period, history yielded diverse and contending perspectives. It is, however, possible to identify what Georg G. Iggers calls the "main tradition of German historiography" that stretched from Leopold von Ranke and Wilhelm von Humboldt in the early part of the nineteenth century to Friedrich Meinecke, whose life and work spanned the last half of the nineteenth and the first half of the twentieth centuries.[5] When we turn to the work of these individuals, we will see clear differences among them, but it will be helpful to make some general remarks before turning to several of the most prominent historians of this tradition.

As the previous chapter indicated, German historicism unfolded within a very particular political context. In reaction to the excesses of the French Revolution, in resistance to the military incursions of the Napoleonic Wars, and out of the processes of nation building in the Germanic lands, a kind of historicism deeply connected to an emerging national identity took shape. It was, in the words of Iggers, "the child of the German national revival and the Wars of Liberation."[6] The German historiographic tradition both reflected and furthered these processes. It pursued a nation-centered history, primarily focused no longer on the "people" (as did Herder) but on the state as the embodiment of national identity, which was elevated above all else. The preoccupation was with the great powers and especially military and political conflicts. Diplomatic history was held in high esteem while social and economic developments and issues were often ignored.[7] Foreign policies and relations took precedence over domestic developments and concerns. Moreover, whereas in other parts of Europe, especially France and England, and in the United States the rights and freedom of the individual were of paramount importance, for the Germans the furthering of the state was central; it was through the development of the state that the individual was advanced, not the other way around. And finally, the values that the state embodied and pursued were not the supposed universal values of the Enlightenment, but national values that came forth from the particular history and character of the German peoples.[8]

Embedded in this approach to history were assumptions and commitments that were, in incipient form, taking shape in the previous century.

Several are important to note again. In particular, what have been called the two great principles or cornerstones of German historicism can be identified in the work of many thinkers associated with this historiographic tradition: individuality and development.[9] As was the case for the early or proto-historicists such as Herder, the nineteenth-century historicists repudiated notions of commonality and sameness in the name of uniqueness, concrete particularity, and diversity. Moreover, individuality could only be understood through the exploration of its development, its coming to fullness in history. In addition, such individuality came to fullness not according to some general rules of development but out of its own distinctive internal norms. Historical studies thus trace not the universal or the same but rather the "sphere of the unique" that is history.[10]

If individuality and development were the organizing principles of German historicism, other assumptions followed from and were embedded in these ideas. A central implication was that conceptualization and generalization were of limited value in historical study. According to Iggers, "The uniqueness of individualities in history restricted the applicability of rational methods in the study of social and cultural phenomenon. The spontaneity and dynamism of life refused to be reduced to common denominators."[11] A historical rationality was the new aim, seeking to acknowledge the distance between past and present, and to find ways to bridge that distance while taking into account the historicity of the contemporary historian. Thus, the hermeneutical notions of *Verstehen* (understanding), empathy, and intuition would come to replace both the universalizing categories of Enlightenment reason and the earlier, religiously grounded traditions of natural law.

As understanding replaced universalizing reason as the form of rationality required by unique historical realities, comparison also became problematic. *Verstehen* gave insight into the individual; it did not provide timeless knowledge of unchanging universals. From the perspective of this work, such reluctance about comparison had a further significant implication: the assumption, echoing thinkers such as Herder, that there are no universal norms by which to evaluate historical occurrences (what is often termed *Antinormativität*). Such relativism not only characterized the work of historians focused on the state and the furthering of its political agenda. It was also strongly present in other modes of nineteenth-century historicism, including Romanticism with its celebration of diversity and in what historian Hayden White terms the aesthetic historicism of the late nineteenth century, in which notions of truth and beauty become increasingly disconnected.[12]

If, as we will explore in the latter parts of this chapter, the relativistic implications of historicism intensified as the century unfolded, most historians of the German historiographic tradition did not come to the conclusion that historical research was not objective and adequate to its objects. Indeed, from Leopold von Ranke onward, historians asserted that the methods of critical historical inquiry were the only ones that yielded objective knowledge of historical realities. In Harvey's words, "Underlying this new science [history] was an almost Promethean will-to-truth. The aim of the historian, it was declared, was to 'tell what really happened.' Description, impartiality, and objectivity were the ideals."[13] No longer beholden to the constraints of religious dogma nor to the prison of Enlightenment abstract conceptualization, equipped with methods appropriate to historical reality, and committed to the professional canons of critical historical inquiry, historians of every ilk, including biblical scholars, sought impartial and objective knowledge.

Humboldt, Ranke, Droysen, and Meinecke

German historical thinkers were numerous in the nineteenth century as historical research and reflection upon the nature of historical thinking took center stage. Several figures stand out, however, as articulators of what would later be referred to as historicism. Among them are Wilhelm von Humboldt, Leopold von Ranke, Johann Gustav Droysen, and Friedrich Meinecke. Together their work spans the whole of the nineteenth and the first half of the twentieth centuries. It is clearly impossible to cover in any adequate fashion all of their work, as it will also be in relation to those thinkers taken up in the remainder of the chapter. We can, however, highlight the guiding assumptions and arguments they made as a way of more fully delineating nineteenth-century historicism and especially as a means of bringing to the fore the kinds of issues that historicism both raised and faced in this period.

Wilhelm von Humboldt

Wilhelm von Humboldt (1767–1835) was an aristocrat and political figure who played an active role in government, diplomacy, and the wider political and cultural debates from the late eighteenth century till his death in 1835. For the purposes of this work, he was especially important as one of the earliest thinkers to set forth the theoretical vision of German historicism. Humboldt's own political views changed over time from an early view of the relation of the state and individual that resembled, at least in part, classical liberalism to a position, in the aftermath of Napoleon's adventurism, that made the state more central. But for us what is more important is that he stressed a number of themes and assumptions that together make the case for German historicism. He, like Herder before and Ranke after, made the notion of individuality the center of his claims about history; that is, concrete reality is composed of individuals that can only be known historically. But for Humboldt there was more to this recognition than a turn from rational reflection to particular concrete reality. He also stressed that these individuals (persons, events, states) develop internally according to their own inner dynamics, but that there is no general scheme or plan to history that is fully discernible to humans. Individuals may have an internal coherence, but history as a whole seems to lack one. History is irrational in that sense and has a chaotic character.[14] While Humboldt, like many other historicists, was optimistic, it was not because he discerned a great teleological pull in history that would bring history to some eschatological conclusion. Instead, Humboldt emphasized history as flux, full of spontaneous novelty, without clear direction or higher purpose.[15]

Humboldt made several other central assertions that were to shape nineteenth-century historicism. Importantly, while he argued for a dynamic, nonprogressive view of history, he did not leave all in complete chaos. Instead, as his thought developed, he introduced precisely that element which later critics of historicism would invoke as a failure of historicist nerve and as proof that historicists were closely aligned with the Western metaphysical tradition that they claimed to repudiate—God. Seeking to give a fuller grounding to his notion of individuality, Humboldt turned to the idea that each individual is the expression and embodiment of an "eternal idea" or essence and that all individuality somehow fits into and reflects the divine mystery from which it came forth.[16] Individuality is thus grounded in divine providence, and God thereby provides the ground for the harmony of diversities.[17] In some ways this seems to contradict the emphasis on the lack of grand schemes that Humboldt also asserted, but he seemed to articulate the notion that the divine plan lies in the diversities and their nonlinear development, not in their abrogation. When Humboldt did not appear to later critics to be an example of discredited metaphysics, he seemed to be the heralder of a "hopeless chaos of values."[18] As we will see, both criticisms have plagued historicism in its various modes.

There is another significant reason Humboldt claims the attention of this work. It is Humboldt who began in earnest to articulate the notion of understanding, or *Verstand,* as central to the comprehension and knowledge of historical reality.[19] For Humboldt, to know the historical one must first engage in the critical, unbiased, and detailed examination of the individual event. Thus, he argued for what would become the hallmark of modern historical inquiry—focus on facts, emphasis upon evidence, attention to documents and sources. This would be the legacy of much of the historicism of the nineteenth century. But Humboldt and other historicists after him did not conclude that such inquiry is sufficient. If true understanding is to be gained, if the historian or knower is to penetrate to the essence of an individual person, event, or state, she or he has to do more than simply assess facts or evidence. Through intuition the inquirer moves beyond mere perception of facts to comprehend, if not fully, at least in part, the true essence of concrete reality. Hence, Humboldt not only focused on dynamic historical reality but also invoked a metaphysical and divine grounding for it and articulated what for him was a historicist theory of understanding. In all these positions, he set the stage for later proponents of German historicism.

Leopold von Ranke

Leopold von Ranke (1795–1886) is widely considered, along with Humboldt, the founding figure of the German tradition of historiography. Ranke, as professor at the University of Berlin for nearly a half century and the author of more than sixty volumes on everything from the Reformation in Germany, France, Italy, and England to a universal history begun when he was eighty-six, contributed immeasurably to the establishment of history as a legitimate and central discipline in the modern university. He, perhaps more than any other nineteenth-century historian, captured and articulated what was meant by a science of history. Leonard Krieger, in his volume *Ranke: The Meaning of History,* develops four main principles that he argues shaped the Rankean ideal of historical reflection and provided the ground for the modern academic discipline of history.[20]

The first principle of Rankean scientific history, according to Krieger, is a commitment to the objectivity of historical claims. The task of history, as a discipline, is to show what actually occurred, neither judging history nor subordinating historical events to purposes no longer relevant to the events themselves.[21] Importantly, for Ranke this meant that the historian in his or her own particularity is to be eclipsed as he or she focuses on the historical event. Critical observation, devoid of prejudices and unclouded by personal or social agendas, is to be the historian's guiding ideal.[22] Georg

G. Iggers captures well this dimension of the Rankean approach to history when he quotes the American historian H. B. Adams, who asserted, in 1888, that Ranke was "determined to hold strictly to the facts of history, to preach no sermon, to point no moral, to adorn no tale, but to tell the simple historic truth."[23] Ranke himself stated that as a historian he had tried "to extinguish my own self, as it were, to let the things speak and the mighty forces appear which have arisen in the course of the centuries."[24]

The best way to ascertain the facts of history is, according to Ranke, the critical use of sources and especially eyewitness accounts of events. The centerpiece of a scientific method of historical inquiry is this turn to sources and documents. According to Ranke, modern history must be based "no longer on the reports even of contemporary historians, except insofar as they are in possession of personal and immediate knowledge of facts; and still less, works yet more remote from the source; but rather on the narratives of eyewitnesses and on genuine and original documents."[25] Whether applied to ancient or modern history, to the Bible or the texts of early pagan cultures, the quest for the earliest documents and for originating sources was undertaken in ever-greater earnest.

This commitment to objectivity is coupled, according to Krieger, with an insistence upon the priority of individual facts. As with other representatives of the Historical School, the focus on particular events, persons, and states or nations is central for Ranke. Importantly, this focus stands over against abstraction and generalization. While a historian might abstract from the particular events of history and make more general claims, these assertions always follow after and emerge from attention to the particularities of history. Historical conclusions and claims are always *a posteriori*, never *a priori*.[26] History follows the facts; it never treats the singular realities of history as embodiments of abstract or general truths. The Hegelian tendency to see concrete history as the embodiment of absolute reason was, thus, highly problematic to Ranke, for it made concrete historical realities "mere shadows or phantoms inflated by this idea."[27] Ranke ruled out not just absolute reason but also theory in general. The prioritizing of facts, for Ranke, implies the need for an unobstructed view, an eye innocent of intervening or distorting theories that comes between the historian and the object of inquiry. The historian is to immerse him- or herself in the reality of the other, grasping the object of historical inquiry. Our contemporary awareness of the presence and importance of theoretical frameworks for any knowledge at all is simply not part of Rankean historicism.

A third principle that animates Ranke's work is the assumption that "every epoch is immediate to God" and hence each is unique and of equal value.[28] This principle entails the insistence that all historical ages have their own unique value and the concomitant refusal to reduce any epoch to a stepping-stone for later developments. The assertion of unique value is one of the hallmarks of the Historical School and set this approach to history over against other views of history, especially speculative philosophies of history that were emerging at the same time. While there may be some forms of progress, in particular material and social development, Ranke was adamant that such progress does not vitiate the value of each historical moment in and of itself. Because every epoch is immediate to God, then "its worth is not at all based on what derives from it but rests in its own existence, in its own self. . . . If I may dare to make this remark, I picture the deity—since no time lies before it—as surveying all of historic mankind in its totality and finding it everywhere of equal value. There is, to be sure, something true in the idea of the education of mankind, but before God all generations of men appear endowed with equal rights, and this is how the historian must view matters."[29] The ramifications of this equivalence of value were significant for nineteenth-century historicism, as it provided the impetus for studying the widest range of historical material. Every age is of interest and has its own contribution to make.

But this principle has further implications. First, it assumes a benign quality to all history, a lack of any sense of the demonic or evil within the historical realm. All of history is "good."[30] And second, it places upon the historian no moral or intellectual obligation to judge history or to engage history critically beyond ascertaining the "facts." The historical thinker thus becomes an objective observer, certain of the positive value of the objects of inquiry and indifferent to any necessity to judge or evaluate what has emerged within the historical realm. While positively resisting the reduction of one age to its utility for another, later age, Ranke simultaneously assumes the radical relativity of all historical phenomena and the moral neutrality of the historian.

A fourth principle or theme that characterizes virtually all the members of the Historical School, and is also central to Ranke, is the importance of politics, especially the activity and workings of the state. States are, like individual humans, living things developing according to their own internal dynamics and laws. Moreover, because of the dominant role played by the state, attention to state activities became the driving goal of much of the Historical

School. Individuals took on a secondary status, and understandings of liberty, freedom, and development applied first to the state and its accumulation of power and only derivatively to individual persons. One ramification of this position for Ranke himself was a conservative political attitude that supported the operations of the state and indeed spiritualized the state (called the thoughts of God) and its quest for power.[31]

Ranke's work has held enormous significance for how the modern academic discipline of history has conceived of itself and how it developed a broadly adhered-to method of source and document analysis and criticism. In many ways Ranke became the model of the objective, scientific, and even positivist version of history. But Ranke also had another side to his understanding of history, what Krieger refers to as the "unscientific counterpoint" to his scientific version of historical analysis.[32] In particular, Ranke continued the theological assumption of the existence of a providential God who harmonizes all historical epochs and events into a unified whole that expresses the divine design in history. Whereas his notion of equivalent uniqueness might lead a nonbeliever toward notions of historical anarchy of values in which anything goes and all is equal, for Ranke the reality of a benevolent God means all exists for the divine good, and history itself is the manifestation of God in and for the world. More than anything, this continuation of Christian faith in Ranke's view of history would lead to the spiritualization of power, the elevation of the state as God's vehicle in the world. Such a view resulted in an optimistic, if not highly progressive, view of history and the avoidance of radical relativism by the invocation of a presumed but not-argued-for theology. Thus, as Ranke critic Charles R. Bambach states, Ranke remained a theological historicist whose assumption of "providential design" was always in danger of unraveling in the face of the modern assault on the self-evident character of traditional metaphysical and theological claims.[33] Iggers alludes to this danger when he comments that "inherent in this type of historicism which Ranke espouses is always the threat that, if Christian faith is shaken, history will lose its meaning and present man with the anarchy of values."[34] It was precisely this threat that was to lead to the crisis of historicism that marked the end of the nineteenth and the beginning of early twentieth centuries.

Johann Gustav Droysen and Friedrich Meinecke

Two other historians also deserve at least our brief attention: Johann Gustav Droysen and Friedrich Meinecke. Droysen (1808–1884) was the founder and leading figure of what came to be called the Prussian School of History.

Not only was Droysen a prolific historian producing studies as varied as works on Alexander the Great and a multivolumed history of Prussian policy, but he also sought to articulate the principles that should guide the practice of history as a discipline.[35] On many counts Droysen's approach echoed Humboldt's and Ranke's, focusing on the state and on the nature of a modern unified Germany. But in important ways he also deviated from their version of historicism. In particular, he distinguished himself from Ranke's overriding fixation on individuals (be they persons, states, or peoples). For Droysen, human knowers are indeed located and encounter the world from their particular place in history. They also know individual parts of history. But Droysen was more convinced than Ranke and Humboldt that such individual units of history are part of a larger coherent and unified world, and that through the knowledge of such particularities the historian can gain some real knowledge of this larger reality and the forces that produced it.[36] Moreover, whereas for Ranke the task and goal of historical inquiry is the individual, for Droysen knowledge of the individual is less a goal and more a means to those forces that are at work in history and that bring about particular historical events and entities. Individualities are entryways to this more profound knowledge.

Thus, Droysen exhibited a great optimism about the possibilities of human knowledge. Moreover, such optimism also characterizes his view of human historical reality, including the state. He asserted a strong theology in which God directs reality, and hence that all that history brings forth reflects a "divine hand."[37] In particular, this means that Droysen asserted a benign interpretation of the state and of power. Evil does not appear to be a real possibility for him, and the state and its operations are inherently good. Historical development seems inevitable and always to be positive.

Friedrich Meinecke's (1862–1954) life and work spanned the last part of the nineteenth century and first half of the twentieth century. He embodied both the convictions of German historicism and their erosion in the face of enormous social and political change. Meinecke's *Die Entstehung des Historismus* (1936) traced the rise and major contributions of historicism and the Historical School.[38] It exhibited his conviction that historicism was one of the greatest developments in human history, especially as it broke the stranglehold of the natural-law tradition in Western thought.[39] For Meinecke, historicism provides the best access to social and historical reality, bypassing the deleterious focus on generalization and abstraction that characterized earlier historical efforts. Moreover, historicism is more than an academic method but constitutes an overarching worldview, "a guiding principle of life" for

interpreting all of human existence.[40] He, like his fellow German historicists, was optimistic about the ability of historical inquirers to maintain a
"disinterested" stance and thus to provide objective knowledge. And he, too,
thought that relativism and a fall into a chaotic "anarchy of values" can be
avoided by linking the human story to divine purpose and causality.[41]

What is significant about Meinecke for us is not so much that he continued to assert many of the convictions that earlier historicists had already
articulated, but that he also deviated from what had become accepted
historicist positions. Over against nineteenth-century Germany, moving
toward unification and celebrating its renewal of national identity, Meinecke confronted a Germany of the twentieth century that engaged disas-
trously in global conflicts and brought about the rapid unraveling of the
relatively recent German sense of identity. Meinecke, like so many other
academics, supported the First World War and the Kaiser's war policies,
interpreting them as "a cleansing of the nation's inner life."[42] And he continued throughout his life to affirm the importance of the state. Increasingly,
however, the historicist assumption about the benign and positive nature
of power seemed problematic. Historicism had linked historical individuality (including the individuality of nations and states), the centrality of the
state, and the assumption of divine direction and control together in an
affirmative theory that power is good and that historical developments are
prima facie positive. By the end of his life Meinecke had come to a deeper
awareness than any of the historians that preceded him of the "problematic
character of power," the disconnecting of any facile bond between ethics
and power and the reality of demonic in history.[43] In the twentieth century,
the historical arena might continue to be the context for human meaning and possibility, but it could no longer be assumed that it is inherently
positive or that the multiplicity of historical values work together in some
divinely coordinated movement of the good. Thus, while Meinecke did
not despair of all meaning in history, the easy optimism of much of the
Historical School was gone forever. As we will see, other developments
and thinkers would erode to an even-greater extent these early assumptions
and hopes of historicism.

Romanticism and Schleiermacher

Romanticism was a quintessential nineteenth-century movement that,
like the Historical School, emerged in significant part out of historicist
impulses. Romanticism, especially as a literary movement, would flourish

across Europe, including in Great Britain, as novelists, poets, and essayists rebelled against the symmetry, order, and appeal to reason that characterized the eighteenth century. For our purposes, the Romantic developments in Germany provide the most important connection between this movement and historicism, especially as it became expressed not only in literature but also in the theology of Friedrich Schleiermacher.

In the German context three intertwined names came to characterize much of Romanticism: Friedrich Schlegel (1772–1834), Novalis (1772–1801), and Friedrich Schleiermacher (1768–1834). Schlegel in many ways played the central role in this group—being friends with both Novalis and Schleiermacher (who knew each other's work but were not otherwise personally acquainted), Schlegel mediated between the two. All the Romantics in Germany were deeply influenced by earlier critics of the Enlightenment and the "age of reason." The writers of the *Sturm und Drang*, with their challenge to Enlightenment rationality, the early Goethe, especially in his work *The Sorrows of Young Werther* (1774), and the historicism of such thinkers as Herder all provided the backdrop against which the nineteenth-century Romantics articulated their emerging position.

A number of themes permeate the work of the German Romantics that both reflect continuity with other historicist developments as well as highlight some of the peculiarities of the movement. Like other historicists, the Romantics placed great emphasis on particularities and individuals. They sought to avoid generalities, focusing instead on the idiosyncratic and the historically unique. Nature and history, in all their vitality and irregularities, now came to the fore. Feeling, intuition, the inner life, friendship (especially with women), memory, and the importance of the past became the themes that appeared repeatedly in the literary journal *Athenaeum,* founded by Schlegel in 1778 and published for three years. Organic metaphors found expression not only in the historiography of the times but also in the literary productions of these writers. Importantly, the Romantics engaged in dialectical thinking, seeking to hold together the polarities of infinite and finite, freedom and conditionedness, and individuality and unity. For our purposes, it is the work of Friedrich Schleiermacher that gave the most influential rendering of these ideas and that would have the most significant impact upon theology and the emergent discipline that would become religious studies.

Friedrich Daniel Ernst Schleiermacher was one of the towering figures of the nineteenth century, and his influence, most notably in theology and hermeneutical theory, continues to be a focus of debate on the current scene. Schleiermacher's work exhibited many of the same influences as did Schlegel's and Novalis's. However, he was also deeply influenced by pietism and by the critical philosophy of Immanuel Kant. This combination of historicist predecessors, critical philosophy, and a strong responsiveness to the feeling dimensions of life so emphasized by pietism resulted in the most innovative religious thought of the nineteenth century.

Schleiermacher shared much with his fellow Romantics. But a central place of difference in the early stages of the movement revolved around religion. While both Schlegel and Novalis would eventually return to religion, early on they were critics of religion who interpreted Christianity as in tension with the very Romantic impulses—the desire for freedom and creativity—that they espoused so enthusiastically. Schleiermacher, while no supporter of an arid orthodoxy, sought to find a way to affirm religion. *On Religion: Speeches to Its Cultured Despisers* (1799) was his groundbreaking effort to articulate a view of religion interpreted not as in opposition to the new spirit of the nineteenth century but as the vital component that allowed that spirit to flourish.[44]

There are several components to Schleiermacher's position that have had lasting effect on the modern understanding of religion. First, he sought to distinguish his own position from a number of other options. For Schleiermacher, religion or piety is not *primarily* concerned with beliefs or with speculative proofs or with behaviors or moral precepts or with institutions such as the church. Instead, religion finds its original wellspring in the affective dimension of life, in "the immediate feeling of the Infinite and the Eternal."[45] As Schleiermacher stated, "true religion is sense and taste for the Infinite."[46] This feeling does not arise from a separate faculty of the human mind or spirit. Neither is it an emotion that comes and goes. Instead, religious feeling refers to "the immediate self-consciousness underlying all our knowing and doing."[47]

Second, for Schleiermacher such a taste and sense for the infinite is universal; it is, as historical theologian Brian Gerrish has put it, "a datum of human consciousness as such."[48] Religiousness is not, therefore, something that only a few persons possess or only one religious tradition might lay claim to while others are automatically to be rejected. Religious feeling and being human become coterminous in Schleiermacher. Thus, as the nineteenth-century world became increasingly aware of the vast multiplicity of religious traditions in the world, Schleiermacher would articulate a position urging tolerance and appreciation for the diverse fashionings of religious sensibilities.

Third, the immediate self-consciousness Schleiermacher associates with religion has a particular character. Ordinary consciousness of the finite world is always characterized by a twofold sense of freedom and conditionedness or dependency; humans always experience themselves, to some degree or another, as both agents and as beings dependent upon and constricted by their world. But permeating such experience of the world, Schleiermacher claimed, is this other self-consciousness, not of the finite but of the infinite in and through the finite. In his later great systematic work *The Christian Faith* (1821–22; revised edition 1830–31) Schleiermacher would call this the feeling of absolute dependence, the immediate self-consciousness of the fundamental relation to God in which no reciprocity, freedom, or creative activity are present.[49] Piety hence becomes identified with this consciousness of absolute dependence, unqualified by any measure of human agency or freedom, and God is interpreted as the Whence of such feeling from which and upon which all finite existence, including the world as a whole, gains its being.[50]

Schleiermacher's appeals to immediate self-consciousness, to the feeling of absolute dependence, to intuition of the infinite and eternal, and to a universalism that makes humanness and religiosity coterminous all appear lacking in historicist insight. Indeed, much of Schleiermacher's heritage, including in theology and the history of religions, has focused on these less-than-historicist dimensions of his work. But Schleiermacher, like other Romantics, sought to balance seemingly incompatible polarities, insisting on maintaining the other, more historical side of these poles. He did so in a number of important ways.

To begin with, while Schleiermacher articulated his understanding of immediate self-consciousness characterized by absolute dependence, he insisted that such consciousness never takes place apart from or in separation from consciousness of the finite world with its dual feelings of partial freedom and partial determination. For Schleiermacher, religious feeling or piety arises in the midst of life and is part and parcel of all finite existence. While the "highest grade of human self-consciousness" is qualitatively distinct from the "lower" grades, they are never separate from each other.[51] Hence, while Schleiermacher argued for a peculiarly religious dimension of human existence, he insisted that this dimension is reached only through the analysis of finite, historical forms of existence. The religious is not found in some separate, isolated realm but is part of every moment of human life.

Moreover, Schleiermacher did not just advocate the analysis of ordinary existence in order to understand the religious dimensions of individuals' lives. He also asserted that humans are fundamentally social and, therefore, that religious feelings always seek expression in community.[52] In the Fourth Speech of *On Religion* he stated, "If there is to be religion at all, it must be social, for that is the nature of man, and it is quite peculiarly the nature of religion."[53] He suggested that pious feeling always seeks "to direct others to the same subject and if possible transmit the impulse."[54] But it is not only the impulse to share that leads to the communal aspects of religion but also the fact that an individual's experience grasps only "a small part" of the religious experience.[55] The religious person must always seek others with whom to share but also from whom to learn. This recognition "urges him to give his religion full expression, and seeking his own perfection, to listen to every note that he can recognize as religious."[56]

While Schleiermacher insisted upon the universal reality of religiousness and came to assert that to be human is to be religious, he also argued that the expression of religious experience is always historical, particular, and located in specific communities and historical locales. Religious sensibility does not express itself in any uniform manner but, as he stated in *On Religion*, "fashions itself with endless variety."[57] The plurality of religions was not a problem for Schleiermacher but a sign simultaneously of the universality of religiousness and the historical and social character of its expression. Schleiermacher thus repudiated claims to "natural religion" or "religion in general" that smooth out the differences among historical communities and ignore as unimportant the cultural specificities of religious communities.[58] The "social union of the pious" is therefore always historically specific, individual, and multiple, and Christianity no less than other religious traditions is thoroughly historical in nature.

In addition and of great importance is Schleiermacher's historicizing of all religious beliefs and with them Christian theology and doctrine. Just as religious traditions and communities are the historic expression in social and communal form of religious affections, so too are the doctrines and theologies that develop within those social contexts. In his view of dogmatic theology, Schleiermacher distinguished himself both from more orthodox theologians who focused on exegesis and on the claims of those who interpreted theology's task as discerning absolute, general, or timeless truth. Instead, "Christian doctrines are accounts of the Christian religious affections set forth in speech."[59] With Schleiermacher, according to Jack Forstman, theology becomes "a descriptive and explanatory science. It describes how people motivated by Christian faith talk about their faith and it explains why they talk this way. . . . Christian theology, as Schleiermacher viewed it, is not a science or knowledge of God, man and world. It is a description of how Christian people talk about themselves, God and world as a result of what they understand to have happened to them."[60] As such, theology is a thoroughly human, historical, and empirical enterprise. It is a task *within* a tradition, concerned with the specificities of that tradition and, thus, forgoes claims to universal validity. Schleiermacher also relinquished the notion that theology, even within a tradition, can ever achieve finality. For Schleiermacher, dogmatic theology offers neither timeless nor unchanging expression of religious affections. Instead, it is the science "which systematizes the doctrine prevalent in a Christian Church at a given time."[61] It is specific not only to a religious tradition, Christianity, but also to a specific and concrete time and place in the history of that tradition. As times change, so too must theology; it must be rewritten for each new age.[62]

Thus, Friedrich Schleiermacher sought to hold together a universalism and historical particularity, a common human religious nature and individual and distinctive human traditions. Those that have followed this significant nineteenth-century figure have often emphasized one side of Schleiermacher's thought to the neglect of the other. Much of theology that identifies with Schleiermacher's vision focuses on the turn to experience and to the supposed universal dimensions of human subjectivity. Many of those thinkers who forged the History of Religion School and the perennialist approaches to religion that assume that religion is a *sui generis* reality distinct from all other modes of existence though universally present built their positions on this assumption as well. For these thinkers, historically specific expressions of religion became secondary, epiphenomenal, and less real. But for historicists Schleiermacher represents another option. He was, as Richard R. Niebuhr has insisted, among the first modern theologians to perceive that Christianity is thoroughly historical.[63] With this recognition, the theological task becomes no longer the pursuit of unchanging truth but the more modest task of detailing and systematizing the convictions of the historical community. It entails, moreover, accepting that the fruits of such work are temporary, finite, and relevant to particular times and places but continually in need of revision and new expression. It is these insights that locate Schleiermacher, at least in part, in the historicist lineage.

Hegel, *Geist,* and History

Another renowned intellectual contemporary, fellow scholar, and rival of the members of the Historical School and thinkers such as Schleiermacher at the newly inaugurated University of Berlin was philosopher Georg Wilhelm Friedrich Hegel (1770–1831). Of all the nineteenth-century developments in philosophy, Hegel's were the most ambitious, far-reaching, and influential. Central to the Hegelian vision was a speculative theory of history that was to reverberate throughout the century and beyond, especially in the critical response of Karl Marx.

Trajectories of thought and historical events similar to those that had shaped the thought of Schleiermacher and the members of the Historical School also influenced Hegel. Hegel's thought was formed out of an appreciation of Greek philosophy, a commitment to autonomous, albeit chastened, moral reason, an interest in Romanticism and its rebellion against religion and the Enlightenment, the French Revolution, and, like Schleiermacher, a commitment to the renewal of Christianity. In Hegel's hands these influences would take a distinctive form that, while making history central, would stand at odds with the assumptions and commitments of many of his historicist contemporaries.

Charles Taylor, in his significant study of Hegel, argues that Hegel's early writings exhibit a confidence that the Romantic desire for unity with nature, self, and other humans, the demands of an autonomous moral reason, and a revitalized Christianity were compatible and able to be harmonized. However, by the end of the eighteenth century, according to Taylor, Hegel had concluded that far from being easily made compatible these stood in tension—indeed, opposition—with one another.[64] It was this recognition of opposition that drove the development of the mature Hegelian philosophy.

Hegel sought to set forth a comprehensive theory of knowledge that took into account and made such opposition not a problem to be denied but the key to understanding the dynamics of knowledge and the possibility of truth. His understanding of the dialectic was foundational for his position. The dialectical process is one in which each claim is incomplete and contains contradictions and tensions. Such internal contradiction gives rise to contrary assertions that also are incomplete and internally conflicted. These in turn give rise to new ideas that contain the possibility of reconciling these differences, not by denying them or choosing one over the other, but by taking up the oppositional truths and preserving them together. In this interpretation of knowing, truth results from a process of development in which truth is emergent, not given; it is to be made, not simply discovered.

Hegel's theory of knowledge was not just a set of epistemological claims. It also the model for articulating a dynamic interpretation of reality, a new metaphysics of history, and a radically transmogrified notion of God now understood as Spirit/*Geist* or Reason. Hegel set forth a philosophy of Spirit or Reason in which all of reality, including human history, is the expression of Spirit coming to its own self-realization and self-consciousness. The world and especially history are the vehicles through which Reason develops, gains self-awareness, and attains absolute truth. Spirit or absolute reason is not something that exists over against the world; rather, the world process or history *is* the dynamic through which Spirit attains its fulfillment.

History, in the Hegelian system, is not just the site of Spirit or Reason's development. Spirit is also the telos that drives history, the internal essence of history that underlies all reality and history and that determines both the process and forms of its development. That which is manifested in all reality and history is Spirit, and Spirit is that which teleologically determines the direction and, indeed, outcome of historical development.

This world process in which *Geist* comes to self-realization and in which history is the vehicle and manifestation of Spirit is also a dialectical process in which Spirit comes to self-consciousness and freedom, not in some linear manner but through a dialectical movement in which *Geist* develops through a process of diremption ("tearing apart"), contradiction, and reconciliation. Spirit's very life and nature are this ongoing expression and reconciliation of opposites, of identity and nonidentity, of the infinite and finite, and nature and freedom.

It is within this larger philosophy of Spirit and dialectical reason that Hegel articulated his more explicit philosophy of history. While the groundwork for his metaphysical treatment of history was laid in his monumental work *The Phenomenology of Spirit* (1807), Hegel's explicit treatment of history came in a series of lectures on the philosophy of history delivered at the University of Berlin and published after his death.[65] In the lectures on world history, Hegel not only set forth this broader vision of history but also offered a comparative analysis of civilizations and detailed what he took to be the stages of development within concrete historical forms.

As is clear from above, for Hegel all of reality is the manifestation of Spirit and its drive to come to full realization. According to Taylor, for Hegel "the universe is his [Spirit's] embodiment."[66] It is especially within human history that Spirit comes to self-actualization; the aim of "world history" for Hegel, "is that the spirit should attain knowledge of its own true nature, and it should objectivise this knowledge and transform it into a real world and give itself an objective existence."[67] For Hegel, this history, too, is a dialectical process in which opposing potentialities come into existence through the various stages of human civilization, with each progressive stage embodying ever more adequate manifestations of reason and the freedom that it requires for successful realization. Hence, every epoch and civilization is to some degree the manifestation of cosmic Spirit. Sometimes such manifestation has a more conscious character as world historical figures articulate new human possibilities. Often, however, history and its central figures fulfill purposes of which they are not fully conscious; the Spirit works through the "cunning of reason" to bring about its ends and to fulfill its goals.[68] History moves on, always serving the Spirit; for Hegel, "each new individual national spirit represents a new stage in the conquering march of the world spirit as it wins its way to consciousness and freedom."[69]

Thus, all civilizations and historical periods are good and have value. However, all are not equal. History is the tale of change and progress in which new possibilities become explicit and concrete and in which old ones are supplanted. Hegel offered a detailed comparative analysis in which he traced the supposed upward development from the pre-Greeks with their union of nature and spirit, through the Jews with a transcendent and utterly separated spirit, to the Greeks and Romans in which the gods are identified with the world, to Christianity in which finally the dialectical coincidence of opposites becomes possible in the incarnation—in a God who pours Godself out into the world without being reduced to the finite. Yet, for Hegel, history has not immediately been fulfilled in Christianity. For that, Hegel turned to the history of the Germanic people, those descendants of the barbarians who superseded the Roman Empire. Here, in the historical trajectory from the Reformation to the nineteenth century, Hegel portrays the final flourishing of Reason and cosmic Spirit. It is *only here* and *finally here* that subjectivity and rational freedom can become manifested and direct not only the life of the individual but can also be embodied in the modern state. Hence, history is not only developmental and progressive; it is hierarchical as well.

It is not only that great world civilizations embody stages of the development of the cosmic Spirit. There are also stages *within* such world movements. Hegel in particular distinguished art, religion, and philosophy as progressive moments in the development of the world Spirit. Just as each civilization manifests a partially adequate dimension of the Spirit, so too do art and religion. Art is the manifestation of Spirit in sensuous form; its aim is "to make the divine immediately perceptible and to present it to the imagination and intuition."[70] Religion, for its part, in feeling and contemplation is a primary means by which "worldly existence becomes conscious of the absolute spirit."[71] Christianity is the highest form of such awareness, for in the incarnation the world Spirit becomes fully manifest in the world. Despite these achievements, art and religion are not the final vehicles for the manifestation of the world Spirit. Both art and religion, including Christianity, represent the absolute in images, pictures, and myths. There must occur another stage of development, and that takes place for Hegel in the move to philosophy, in which the truth of the incarnation, the unity of the infinite and finite, of the absolute with that which it is not, can take full conceptual form. In philosophy, specifically Hegel's philosophical system, Spirit comes to full self-knowledge and is made fully manifest in history. In the sense of completion and realization, history has now reached an end. Hence, the realization of the world Spirit, absolute knowledge, and rational freedom have all coalesced in this fullness of the historical moment.

For the purpose of locating Hegel's philosophical treatment of history in relation to historicism, it is important to highlight several dimensions of his theory. Hegel shared with many historicists a dynamic view of history in which change is central and in which any understanding of human subjectivity is tied to such historical development. But his views differ greatly as well. Whereas the theorists of the Historical School, such as Humboldt and Ranke, asserted the primacy of individual concrete facts and argued that it is with empirical realities that all understandings of history begin, Hegel prioritized the notion of Absolute Spirit from which alone an interpretation of history emerges. Moreover, while Hegel demonstrated interest in the sweep of civilizations, he had little interest in the idiosyncrasies that actually make up real history, the details of lived lives. From Hegel's perspective many of the historicists dealt with a "motley assortment of details, petty interests" and hence were incapable of discerning "a whole, a general design."[72] And for the scholars of the Historical School, Hegel's system was speculative, not empirical, imposing interpretations on history without real attention to its concrete forms. Real history appears, to Hegel's critics, as epiphenomenal and secondary.

Another point of contrast lies in Hegel's strong sense of history as progress in contrast to the more chastened view of many other historicists. In the Hegelian vision each moment is an element in the upward, if indirect, movement of reason. Furthermore, history unfolds in a necessary manner; its stages are inevitable and predetermined by the teleological pull provided by Spirit. For thinkers such as Humboldt, history has a more chaotic character and lacks such a clear telos.

Significantly, Hegel's hierarchical interpretation of civilizations and periods also is a point of contrast with many of the historicists. Whether it was Ranke's notion that all stages of history are equidistant from God or eventually Troeltsch's rejection of the attempt to prove the superiority of Christianity, other historicists offered at least partial alternatives to the Hegelian notion that in nineteenth-century German thought and society history had reached its completion. While many shared Hegel's claim that his own time represented the "birth of a new era," the accompanying assertion that this era represented the end of history, the full self-realization of the divine, seemed more problematic.

While Hegel was at odds with much of the rest of nineteenth-century historicism, he, like many other nineteenth-century historicists, did not leave religion aside. Indeed, from beginning to end, he sought to revitalize a form of Reformation-born, especially Lutheran, Christianity. So, for him, like the members of the Historical School and Schleiermacher, history gains its meaning and positive potential from God. However, while Humboldt and Ranke invoked God after the fact, so to speak, in order to mitigate the seemingly anarchic repercussions of historicism and to harmonize the chaotic impulses of diversity, Hegel, through his metaphysical treatment of history, offered a philosophical vision that made providence, predestination, and a secularized theodicy central themes. For Hegel, "reason rules the world,"[73] and hence all that emerges does so inevitably, necessarily, and benignly. The movement of reason may be indirect and its operations "cunning," but its purposes are unwavering and its outcomes are never in doubt. What appears as evil represents just one partial moment that is necessary but not final in the larger drama of historical development. Thus, Hegel developed the most articulated metaphysics of history found in the nineteenth century. As we will see, it is precisely these metaphysical pretensions that would invoke both the criticism and the continued appeal of Hegel as the nineteenth and twentieth centuries unfolded.

Ludwig Feuerbach

If the influence of Hegel has been enduring and widespread, so too have the critical reactions to his philosophical theory of history. The speculative character of his system, the epiphenomenal status of concrete history, the lingering religious and indeed mystical assumptions, the hierarchical ordering of history and its colonial ramifications, and the assumption of progress have all come under attack by later historicists and nonhistoricists alike.

There were two primary figures in the nineteenth century, Ludwig Feuerbach and Karl Marx, who challenged Hegel on many of these points while appropriating central motifs of the Hegelian corpus. These transformations of Hegel's positions have carried immense repercussions and, importantly for our purposes, contributed to the developments of historicism in the twentieth century.

Ludwig Feuerbach (1804–1872) began his academic studies as a theological student at Heidelberg but moved to philosophy albeit with a consuming interest in religion and theology. He studied at the University of Berlin, hearing both Schleiermacher and Hegel lecture. It would be Hegel, however, who captured his interest and, originally, his loyalty, influencing a number of his early writings. Eventually, however, Feuerbach became a critic not only of religion and theology but especially a challenger to Hegel's philosophy.

Feuerbach's work *The Essence of Christianity* (1841) plays the pivotal role here.[74] With this work, Feuerbach became famous and founded a new philosophy of religion that stood in opposition to Hegel's understanding of Absolute Spirit. As noted above, Hegel developed a speculative method that grounds his philosophy of history in the notion of the Absolute Spirit developing through history, including in and through the stages of religion. History is the manifestation of Spirit or Reason as it drives toward full realization and self-consciousness. Feuerbach offered a vision that essentially turned Hegel's position on its head.

First, Feuerbach argued that Hegel's understanding of the Absolute as the beginning and end of all things in reality reduces the significance of real history and even denies the importance of humanity. In contrast to Hegelian idealism, Feuerbach urged a turn to empiricism and the empirical method as the only adequate method for understanding and interpreting history. To understand history one must start with concrete material history, not abstractions or ideas.[75]

When Feuerbach applied his empirical and materialist method to religion, the result was a thoroughly naturalist and secular interpretation of religion with what, for many, seemed like clear atheistic overtones. Feuerbach asserted that what gives humans their distinct character in contrast to animals is consciousness, but of a very specific kind. The dividing line is consciousness of humans not as individuals but as members of a species, as humans; for Feuerbach, "consciousness in the strictest sense is present only in a being to whom his species, his essential nature, is an object of thought."[76] Out of this consciousness humans develop religion.

Feuerbach suggested that as individuals humans are faced with limits, are finite, and, especially, die. But as a species, he insisted, there are no such limits. Feuerbach claimed that what one person lacks another has, what one age fails to develop another does, and, in a burst of nineteenth-century optimism that could not imagine the destruction of the human species, he asserted that while every individual dies new persons are born and the species continues without end. What takes place in religion, according to Feuerbach, is an imperfect and distorted form of the human awareness of this limitless species nature. In religion, human beings, out of their awareness of limitation and finitude, and the fears and needs this awareness brings, project their own image as a species beyond themselves and then reify and deify the image and call this projection God or the divine. Whereas Hegel had made history, including religion, the manifestation of Spirit, Feuerbach claimed the opposite, asserting that the divine is the projection of historical humans and their nature.[77]

In this brief analysis of Feuerbach, three more significant elements are important to note. With Feuerbach there is not just a turn to the empirical method but an insistence that what the empirical method investigates is historical, social, and material reality. He was an early advocate of both a social anthropology and of the recognition of the material and bodily nature of human life. Feuerbach's famous dictum "you are what you eat" expressed his point clearly; it is concrete, material, sensuous existence that should be the focus of attention for understanding humanity. Later historicists often neglected such material and bodily existence and have only recently begun to think through what a fully materialist historicism might look like.

Another element that has had long-term repercussions both for historicists and many others has been Feuerbach's insistence that religion be interpreted naturally and without recourse to supernaturalistic assumptions or the covertly religious metaphysical assumptions of Hegel and others, such as representatives of the Historical School. History is not, for Feuerbach, the outcome of divine providential action à la Ranke, Humboldt, or Hegel; the notion of divine providence is the outcome of human needs, history, and action. Feuerbach, in his later works *The Essence of Religion* (1846) and *Lectures on the Essence of Religion* (1851), rejected what had come to look like another abstraction, turning away from the notion of species consciousness and insisting that religion emerges out of the human need to interpret its place within and in relation to nature. But even with this turn to nature, Feuerbach maintained his emphasis on the human need to interpret imaginatively humanity's place in reality and the importance of claiming such a historical process as humanity's own.[78]

Going along with the Feuerbachian claim of the human character of religious reality and our ideas of the divine, Feuerbach also stressed that the outcome of failing to recognize and claim these human productions results in alienation. In *The Essence of Christianity*, when God is seen as over against and different from the world, then the result is "an impoverishing of the real world."[79] In a classic statement Feuerbach observes, "to enrich God, man must become poor, that God may be all, man must be nothing."[80] In his later works Feuerbach was even more critical of religion, especially Christianity, for he saw in its otherworldly orientation a negative evaluation of finite reality and an inability to claim nature and history as our human home. It is the task of reclaiming and affirming the earth that Feuerbach set forth.

Karl Marx

Karl Marx (1818–1883), as a student at the University of Berlin, was deeply influenced by the Hegelian currents that persisted in shaping the generation of thinkers who continued Hegel's work after his death. Like Feuerbach, he identified early on with Hegel and the young Hegelians that perpetuated Hegel's legacy. But also like Feuerbach and for similar reasons, Marx would develop his own position in opposition to the fundamental assumptions of Hegelian philosophy. The result was an anthropology, a philosophy of history, and a social and an economic theory that came to be one of the most important influences on the modern period.

Over the last century there have been numerous debates about the relation of the early, more philosophically oriented Marx and the later Marx of economic and political theory fame. In relation to historicism, both require attention, but it is especially the Marxian articulation of a historically minded anthropology that reflected and contributed to historicist developments.

Underlying much of Marx's critical analysis is a theory of the human. For Marx, human nature is primarily social and historical. In contrast to the Hegelian idealists who began with notions of Spirit, Marx insisted that adequate interpretation of the human must begin with concrete, living, corporeal, and sentient human beings. And to begin here means to start with humans as historical agents who construct themselves through activity or labor. Marx concurred with the modern notion of humanity's self-creativity but interpreted this in sociohistorical terms instead of rational ones. Marx interpreted agency or creative self-activity in terms of labor rather than mental or rational processes.[81]

Human self-activity or labor emerged over time out of the necessary efforts of humans to come to terms with nature and all the forces beyond human control. Through these efforts, especially as they issued forth in the development of tools, humans created both themselves and history. As Erich Fromm has stated, for Marx, "history is the history of man's self-realization; it is nothing but the self-creation of man through the process of his work and production."[82]

Productive activity or labor is thus humanity's primary form of relationship with itself and with the rest of the world. But increasingly such labor becomes a form of alienation in which labor and its products are separated. Such alienation has existed throughout history and, according to Marx, has its roots in the division of labor, beginning with sexual distinctions between males and females. But despite its presence throughout history, alienation has reached a peak in capitalism with the complete division of labor, the primacy of private property, and rigid class distinctions and conflicts. Labor is no longer an expression of human self-creation but has turned into a meaningless process in which the products of labor exist over against their makers. Labor has become, for most humans, a matter of dehumanization and depersonalization, and estrangement is now at the heart of the social process.

Several elements in Marx's vision are important to highlight. First, Marx, on a twist of the Hegelian dialect, saw history as developing through this process of alienation and conflict and their being overcome. Conflict, especially among classes, is central to historical development.

Second, the Marxian dialectic differs from the Hegelian one in that it is material forces that drive it, not idealist ones. While Hegel also stressed diremption, conflict, and continual transformation, these are driven by developments within consciousness. For Marx, in contrast, consciousness is the result of material, primarily economic, forces, not the other way around. Often Marx sounded a deterministic note; humans create themselves and history through self-activity or labor, but such labor always takes place within the constraints of economic forces. Marx expressed this frequently in terms of his claim that the economic or material base or foundation conditions and determines what he termed the superstructure of society, including its ideological elements. Hence, Marx stressed both the agential character of human historical existence and its conditioned character. Early Marxian thought articulated more of the former, and the economic determinism of later Marx gave more weight to the latter.

Third, Marx not only had a deterministic outlook concerning developments *within* historical processes but also tended to sound, like Hegel, as though the very direction of historical development is necessary as well. Hence, capitalism, as did earlier economic forms, contains its own seeds of internal conflict that will lead to its dissolution and the emergence and eventual victory of communism. If, however, history unfolds through a kind of internal logic, its development is nonetheless a tale of progress. Conflict, tension, and alienation in the Marxian view, as in the Hegelian one, are progressive processes, leading ineluctably toward progress.

Importantly, Marx, like Feuerbach, interpreted religion as a form of human alienation. Indeed, Marx asserted that with Feuerbach's analysis the criticism of religion was complete. Where they differed was that Feuerbach interpreted religion as the source of all alienation and assumed that with its criticism human history might move toward nonalienated forms. Marx, in contrast, interpreted religion as an expression of alienation, not its source; religion reflects and protests against an alienated order. Through promises of otherworldly reward and the justification of worldly suffering, religion contributes to alienation's continuance without being its real cause. Religion's abolition is therefore necessary for the overcoming of alienation, but it is not sufficient. The real abolition of alienation requires the transformation of an alienated world order. As Marx states, "the abolition of religion as the *illusory* happiness of the people is required for their real happiness. The demand to give up the illusions about its condition is the *demand to give up a condition that needs illusions.* The criticism of religion is therefore *in embryo the criticism of the vale of woe,* the *halo* of which is religion."[83] Thus, for Marx, the real task is the one that explicates and uncovers the sources of alienation and the relation of religion to these sources. Where Marx and Feuerbach were in agreement, however, is that religion is a human product and that it reflects the realities of human historical existence.

Many elements of Marxian thought have been important for subsequent historicism. They include his insistence on the agential quality of human existence (the proclamation that we are what we make) balanced by his assertion that such agency is not free-floating but always takes place within materialist, historical, and social constraints; his emphasis upon the importance of the material conditions of life; his claim of the dependent relation of consciousness upon those conditions; and his complementary conclusion that religion, as part of the ideological superstructure that reflects those conditions, is both human and, like its causes, distorted.

As with other nineteenth-century thinkers, Marx's work has been widely assailed. On the one hand his economic theory, his views of capitalism, socialism, and communism, as well as his claims concerning the historical role of the proletariat contributed not only to intellectual debates but to actual historical movements and change; hence, his famous argument that the task is not to explain the world but to change it has had living embodiment. However, the inadequacies of much of his theory and the failure of his seemingly predictive pronouncements to materialize left Marx open to endless attacks. Still, he bequeathed much to the historicist-oriented among those that have followed, including the recognition that historicism must account for the material—including economic—dimensions of human existence; the assertion that human agency takes place within the constraints not only of tradition and language but in relation to such material forces; and the Feuerbachian-inspired insight into the human character of religion and its potential for alienation and collusion with the dynamics of power and dispossession.

Importantly, later neo-Marxist thinkers appropriated Marx's insights but creatively reworked his claims to avoid many of their particularly problematic aspects. Prominent among this group were the members of the Frankfurt Institute, which existed first in Germany and, subsequently, in exile in the United States from 1935 to 1950. Thinkers such as Max Horkheimer, Theodor Adorno, Herbert Marcuse, and Erich Fromm rethought Marxian insights while also finding vehicles to promote progressive social agendas. More recently the Birmingham School in England, through the work of such persons as Raymond Williams and those influenced by Williams, has set forth more dynamic and reciprocal notions of the relation of material forces and culture, including its ideational forms.[84] They have forsaken notions of history as inevitable progress and have developed interpretations of culture as conflictual, power-laden processes whose outcome is neither necessary nor predictable. Contemporary historicists, including theologians, have been especially appreciative of these historicized interpretations of culture that have sought to link culture and the nonideational dimensions of human existence, including economic and other material realities.[85] Hence, while Marx's fortunes have been less than stellar, both intellectually and politically, his legacy has continued to force the historically minded toward an ever-more holistic, dynamic, and nuanced interpretation of historical existence.

Biblical Criticism and David Friedrich Strauss

Commitments to historical-critical methods of inquiry and interests in philosophical versions of historicism continued to shape various intellectual disciplines and locales in the nineteenth century. Sometimes these various historicist approaches conflicted and competed with each other, as was demonstrated by the tensions between the Historical School and Hegel's metaphysics of history. At other times, scholars sought to combine the commitment to critical historical methodology and philosophical orientations to history. Biblical scholar David Friedrich Strauss was perhaps the greatest and most controversial example of such an attempt to carry forward critical methodologies in biblical criticism while simultaneously embracing philosophical, in his case Hegelian, visions of the nature of history. In so doing Strauss both embodied the historicist agenda in biblical studies and raised questions concerning its limits, especially as a resource for religious faith. Strauss's work marked a culminating point in nineteenth-century biblical criticism and brought into sharp relief the tensions engendered by historicism.

Many of these tensions had been building in the field of biblical criticism for decades. Continuing earlier developments in the study of the Bible, biblical criticism had sought its place in the modern university, reflecting its canons of research and academic ideals. Here, as in other disciplines, such commitments to critical norms functioned to complexify the relation between the study of the Bible and religious beliefs and practices. On the one hand, as John Drury states in his book *Critics of the Bible 1724–1872*, "historicism was biblical criticism's charter of freedom from ecclesiastical control."[86] On the other hand, such freedom opened up difficult questions about the nature of the past and its relation to contemporary religious realities.

The repercussions of historicist commitments were seen in the study of both the Hebrew Scriptures and the Christian Scriptures. Wilhelm Gesenius (1786–1842) pursued philological and comparative work in a manner that pushed other scholars to work with original sources. Other figures, such as W. M. L. de Wette (1773–1859), contributed to biblical criticism by utilizing critical historical methods to call into question the purported historicity of many texts, including Deuteronomy and Chronicles. Julius Wellhausen's (1844–1918) work signaled, in the words of biblical historian R. E. Clements, "a triumph of the historical movement in biblical studies" as he, like the Historical School, stressed the significance of national identity and development in the history of Israel.[87] Source criticism, literary criticism, form criticism, and redaction criticism all owe much to these nineteenth-century thinkers.

In New Testament studies the impact of historicism was also felt. This is especially the case in what is termed the Quest of/for the Historical Jesus. In many ways this first Quest (often dated from Reimarus to Albert Schweitzer) is the embodiment of the conflicting trends and commitments of nineteenth-century historicism.[88] There were what many have called the positivistic concerns of the quest, whereby biblical scholars sought to identify historical materials, original sources, eyewitness accounts (which increasingly proved to be elusive), and on the basis of such critical study to make empirical claims about Jesus and the origins of Christianity. But, while espousing positivist dreams of objective historical inquiry, many biblical scholars sought the historical Jesus for religious purposes, seeking to determine how he was the originating event that precipitated Christianity and how he was relevant for the modern period. Often, in ways not acknowledged, these two dynamics shaped the quest and colored the resultant Jesuses that the nineteenth century claimed to have discovered. Throughout the Quest's first phase many tensions were exhibited: between history as an empirical science versus religious assumptions and purposes; between the historical character of the past and the needs of the present; between the focus on individual facts and the theoretical framing that shaped the interpretive approaches to their study; and between the significance of Jesus within Christianity and the growing body of knowledge about the ancient Near East and about other ancient cultures and traditions that offered figures, scriptures, and religiously important heritages of their own that belied Christianity's traditional claims to uniqueness. And haunting the whole process were the lurking relativism and anarchy of values fed by historicism's challenge to timeless truth and to the possibility of transcultural and transtemporal judgment both within and across historical traditions.

The biblical scholar who stands out in the nineteenth century as the embodiment of many of these tensions is David Friedrich Strauss. In 1835 Strauss published his two-volume work *The Life of Jesus Critically Reexamined.* This work unleashed, as Albert Schweitzer would note, a firestorm that both "made him famous in a moment and destroyed his prospects."[89] Strauss followed the mandates of historicist thought as he sought to identify the "really historical" in the New Testament accounts of Jesus and to thereby separate the historically accurate depictions from mythic expressions of religious truth. As biblical theologian Dennis Nineham has stated,

Strauss's endeavor distanced him from both the supernaturalists who refused to problematize fantastic events, and the rationalists who attempted to clean up the biblical stories and render them in terms acceptable to modern persons. Instead, "Strauss suggested that many of the supernatural traits in the Gospels were neither to be accepted *au pied de la lettre* as the orthodox supposed, nor yet regarded with the rationalists as misinterpretations of quite ordinary occurrences, but seen as entirely legendary constructions."[90] Thus, in many ways Strauss is important for his close application of historical-critical methods and his refusal to name as historical what could not pass the muster of historical analysis.

However, Strauss did not just label much of the New Testament as myth or legend and leave it at that. He was deeply influenced by Hegelian thought and positively embraced it in contrast to Feuerbach and Marx. Strauss came to argue that myths are not just false history or bad science, but instead they embody religious truth. Strauss, perhaps more than many other questers for the historical Jesus, made a self-conscious philosophical attempt to salvage the importance of Jesus in the face of the erosion of historical claims about him. In Strauss's view, the religious truth, clothed in the mythological forms of Jesus' day, remains significant when abstracted from those forms. This truth, the Hegelian assertion that the divine entered history resulting in the divinization of the historical realm, remained even as Jesus was shorn of his historical status. The negative reactions to Strauss's work were legend, as many thinkers concluded that the philosophical salvaging of Jesus' significance was not an acceptable solution to the problems of Jesus' historicity. Thus, the Quest has continued but without resolution and often without consciousness of the various issues that plagued the first forms of historicism and continue to haunt their successive expressions.

Wilhelm Dilthey

A number of other thinkers contributed to the development of reflection about history and historicity in the nineteenth and early twentieth centuries, including Benedetto Croce (1866–1952) in Italy and R. G. Collingwood (1889–1943) in England. But two historicist figures stand out as consolidators of historicist insights and as thinkers who set the historicist problematic for the twentieth century. The first of these is Wilhelm Dilthey.

Wilhelm Dilthey (1833–1911), like so many of his predecessors, began his studies in theology but soon segued into philosophy and history. He held academic positions at Basel, Kiel, Breslau, and, finally, the University of Berlin. His work was influential in many disciplines, including philosophy, literary criticism, history, psychology, and sociology and the other social sciences. Later thinkers such as Martin Heidegger, Max Weber, and Talcott Parsons all acknowledged the importance of his work for their own understandings of human historicity and temporality and for the methodological formulation of the human sciences. Contemporary theological historicists such as Gordon Kaufman have also acknowledged the influence of Dilthey on their work.

For our purposes, there are several key historicist assumptions that find significant articulation in Dilthey's work. The first idea is his notion of a philosophy of life (*Philosophie des Lebens*). For Dilthey, the term "philosophy of life" refers to the most expansive and inclusive human project—that is, all of human activity, from the most individual to the most complex social and cultural reality. Nothing human is to be left out. But if Dilthey proposed an inclusive project he also saw the philosophy of life as severely delimited. Human reflection is to deal with human historical reality. Its concern is not timeless truth, metaphysical realities, some pure mind or realm of ideas; it is humanity and humanity alone in its manifold historical and social existence. "Life," for Dilthey, "does not mean anything other than itself. There is nothing in it that points to a meaning beyond it."[91] There is no starting point or end goal beyond human knowledge of finite human existence and its expressions; indeed, "knowledge begins in the middle," in the midst of historical existence.[92] "Every beginning is arbitrary" according to Dilthey.[93] Philosophy hence was to take its place among the other human sciences and become anthropologically centered.

To begin with experience in its various and manifold forms meant for Dilthey, like other historicists, attention to the individual and unique manifestations of life. But Dilthey was also convinced that humans do not just experience and hence know life chaotically and randomly. Humans experience and, indeed, continually create a meaningful world. As many twentieth- and twenty-first-century historicists would also argue, humans, for Dilthey, constantly organize their experience through human-created categories; art, culture, law, moral precepts, religion, literature, social systems, and so forth are all manifestations of this meaning—creating, valuing, ordering, and interpretive activity of historical human beings.

Moreover, humans do not just interpret locally, so to speak. Humans also develop overarching and comprehensive frameworks of interpretation or worldviews (*Weltanschauungen*) that give expression to an individual's and a community's basic assumptions about reality and about humanity's place in the world. Dilthey was one of the first thinkers to understand these schemes as the product of human creative historical activity and to claim for them the status of finite historical ideas. Dilthey suggested that there were three basic worldviews, which he labeled (1) naturalism or materialism (Democritus, Lucretius, Epicurus, Hobbes, modern materialism, and forms of positivism); (2) an idealism of freedom (Plato, Hellenistic-Roman philosophy, Christianity, and Kant); and (3) objective idealism (Heraclitus, forms of Stoicism, Spinoza, Leibniz, Goethe, Schelling, Schleiermacher, and Hegel).[94] Each of these provides a different interpretive approach to life, and they cannot be reduced to one another; they are alternative visions of reality, not variations on the same theme. Each is thoroughly historical, arising in history out of the human necessity to interpret life and endow it with significance and order. As historical systems, none can claim some absolute status or be proven to be finally true, correct, or adequate. For Dilthey, "philosophy is not able to grasp the world in its essence through a metaphysical system, demonstrated with universal validity."[95] Hence, all are relative, partial, and represent the most human of efforts to make sense of life. It is this historical life with which we begin and end and it is that "behind which we cannot go."[96] Dilthey's version of worldviews heralded a farewell that had been in the making throughout the nineteenth century to the quest for absolute truth or metaphysical finality.

Wilhelm Dilthey's articulation of a philosophy of life was accompanied by his preoccupation with delineating the character and methods appropriate to the human sciences in contrast to the natural sciences. As Hayden White has stated, "the intellectual history of nineteenth century Germany, if indeed not all of Europe, may be conceived as centering on the problem of defining the relation between the human sciences (*Geisteswissenschaften*) and the natural sciences (*Naturwissenschaften*)."[97] This distinction and its repercussions were of concern for many historicist thinkers of the era. But Dilthey was singular in his pursuit of the issue. According to him, the natural and social sciences share much in common; they are involved in empirical analysis, inductive methods, and so forth. But the human sciences have a fundamentally different subject matter—human life and experience. And this subject matter requires its own methods.

In developing his views of the human sciences, Dilthey first reiterated a distinctively historicist claim heard first in Vico: humans can understand human existence because it is human-made and the human inquirer exists as a participant within human history. We can know other persons, places, and times because we know our own experience; human inquirers are always already part of their subject of study; they are "familiar" with their own human history and hence can know other human history. As we will see, Ernst Troeltsch will make a similar claim that historical knowledge is possible because of the possibility of analogy—like recognizing like. But this familiarity is never complete, which is why humans are always engaged in a process of creative interpretation. What is familiar is also different and strange. Dilthey stated, "Interpretation would be impossible if expressions of life were completely strange. It would be unnecessary if nothing strange were in them. It lies, therefore, between these two extremes. It is always required where something strange is to be grasped through the art of understanding."[98]

Hence, for Dilthey knowledge of the human world is possible because the knower is immersed within history and is a historical being him/herself. Because of that we not only *can* but also *must* engage that which is simultaneously familiar and strange, and we do so through the process of interpretation or understanding (*Das Verstehen*). Such interpretation requires empathy (*Einfühlung*), in which the interpreter can enter into the world of the other, for such a world has its own value and exhibits its own coherence. And the interpreter can make such a leap because she/he too is historical and shares a common humanity with the other no matter how different. As philosopher David Couzens Hoy argues, in Dilthey's view, when interpreting the past, especially a text from the past, "the interpreter must transpose himself into the author's horizon so as to relive the creative act. The essential link between author and reader, no matter how great the time distance, is a common humanity, a common psychological makeup or genetic consciousness, that grounds the intuitive ability to empathize with other persons."[99]

But understanding also requires several other important elements. For Dilthey, to understand the past or that which is different means to recognize the context in which events took place, ideas emerged, or cultures arose. Empathy alone will not suffice. Understanding always entails contextualization. The notion of abstract ideas, not historically located, was thoroughly rejected by Dilthey.

Of equal importance is Dilthey's rejection of a detached knower, the "extinguished self" of Ranke. Dilthey's empathetic knower is also thoroughly historical, located within the horizons of his/her own time and place. The knower's own historicity is as paramount as that of what is known. As literary critic Claire Colebrook states, for Dilthey "the historian's task would always be conditioned and delimited by his or her own historical position which would not in itself permit of ultimate explication."[100] In the twentieth century, Hans-Georg Gadamer, perhaps more than any other thinker, would take up these issues most fully in his analysis of hermeneutics or the processes of interpretation, in which the horizons of the knower and the object of interpretation are different and there is no such thing as a presuppositionless knowledge. And Gadamer would, like other twentieth-century historicists, take Dilthey's recognition of difference more seriously than his emphasis on empathy as well as extend Dilthey's acknowledgment of the situated character of all interpretation.[101]

Dilthey's legacy is therefore somewhat ironic. He wanted to develop a clear understanding of the human sciences as *science*. He distinguished their subject matter and methods and asserted, through his epistemological investigation, that historical knowledge is possible; indeed, for him, the last word is not the relativity of our claims or our worldviews but, as he puts it, "the sovereignty of the mind over against every single one of them."[102] But despite this expectation that humans can "present systematically the relation of the human mind to the riddle of the world and life," he also continually undermined any claims to absolute validity, even of these speculations concerning human historicity.[103] The overwhelming implications of Dilthey's historicist claims are relativistic in nature. No human experience and no human claim about experience escape time and place and the limited and incomplete nature of history. Philosophy, religion, art, law, and so forth are all human constructions, attempts to endow life with meaning and value. They will never be otherwise. Thus, Georg Iggers suggests that "a very disturbing contradiction runs through all Dilthey's writings. . . . On the one hand, he attempted to provide historical and cultural studies with firm epistemological foundations, and throughout his life he maintained the firm conviction that this could be achieved. On the other hand, his examination of consciousness led him to the conclusion that all knowledge is radically subjective."[104] Or, again, as Charles Bambach notes, "Dilthey's work is marked by this persistent tension between the claims of scientific knowledge for universal validity and the finitude of temporal, historical being."[105]

The implications of Dilthey's dilemma contributed to the crisis that historicism engendered. Indeed, throughout his own work the language of "crisis, anarchy, contradiction, and anxiety" are found.[106] Twentieth-century and now twenty-first-century thinkers have struggled with a variety of ways to reconcile the historicity of ideas with desires for validity and adequacy, the locatedness of knowers with the quest for understanding of others, and the need for judgment and evaluation in a world without absolute norms. We will soon turn to those developments, but before doing so we must explore the figure who in many ways represented the culmination of this phase of historicism and whose work accentuates, especially for those interested in religion and theology, the crises that historicism engendered.

Ernst Troeltsch

Ernst Troeltsch (1865–1923) represents in many ways the final and fullest expression of historicism as it entered the twentieth century. A prolific writer in many fields, Troeltsch was to become influential in theology, history, social history, sociology, and ethics. His impact has been especially strong in the study of religion and theology. As theologian John Cobb has put it, "Troeltsch became, reluctantly, the first great Christian relativist," bequeathing to those who followed the full relativistic implications of historicism.[107] Much of twentieth-century thought was an attempt to come to terms with or evade those implications.

Troeltsch studied first at Erlangen but found the theology there too traditional. He moved to Göttingen where the great liberal theologian of the late nineteenth century, Albrecht Ritschl, held court. Ritschl argued strongly for a this-worldly, ethical Christianity in which God and the world are not separated, and the goal of Christian belief and action is the transformation of the concrete historical world, the bringing of the kingdom of God on earth. Ritschl based his claims upon normative dogmatic assumptions and, while oriented toward history as the realm of Christian life, he did not see history as the place that yielded the normative vision in the first place. Troeltsch would find the Ritschlian emphasis upon ethics and the world impressive, but he would strenuously repudiate the perspective's dogmatic orientation.

A second influence at Göttingen was the emerging History of Religion School, whose influence would be evident throughout Troeltsch's life. These thinkers, including professor of Oriental languages Paul de Lagarde, and Old Testament professor Bernard Duhm, sought to move toward a study of religion not beholden to the dictates of dogmatic theology. They stressed a growing interest in comparison and in the treatment of different religious traditions in a similar fashion. The dogmatic orientation of Ritschl and his followers was rejected, and there was a decisive turn to history. However, the History of Religion School also exhibited another idealist and nonhistoricist strain that Troeltsch both resisted and also continued to embody throughout his work. For the loose members of the History of Religion School, religion was seen as the history of Spirit as it "manifested itself in the great 'web of history' in the religious experiences and personalities of the past."[108] The emphasis continued the earlier nineteenth-century interest in piety, inwardness, and primordial and immediate experiences.[109] Such an emphasis, which stretched from Schleiermacher to the History of Religion School to thinkers such as Rudolf Otto and Mircea Eliade, has come to be seen by many contemporary thinkers as a profound betrayal of more historicist assumptions. As we will see, the tension between these assumptions and what theologian Mark Chapman has called the "mystical solution" plagued Troeltsch's work as well.[110]

For Troeltsch, the defining characteristic of the modern age was the emergence of historical consciousness and with it the development of a historical method for approaching all things human. There are no areas of human life that are not affected by this way of viewing human reality. But while nothing human escapes the repercussions of historicity, the impact of recognizing such historicity was devastating for religion in general and especially for the traditional claims of Christianity, leading to "the disintegration of the Christian world of ideas."[111] According to Troeltsch, "once applied to the scientific study of the Bible and church history, the historical method acts as a leaven, transforming everything and ultimately exploding the very form of earlier theological methods."[112]

Troeltsch gave early expression to this method in an essay attacking his Ritschlian opponents and their dogmatic orientation. The early essay "Historical and Dogmatic Method in Theology" (1898) set out to undermine the dogmatic case and to articulate the central principles of the historical method. According to Troeltsch, the Ritschlians dealt with the challenges of historical criticism by focusing on particular problems, but they utterly failed to grasp the larger challenge that historical consciousness raised for religious claims. His opponents, in this case Ritschlian theologian Friedrich Niebergall, took the "authoritarian concept of revelation for granted" and regarded "anything beyond Christianity as merely 'natural décor.'"[113] In contrast, the recognition of historicity and the methodological implications that follow required a new attitude and approach: "Like the modern natural sciences, [the historical method] represents a complete revolution in our patterns of thought vis-à-vis antiquity and the Middle Ages. As these sciences imply a new attitude toward nature, so history implies a new attitude toward the human spirit and its production in the realm of ideas."[114]

This new attitude was given expression in the historical method that Troeltsch argued is best described through the explication of three major principles. The first aspect of Troeltsch's historical method is what he termed the "habituation on principle to historical criticism."[115] Such an approach brings all traditions under historical scrutiny, refusing to protect or elevate any beyond the reach of historical inquiry. The result of this approach is the loss of the capacity to make certain or absolute claims. Troeltsch voiced this principle by arguing that historical criticism "brings a measure of uncertainty to every single fact."[116] The relation between the present and past events is real but always "partly obscure."[117] To base religious belief on any single event in the past becomes, therefore, impossible; the relationship between contemporary believers and earlier persons and events is always mediated through the present; it is never direct or certain.[118] Probability, not certitude, is the hallmark of critical historical reflection in relation to religion as it is to all other historical realities.[119]

The second aspect of historical method that Troeltsch raised up is two-sided. On the one hand, he asserted, as did so many other historicists, the unique character of historical events and facts, "the originality of the particular historical fact."[120] But such originality does not rule out, on the other hand, the possibility of historical knowledge. Rather, through the process of analogical thinking, contemporary historical critics recognize both that original events in the past are analogous to similar ones in their own context and to ones in other historical eras and milieux. What this means for Troeltsch is that, indeed, historical knowledge is possible but that the isolation of any historical event or personage as somehow transcending the vicissitudes of history is ruled out. The dogmatic moves of claiming the complete distinctiveness of Jesus or of the originating events of Christianity are no longer acceptable for those committed to the historical method.

The third dimension of the historical method also rules out the strategies of isolation so often utilized by traditional Christian theology. This principle, what Troeltsch termed *correlation*, insists that all historical events, while particular and individual, are also interconnected and that "their evaluation and judgment no less than their explanation and descriptions must begin with the total context."[121] Again, with this principle Troeltsch resisted what he took to be the dogmatic removal of religious events and personages from history and the attempt to guarantee their truth by appeal to explicit and sometimes covert supernatural sources.[122] The historicist perspective, in contrast, locates all historical events within the matrix of interconnected historical existence, and any claims for validity must thus be made without recourse to the supernatural or through the vitiating of history itself.

When these principles have been applied to Christianity and especially to its dogmatic defenders who assume its uniqueness and superiority on nonhistorical bases, the result is devastating. Rather than being unique or self-evidently true, "Christianity, too, must be regarded as an entity to be explained and evaluated in relation to the total context of which it forms a part."[123] Whatever judgments are to be made must be historically informed judgments in which "standards of value cannot be derived from isolated events but only from an overview of the historical totality."[124] Hence, Christianity and other religions are thoroughly historicized, viewed comparatively, and evaluated within the context of a broad and inclusive history. Thus, theology, for Troeltsch, takes its place within the history of religion and forgoes the pretensions of traditional dogmatic orientations.[125]

Troeltsch continued his assault on nonhistorical approaches to religions, including Christianity, in *The Absoluteness of Christianity and the History of Religions*.[126] According to Troeltsch, the modern view of history provides a "comprehensive view of everything human."[127] It orients us to "the development of peoples, spheres of culture, and cultural components."[128] Importantly, it "dissolves all dogmas in the flow of events."[129] When modern persons adopt such a historical perspective, the results are far-reaching, especially for the claims of superiority, uniqueness, and absoluteness proffered by the representatives of religions, specifically Christianity.

Troeltsch directed his critical eye toward two main attempts to claim a special status for Christianity. The first approach to be repudiated is the supernatural apologetic of traditional dogmatic theology, which he had already challenged in his seminal essay on method. This approach predicates its claims about Christianity on nonhistorical events, such as miracles, revelations, and subjective, nonpublic experiences. Dogma takes precedence over history, and truth is taken to be derived directly from God, not history. Modernity, with its historicist commitments, can no longer, for Troeltsch, advocate such a perspective: "Thus the modern idea of history marks the end of dogmatic conceptualization which hypostatizes naïve claims to validity with a few comparatively simple notions such as revelations or truths of natural reason."[130] The apologetic strategies that isolated Christianity are now ruled out, and Christianity must be seen as one religion among many.

But it was not only the attempts to isolate Christianity by appeal to nonhistorical bases that Troeltsch rejected. With equal strength, albeit more sympathy, Troeltsch also repudiated the attempts to safeguard Christianity's absoluteness by other modern thinkers, such as Hegel and Schleiermacher, who simultaneously invoked history and at the same time introduced nonhistorical principles into the analysis. Troeltsch labeled this approach, widespread in his era, the evolutionary apologetic. This perspective seemingly embraces history. History is treated as "causally and teleologically as a single whole."[131] Within history the religious principle (for instance, Hegel's Spirit) moves ever forward, unfolding through various historical moments or eras, until it reaches fruition and completion at the final stage of history, especially, for Christians adopting this view, in modern Christianity. All religions have value, while at the same time Christian absoluteness can still be confirmed. For Troeltsch, this approach only pretends to take history seriously. Over against this modern approach, Troeltsch maintained the problematic nature of the notion of a universal principle that governs individual historical realities.[132] He rejected the idea that religions develop through graduated forms, each new one advancing on the last in a linear fashion. Instead, he insisted that cultures and religions developed in parallel fashion, not like rungs on a ladder. Importantly, Troeltsch asserted, Christianity is, like other religions, a historical phenomenon, whose various forms reflect the conditions of its location in space and time. Thus, he could state, "it is also evident that Christianity in every age, and particularly in its period of origin, is a genuinely historical phenomenon—new, by and large, in its consequences, but profoundly and radically conditioned by the historical situation and environment in which it found itself as well as by the relations it entered into in its further development."[133] For Troeltsch, the result of a historicist approach is the recognition that "history is no place for 'absolute religions' or 'absolute personalities.' Such terms are self-contradictory."[134]

While Troeltsch critically distanced himself both from traditional dogmatic efforts and from the evolutionary apologetics of liberal theology, he did not conclude that there are no criteria by which to judge historical realities. Instead, he argued for the historical and comparative analysis of religions, which he believed would yield a set of relatively few values and norms that then in turn might be used to make judgments. Quickly dismissing, like most of his fellow European thinkers, polytheism and other "lower stages of religion," Troeltsch narrowed the higher historical possibilities to the "personal" religions of Judaism, Islam, and Christianity on the one hand and the "impersonal" religions of Hinduism and Buddhism on the other. And finally, for Troeltsch, such comparative analysis can yield the judgment that Christianity is the highest religious truth, embodying the possibilities of the highest religious life revolving around the ideas of God, the world, soul, and the higher life beyond this world.[135] Importantly here, Troeltsch sought to hold together the historicity of such religions while also pointing to tendencies toward an absolute goal. In other writings Troeltsch utilized language of a religious *a priori* or *essence* that somehow is present in the relative historical moment. Such language, hearkening to the history-of-religion essence talk and the Hegelian notion of Spirit, Mark Chapman suggests represents an ongoing tension in Troeltsch that was never fully resolved.[136]

But even when Troeltsch used this language of essence or religious principle, he often applied a caveat that, when thoroughly carried through, pushed his position away from unifying notions and toward ever-greater particularities and the relativity of values these imply. In *The Absoluteness of Christianity and the History of Religions* he argued that while comparison is possible, and while a criterion would emerge from "the religion that is strongest and most profound,"[137] there is always an element of decision and personal conviction in discerning this criterion. Human historical beings are always engaged not only in discerning value in history but also in subjectively deciding value for themselves. Hence, for Troeltsch, humans can "obtain a criterion that will enable us to choose among competing historical values," but such choice is always "a personal, ethically oriented, religious conviction acquired by comparison and evaluation."[138]

Troeltsch's grappling with the issues presented by historicism was further explored in the collection of his writings on the philosophy of history published in 1922 as *Der Historismus und seine Probleme (Historicism and Its Problems)*. In this work, the third volume of his collected writings, Troeltsch sought to balance the reality of contingent history, with all its finite particularities, and the ongoing concern for more transcendent and universal norms and criteria of judgment. This lingering desire to hold together transcendent and less-than-historical values and norms with the contingencies of history embodied the crisis that came to confront historicism and, simultaneously, the failure of its proponents to overcome this crisis. These Troeltschian efforts both illustrated the growing challenges posed by historicism and also pointed to the less and less acceptable theological and metaphysical attempts to avoid the full implications of historicism.

By the end of his life Troeltsch would voice significant doubts about the comparative project that had engaged him earlier and about the possibility of discerning norms in history, or beyond history, that can be applied across traditions. In the essay "The Place of Christianity among the World Religions," written shortly before his death in 1923 and published post-humously, Troeltsch reviewed the arguments of his earlier book on the absoluteness of Christianity and found his own resolution of the problem lacking.[139] He was more and more convinced of the historically particular character of traditions and less assured that these hold much in common. What emerged from within history are the particular values of individual cultures and traditions, not norms and criteria that inform all higher religions that can be applied across time and space. Humans can make judgments about the validity of a tradition "for us," but the possibility of transcultural or transreligious judgment seems remote. Troeltsch's legacy finally stressed not the metaphysical solution to the challenge of historicism nor his more historicist attempts to solve historicism's problems but the multiplicity of historical values, the particularity of their formations and expressions, and the difficulty of establishing anything other than local judgments. Thus, the various solutions Troeltsch articulated throughout his life would seem for his heirs less and less plausible as the twentieth century witnessed the full anarchy of historical values, and he, therefore, bequeathed to those who followed not the overcoming of the crisis of historicism but its burdens.

The Crisis of/in Historicism

This chapter has demonstrated that historicism, in its myriad forms, came to permeate much of the nineteenth century in Europe, especially Germany. By so doing it marked deep and pervasive changes in Western thought. While many of the assumptions and commitments formulated during the Enlightenment continued to influence Western understandings of reality and to drive the modern Western project, they were now joined by alternative interpretations that shaped a different mode of modernity, a form steeped in the recognition of human historicity and its implications for all areas of life. The negation of the past and of tradition prevalent in the Enlightenment was replaced by a profound sense of the role of the past in human experience. The general and the universal were repudiated in the name of the particular and the individual; commitment to universal values was now replaced by adherence to the traditions and values of the nation and the *Volk*, and inhabitants of particular locales, languages, and histories replaced the cosmopolitan world citizen. The search for timeless truth and absolute certainty was increasingly forgone as the historicity and relativity of human claims to truth were acknowledged. And the methods of science were now complemented by the historical methods of the emerging disciplines of history and other social sciences.

The implications of these developments for many areas of intellectual life including philosophy, theology, and the growing study and interpretation of religions other than Christianity, were far reaching. While the importance of the past, of origins, and of founding documents and figures increased, simultaneously their accessibility seemed problematized as critical studies raised questions about the authenticity, the conditions of production, and the capacity for contemporary interpreters to know and understand the past. Precisely as the past was rehabilitated its authority was being undermined. Accompanying these challenges to the authority of the past, demonstrated by the humanizing of Jesus and the broad-based criticism of the historical reliability of biblical texts, was the ever-intensifying attack on the remnants of the supernaturalistic worldview that had characterized so much of earlier Western history. Modern science, especially as it articulated an evolutionary set of presumptions, and nineteenth-century historicism collaborated in a double-pronged assault on lingering appeals to nonhistorical revelation, miraculous forms of inner experience, and transtemporal divine realities. Moreover, as the Western world's colonial ambitions expanded the presence and role of the European powers around the globe, the side effect was greater knowledge of other cultures and religions and, with this, the inevitable questioning of Christianity's uniqueness and superiority. Theology, reflecting and responding to these trends, began, from Schleiermacher onward, to formulate a self-understanding in more historicist terms, now no longer preoccupied with the search for absolute truth but for contemporary expressions of religious insights, experiences, and practices that were to be seen as historically relative claims pertinent to their own time and place.

Nineteenth-century German and European historicism contributed in a major manner to the recognition of the conditioned, located, particular, and relative character of all human thought and experience. But for much of the century the great thinkers of the nineteenth century did not follow through on the most challenging of the implications of historicism. When the historians of the Historical School confronted, for example, the sheer multiplicity of human values, they repeatedly invoked a benign divine reality to harmonize history. Or again, in the monumental philosophy of history of Hegel, the telos of divine power continued to motivate the development of the historical process. Divine providence continued, despite the historicist undermining of nonhistoricist renderings of God, to haunt historicism from Herder to the mystical side of Troeltsch.

Going along with the continued invocation of divine providence to rescue history from anarchy and chaos was an almost inexplicable failure to apply the full impact of historicism to the situation of contemporary knowers. Hence, the scholars of the Historical School contextualized all objects of their study, relativized the ancient peoples and texts they scrutinized, and simultaneously upheld their own claims to objectivity and neutrality. While thinkers such as Troeltsch called for the historicizing of all human experience and knowledge, the implications of this call for the status of historicists' own claims were often lost.

By the end of the nineteenth century and the beginning of the twentieth century the full implications of historicism had begun to be felt. Historicism began to be experienced not as the cause of celebration and the grounds for at least a cautious optimism about humanity's ability to control its destiny but as the instigator of a crisis that it no longer had the means to overcome. History, which decades earlier provided the source of art, humanistic scholarship, and cultural identity, now emerged as a burden. Divine providence, metaphysics, rationality's capacity for objective knowledge, history as an arena providing its own clear-cut criteria for judgments of cultures, religions, and political organizations—all these became less and less compelling. As historicism and progress had once been linked, now historicism and crisis seemed inevitably intertwined. And by 1914 the celebration of the particular in the form of national cultures devolved into the ascendancy of German nationalism and world war.

The crisis of historicism had many ramifications. For our purposes, the theological response known as neoorthodoxy, epitomized in the work of Karl Barth, is the most significant development that occurred in European theology. Barth repudiated the nonhistoricist side of nineteenth-century liberal theology in its Schleiermachian appeal to religious experience. He maintained the radical relativism of all human experience and claims to knowledge that Schleiermacher had moved toward. But rather than grounding those relative claims in some ahistorical experience, Barth sought a new certainty in an appeal to a thoroughly nonhistorical, radical revelation. The crisis engendered by historicism was, for Barth, resolved by a renewed invocation of supernaturalism and of an utterly transcendent God untainted by the relativity of history. What history could no longer provide, radical revelation offered, though in a manner that would undermine all human arrogance about humanity's own capacities.

Barthian thought and neoorthodoxy remained powerful responses to the developments of the nineteenth century for much of the twentieth century. But eventually the Barthian appeal to ahistorical sources for truth and meaning would erode in the face of the submerged but lingering forms of historicism. And while neoorthodoxy found significant expressions in the United States, there were other, far more historicist developments in America that embodied historicist perspectives and alternative forms of historicism, which lacked many of the problems of their German progenitors. It is to these early twentieth-century developments in the United States that we now turn.

3

Historicism in America

The American Context

Many accounts of historicism focus exclusively on Germany and, occasionally, on the wider European context of the nineteenth century. As the previous chapter has demonstrated, historicism did indeed flourish in those milieus. Europe was not the only site of historicism's development, however, and German historicism was not its only form of expression. In America, too, historicism came to take root and, in this context, different versions of historicism rose up providing both resources and challenges for today.

The nineteenth century in Europe and especially in the emerging German nation-state played a pivotal role in shaping historicism's rise and contours. So, too, did the realities of the United States of America contribute to what historicism would come to look like on these shores. American historicism had deep roots in America's history, but it came to the fore in the aftermath of the Civil War as the nation struggled with its identity in the face of widespread civil discord and devastation. New economic realities confronted the United States and large shifts in demographics occurred as people moved from rural areas to cities and significant waves of immigrants changed the American population.

These contextual particularities issued forth in a particularly American brand of historicism. It was a historicism explicitly linked to the emerging American philosophy of pragmatism, a philosophy in which classical metaphysics was foregone in lieu of a practical focus on time- and place-bound results and a creative sense of problem solving. American historicism was respectful of the past but steadfastly oriented toward a new and emerging future. This form of historicism also came to be aligned not only with pragmatism but also with the open embrace of modern science and, with it, a new naturalism. While the Germans often bolstered their historicism with appeal to an increasingly discredited supernaturalism, the American historicists openly argued not only for a new view of philosophy but also for new views of theology and especially for the reconstruction of ideas of God along naturalistic lines that cohered with evolutionary science.

The proponents of historicism, pragmatism, and naturalism also over-whelmingly associated their views with what they took to be central to the American project: a commitment to democracy. Such a commitment was not always easily or fully realized as thinkers such as W. E. B. Du Bois, John Dewey, and Mordecai Kaplan asserted in their struggles to enlarge the democratic pro-cess in the face of legacies of racism, anti-Semitism, and a host of exclusionary beliefs and policies that haunted the United States as it moved toward a more racially, ethnically, and religiously diverse twentieth-century nation. Yet for each of the thinkers we will examine in this chapter, historicism, pragmatism, and naturalism also entailed a commitment not to the appeal to supernatural truths or to the historically enshrined power of the few but to an ever-widening empowerment of the many to debate and decide the future.

Finally, the Americans, working within a more diverse context than Europe, in a nation of immigrants, former slaves, and native inhabitants, came to have a far more global perspective than did the Germans. Identity and affiliation would remain particular and concrete but would transcend the confines of soil and blood. Internally, America was diverse and ever-increasingly so as wave after wave of immigrants migrated to this nation. But thinkers such as Du Bois would insist as well on the importance of a wider global context of modern capitalism and the dynamics of empire. Both because of the internal realities of the United States and the growing recognition of global interconnections the analysis of power also came to play a much greater role in twentieth-century American historicism than it did in the nineteenth-century-inspired historicism of Germany and Europe. Thus, historicism, pragmatism, and naturalism would be linked on the American scene with a commitment to democracy and to radically inclusive and liberative processes. It is to this American version of the his-toricist project that we now turn.

William James, Historicism, and the Emergence of Pragmatism

William James (1842–1910) has been a towering figure in American thought. The product of an unconventional and eclectic education in the United States and Europe, the son of idiosyncratic religious thinker Henry

James Sr. and sibling of Alice James and Henry James Jr., James was exposed to many of the developments in American thought, including the Emersonian transcendentalism that shaped the early to mid-nineteenth century. James, moreover, came of age as the Civil War raged in the United States, as science, especially Darwinian evolutionary theory, challenged older conceptions of reality, and as the rising middle class in the United States sought new interpretations of the individual, nature, and the social realm. In his education and his life James incorporated many of the currents prevalent in his age. Recipient of a medical degree from Harvard, James never taught or practiced medicine. Instead, he went on to teach, successively, physiology, experimental psychology, and eventually philosophy. He became well known not only in these fields but in particular as an interpreter of religious experience and as an articulator of the emerging philosophical perspective known as pragmatism.

James, in a manner somewhat analogous to Schleiermacher, holds an ambiguous place in any recounting of historicism. As we will see, James had a profound sense of the historicity of experience and of ideas that led him to emphasize contingency, fallibility, and the need for ongoing revisions in all arenas of human life. Such a sense would also lead him to propose pragmatism as both the best method for adjudicating disputes and for interpreting the meaning of truth. This linking of historicism and pragmatism is an important development that will be seen to continue especially in contemporary theological reflection. However, James also set forth a metaphysical vision, labeled radical empiricism, which, especially when linked to more mystical versions of religious experience, has appeared to many contemporary thinkers to be a repudiation of historicist insights and one more strategy for protecting religion from critical and historical analysis and understanding. We will turn first to James's more historicist understanding of ideas and his pragmatist theory of truth and then explore his articulation of radical empiricism.

Historicism and Pragmatism

William James was, in relation to every dimension of his thought, a thinker profoundly focused on experience in its fullness, plurality, and concreteness. James, in his essay entitled *Pragmatism* (1907), urged not an interest in some supposed unchanging or eternal truth but attention to "this broad colossal universe of concrete facts, on their awful bewilderments, their surprises and cruelties, on the wildness which they show."[1] In contrast to what he labeled the "simple, clean, and noble" world of the philosopher, he commended the more chaotic world of the "street," the world of lived experience.[2] "The world of concrete personal experiences to which the street belongs is multitudinous beyond imagination, tangled, muddy, painful and perplexed."[3] James argued that it is to "this actual world of finite human lives" that our reflection must turn and to which we must make some "positive connection."[4]

When James turned to this concrete world of experience, he found a historical world. In his work *A Pluralistic Universe* (1909), James proclaimed, "I am finite once for all, and all the categories of my sympathy are knit up with the finite world *as such*, and with things that have a history."[5] The world of finite creatures is the historical world in which there is nothing, including God, which "is great or static or eternal enough not to have some history."[6] This focus on the world of finite reality led James to argue for letting go of categories such as the absolute and philosophical perspectives such as idealism and rationalism that ignore the fundamental historicity and finitude of existence. Thus, he called for "exorcising the absolute" that "de-realizer of the only life we are at home in," and for developing an empirically minded philosophical outlook appropriate to human historical existence.[7]

When we turn "toward facts," how are we to understand our ideas, concepts, and beliefs? It is in relation to how we know the world and how we should understand our ideas about the world and our experience that James sounded his strongest historicist note. First, James always maintained something of a realist stance. He took it for granted that humans encounter and exist within a real world that exerts pressure and limitations upon any interpretation of it. Though often accused of portraying a world of our own invention, James repeatedly asserted that he was an epistemological realist and stated in his work *The Meaning of Truth* (1909) that "there could be no truth if there is nothing to be true about."[8] Having argued this, however, James continually repudiated notions that ideas mirror an unchanging reality and that truth consists in the correspondence between human ideas and the reality they reflect. He noted that up until the 1850s notions of ideas as copies of reality were prevalent but that as the modern era emerged with the multiplication of theories such "replica" notions of truth were undermined.[9] In their stead, he offered an understanding of human ideas and human knowledge, including what humans call truth, in terms that echo clear historicist sentiments.

For James, ideas, concepts, and beliefs, including both scientific and religious ones, are thoroughly human and, as such, finite, contingent, and fallible, just like the world of which they are part. In particular, James saw these as human constructions that emerge in history and in turn contribute to ongoing developing reality. In relation to our exploration of historicism James can be seen to have developed a number of important insights in relation to this process. First, he had a deep sense of the importance of tradition and the past. For James, human ideas do not spring *de novo* into existence. Instead, they develop over time and change and are transformed as experience stresses them, demanding revision. Humans, according to this perspective, build up stores of ideas, beliefs, and theories through which we interpret our world. As historical beings we are always inheriting the ideas that came before us. But in a dynamic, historical world of ongoing change, experience is always straining, contradicting, stressing our ideas. New ideas, new versions of the truth, emerge as humans amend and revise their inherited traditions in light of new experiences. Here James assumed the importance of inheritance and suggested the importance of continuity: "New truth is always a go-between, a smoother-over of transitions. It marries old opinion to new fact so as ever to show a minimum of jolt, a maximum of continuity."[10]

But while this interpretation of the knowing process points to the importance of the past, to the funded character of experience, it does not rule out novelty or revision. Indeed, ever-new ideas and new conceptions of truth are the product of this ongoing interplay of experience and human interpretive activity. In the Jamesian view of things, novelty and continuity are not contradictory but are co-implicated, requiring each other in a historical universe. The new is grafted on the old, but it is indeed new, creative, and novel.

James stressed as well what might be termed the perspectival character of historical experience and knowledge. Humans do not know everything equally or passively reflect what is before us. Instead, we attend to some things while ignoring others, highlight certain realities while downplaying others that might as well have demanded our attention. The ideas through which we interpret reality, the theories we utilize to order and arrange it, the nouns and adjectives we use to describe experience all determine in part what we experience and know, and they do so not out of some neutrality but out of the interests, desires, and needs of the human knowers and experiencers. Therefore, James proclaimed, "What we say about reality thus depends on the perspective into which we throw it."[11] According to James, it is impossible to eliminate this "human contribution."[12] "Our nouns and adjectives are all humanized heirlooms, and in the theories we build them into, the inner order and arrangement is wholly dictated by human consid-erations."[13] This is the case even for mathematics, logic, and physics; these, too, are "fermenting with human arrangement," following "massive cues of preference."[14]

James thus suggested that human experience and knowledge are fraught with interest and that these shape all we know and experience: "Human motives sharpen all our questions, human satisfactions lurk in all our answers, all our formulas have a human twist."[15] James never carried out a full examination of human motivations and interests in terms of what later historicists would see as the interlocking of power and knowledge, of inter-ests in a less benign interpretation. Nor did he tie such human processes to social context to the extent that later thinkers would. Nonetheless, his asser-tion that "the trail of the human serpent is thus over everything" has stood as a profound historicist insight.[16] It is also one that pushed James in the direction of a pragmatic method and a pragmatic interpretation of truth.

In many ways, James's significance for historicism lies in his articulation of pragmatism. Charles Sanders Peirce was the originator of both the term *pragmatism* and the pragmatic method. For Peirce, this method related most centrally to science and entailed a method for ensuring scientific pre-cision in the laboratory. He did so by identifying the meaning of a concept through the explication of its possible effects. James had a broader and, indeed, looser understanding of pragmatism, an understanding from which the more strictly scientifically minded Peirce would distance himself.

For James, pragmatism, as a method of inquiry, is particularly helpful in settling metaphysical disagreements. These arguments about the nature of reality itself cannot be settled by comparing competing theories to some readily available world in order to see which theory corresponds more closely. If this is difficult about individual concepts, it is impossible about metaphysical systems. Instead, James suggested that humans must ask not about correspondence nor about such matters as the origin of ideas but, rather, what difference to lived experience does holding one vision of real-ity make in contrast to holding another interpretation. As contemporary pragmatist Richard J. Bernstein has stated, the question is, What is the difference that makes a difference?[17] If the effects of espousing and living out of different assumptions about reality are negligible then these disputes are, as James put it, "idle."[18] If, however, there are different ramifications for concrete life and action then we have significant disputes. Philosophy should thus turn its attention to these concrete effects in understanding what is at stake in philosophical (and theological) disputes. The pragmatist thinker turns away from abstractions, from "verbal solutions, from bad *a priori* reasons, from fixed principles, closed systems and pretended absolutes and origins. He turns towards concreteness, adequacy, towards facts, towards action and towards power."[19]

This Jamesian method sets ideas to work. It sees ideas, concepts, beliefs, and larger theoretical frameworks not as mirrors or forms of duplication, as argued above, but as tools for interpreting reality and contributing to experience. Ideas and the theories that grow up out of them become, in this pragmatic scheme, instruments, "*not answers to enigmas, in which we can rest.*"[20] When they are seen as such then the locus of inquiry is altered. Pragmatist thinkers no longer concern themselves with "first principles" or supposedly necessary truths. Nor are they concerned about historical origins that are somehow pristine or elevated above other historical claims. While pragmatists, as noted above, acknowledge the funded character of human ideas, such origination in the past does not decide the value of particular visions and beliefs. Rather, the pragmatist is firmly turned toward what James refers to as "*last things, fruits, consequences, facts.*"[21] It is the work that human ideas, beliefs, and theories do, the action they engender, that matters.

While James first espoused pragmatism as a method, he went on to expound it as a theory of truth, an unpacking of what humans mean when we refer to true ideas or beliefs. Virtually gone for James is the age-old obsession about eternal truths—about the world as it "really is." Instead, in the historicist and pragmatist mode of thought he developed, ideas are true insofar as they contribute to experience in a fruitful manner; they are true to the extent that they "*help us to get into a satisfactory relation with other parts of our experience.*"[22] True ideas or theories are not eternal unchanging templates that we somehow discover. Rather, they are the products of human history that work in relation to other dimensions of experience, including other ideas. James used all sorts of dynamic terms to indicate what he meant by truth; true ideas "lead" humans to experience, they are "instruments of action," they "fit" experience.[23] A number of important claims accompany this approach. Truth, for James, is not a "stagnant property" inherent in ideas.[24] Instead, truth is something that happens to ideas as they work for humans, as they allow humans to enhance and enlarge their experience. Ideas *become true* through a process of contributing to more satisfactory experience. Truth is not discovered but invented. It is not an unchanging attribute of an eternal idea but an event and a process by which historical human ideas are verified in experience and action.

This account of truth as dynamic, historical, and becoming led James to make other claims as well. Truth is not singular in nature. For James, truth always means plural truths, plural ways of leading that compete with each other. The great contrast for James is not truth and falsity, as though these can be distinguished for all time, but a world of competing truths, enabling different outcomes. There is no "The Truth" for James. Such an idea he dismissively called "a perfect idol of the rationalistic mind."[25]

James did occasionally refer to what he considered the ideal notion of absolute truth. But such an idea points to some vastly distant future that is unlikely ever to come into being. As an ideal, the notion of absolute truth is a "regulative notion of a potentially better truth" at a later time.[26] Such a potentially better truth is a critical principle that functions to keep humans open to new possibilities and new truth and to the need to jettison those claims that no longer work. In a historical world of finite, limited creatures "we have to live to-day by what truth we can get to-day, and be ready to-morrow to call it falsehood."[27]

James thus developed a picture of historical existence in which human ideas, beliefs, and theories are always in the process of making and remaking. Truths become true and sometimes die. They enhance experience and then no longer function satisfactorily in relation to new experiences. In practice humans are always testing their beliefs against other beliefs and in terms of the experiences they permit or inhibit. Such ideas are not passive duplications of reality standing outside of the world. Rather, they are part of experience, additions to the ongoing sum of reality. They not only describe the world; they add to it, becoming part of the world's experience as humans and the rest of finite reality move ever into an open future.[28]

Radical Empiricism

Many contemporary historicists and pragmatists have found James's historicized renderings of truth compelling. However, James made further claims that have been a matter of contention for many thinkers who followed. In particular, he developed a metaphysical vision of reality that has remained controversial. The recognition that human ideas, beliefs, and theories are historical artifacts that function for human purposes and the concomitant insight that the quest for absolute truth or some sure ground for human claims is fruitless and wrongheaded has led philosophers such as Richard Rorty to draw the conclusion that the development of metaphysical or ontological pictures of reality is to be forgone. Thus, for Rorty, any metaphysical speculation, *no matter its content*, is no longer of interest.[29] James, however, drew another conclusion. He understood metaphysical visions of reality, large, overarching interpretations of the nature of reality, to be hypothetical proposals that can both be tested against experience and, like other human ideas and schemes, contribute pragmatically to human life. The important thing to note about his metaphysical speculations is that, for James, these are imaginative hypotheses, open, like all other ideas and theories, to challenge and revision. They are working interpretations of reality and have the same fallible status of other human constructions.

James saw his own historical moment as being divided by attraction to two contrasting metaphysical visions: *theism*, which he often linked to forms of rationalism and idealism, and *materialism*, which he located as an offshoot of empiricism. Both of these approaches, James suspected, can be used to explain past reality.[30] What he was interested in, however, is what basic assumptions about reality might engender in the present and the future, what kinds of experience would be encouraged by such visions of reality. James found both materialism and theism lacking when humans looked forward instead of backward. Theism, both in its form as dualistic supernaturalism and in its monistic modes, gives humans confidence in a meaningful universe but fails to support human freedom and action or a truly open future. Materialism, for its part, also undermines free will and offers us a world of multiple but unconnected realities. James, over against these, sought to articulate a mediating position that he came to term *radical empiricism*, which offers a portrayal of a pluralistic universe of multiple but connected concrete realities.

The vision James developed was of a universe composed of a multiplicity of particular realities. Empiricism also emphasized an interpretation of reality composed of discrete perceptions.[31] Where James differed was to insist that these multiple individual realities are always in relation with one another; they are not separate entities existing side by side but without connection. Instead, the universe *is* the dynamic conglomeration of units of reality and experience that are connected with one another without losing their individuality. The universe is not a container holding static realities. Instead, it *is* the very flow of experience, the dynamic interaction of concrete realities. James thus used words like *flow, flux,* and *pulses,* and he repeatedly referred to the continuous changing character of reality. "What really exists," for James, "is not things made but things in the making."[32] Reality, for him, "buds and bourgeons, changes and creates."[33]

James's radical empiricism was, however, not just a speculative vision of a dynamic universe. James made other important claims that, according to him, supported his historicist and pragmatic positions and, to his critics, has seemed to strain those understandings. A central claim James made in relation to this multiverse was that the individual units of experience are connected to one another and that relations between concrete realities are as important and real as the units themselves. In *The Meaning of Truth* James declared that "the relations between things, conjunctive as well as disjunctive, are just as much matters of direct particular experience, neither more so nor less so, than the things themselves."[34] Relations hold the multiverse together, avoiding the sheer chaos of a pluralistic but unconnected universe while also providing the mechanisms by which reality changes, grows, and dies. Such a universe requires no supernatural, utterly external reality to hold it together; rather, parts of experience "hold together from next to next by relations that are themselves parts of experience."[35] There is no need for an external God or some other unifying agency.

James did not stop with his assertion of the reality and significance of the importance of relations. He clearly saw this version of reality as a hypothesis that commends itself because it offers an interpretation of an open and dynamic multiverse to which human agency can contribute and hence fit with human historical experience in a fruitful manner. But James thought that radical empiricism has more than theoretical worth. He thought it resonates with dimensions of human experience that other theoretical proposals ignore or deny. In particular, it asserts, over against the British-style empiricism that was thoroughly focused on sense experience, that humans literally experience these relations that hold the multiverse together but do so in a nonsensual fashion and on a subconscious level. Beyond the experience of our senses there is what James termed the "felt-dimension" of life. Here experience is by "direct acquaintance," not through the mediation of our senses or language.[36] It is on this level that we experience reality's "thickness," where humans "dive back into the flux itself."[37] In philosopher of religion Nancy Frankenberry's words, "radical empiricism is defined by the understanding that sense-perception is neither the only nor the primary mode of experience, but is rather derived from a still more elemental and organic togetherness of the experiencing subject and the experienced environment."[38] Experience, mediated through the senses or through linguistic forms, is a more developed and indirect form of interaction with the world. What is central to radical empiricism is that it refuses to reduce experience to these levels and insists on broadening experience "from a mere modality of cognition to an inclusion of experienced relations, felt transitions, and qualitative feeling."[39]

For many contemporary historicists who have become focused on the mediating role of language and culture, such direct experience seems like a repudiation of historicist insights. For James, however, experience mediated by consciousness and language are not denied by his radical empiricist claims but are complemented. While he had a profound sense of the role language played in much of experience, James also wanted to escape "the conceptual decomposition of life."[40] As Richard J. Bernstein has stated, for James "conceptual thought, despite its practical or theoretical efficacy, stays on the surface of things. It is knowledge *about* things; it does not penetrate the inner life of things and reality's continuously changing character."[41] James offered what he took to be a more holistic interpretation of reality in which humans traffic with the world not only through the mediation of language but also with our bodies and through the felt dimension of experience. While his turn to this other dimension of experience has long troubled historicists, his position remains a challenge to those thinkers so thoroughly focused on language and culture to the detriment of other dimensions of experience, especially bodily experience. Bernstein notes that "James was among the first contemporary philosophers to insist that much of western thought has been based upon a misguided revulsion and denigration of the human body and sensual experience."[42] As such, James remains a challenge to forms of historicism that ignore bodily experience, nature, and the material world.

Religious Experience

But if James's claims to an experiential level not subordinated to language and consciousness have proved problematic in historicist circles, so too has his linkage of this level of experience to claims about religious experience and God. James, though not a member of a particular religious tradition, had strongly sympathetic sentiments toward what he considered the religious dimensions of human experience and is perhaps best known for his analysis of religious experience. James took up the topic of religious experience in a variety of writings. In *The Will to Believe* (1897) James defended "the legitimacy of religious faith."[43] He did so not by making claims of certitude about religious matters but by emphasizing, as always, the hypothetical and pragmatic character of our religious convictions and asserting that humans have the *right* to hold such assumptions at their own risk. Moreover, he stressed that in religious matters, like other aspects of life, the process for determining the legitimacy of these beliefs lies not in some rationalistic proof or revelation outside of history but in the lives these beliefs make possible. Thus, James stated, "If religious hypothesis about the universe be in order at all, then the active faith of individuals in them, freely expressing themselves in life, are the experimental tests by which they are verified, and the only means by which their truth or falsehood can be wrought."[44] For James, religious beliefs, like other fundamental convictions about reality, are historical hypothetical conjectures about which we should let go any "rationalistic and authoritative pretensions."[45] Instead, humans should see them as the expression of our ideals and what he calls "over-beliefs" and should focus on the forms of life to which they give rise as the sites for testing their validity.

James took up these themes again both in the set of lectures published as *Pragmatism: A New Name for Some Old Ways of Thinking* (1907) and in the Hibbert Lectures delivered at the University of Manchester in 1908 and later published as *A Pluralistic Universe*. In the former he again argued for the legitimacy of religious hypotheses by focusing on their consequences, stating that according to pragmatic principles humans cannot reject these out of court "if consequences useful to life" flow from them.[46] But having asserted that religious visions in general should be considered legitimate, James also outlined his own religious hypothesis. In particular, he set himself against notions of an absolute in which all things are already decided, including what might be termed salvation. In contrast to a world anchored in some absolute, James portrayed a world of possibility in which no outcome, for good or ill, is determined ahead of time. The world of real experience is, James thought, a world of uncertainty but also possibility, a world in which nothing is guaranteed but there always remains the potential to contribute to the enhancement of experience. The religious belief in some sort of salvation in this view does not mean a promise of the inevitable but the belief that humans and others, including, as we will see, God, can contribute to enhancing reality. Thus, for James, to be religious in this manner means "I find myself willing to take the universe to be really dangerous and adventurous, without therefore backing out and crying 'no play.' . . . I am willing that there should be real losses and real losers, and no total preservation of all that is."[47] For James, this sort of religious vision is of what he called "an epic universe" in which humans accept "loss as unatoned for" and vigorously set our lives toward ameliorating the suffering and evil that are real in the world and commit ourselves to improving the prospects for the future.[48]

James expounded his own religious orientation again in *A Pluralistic Universe*, putting forth a notion of God interpreted not as some supernatural absolute controlling all of reality nor as a pantheistic whole of reality. Instead, he proposed that God is the name for the ideal tendencies in things, the ideal portion of reality.[49] At other times in the Hibbert Lectures he argued that he was positioning himself between a naturalism where human consciousness is the highest form of consciousness in the universe and supernatural theism where there is a greater consciousness but it is outside of and discontinuous with the rest of reality.[50] Instead, he proposed a "More," but a More that is finite and thoroughly implicated in the multiverse that is all that finite creatures know and experience. According to James, "if there be a God, he is no absolute all-experiencer, but simply the experiencer of widest actual conscious span."[51] Gone is the absolute God of the Western tradition and gone is the God of the German historicists who somehow guaranteed history: those Gods are replaced, by James, by a finite More that, with us, contributes to the ongoing unfolding of creative potential in a pluralistic universe.

James thus historicized and rendered finite his conception of God. Notions of omnipotence, timelessness, and supernatural transcendence are all jettisoned to suggest an idea of God that resonates more with the Jamesian vision of a finite, open, and dynamic universe. These kinds of claims have also appealed to later historicist-minded theologians. However, James suggested that these ideas are not just imaginative hypotheses that organize human experience (a position frequent in contemporary historicist approaches). Nor did he only propose pragmatic criteria for assessing their validity. At various points James also linked them with his assertions about radical empiricism and about the felt dimensions of life and explored the religious attitudes that accompany these felt dimensions of life. In these claims James suggested we experience the More and our relationship to it at those vague borders of human consciousness where we feel life more than we consciously know it. Hence, James not only explored the pragmatic functions of our religious sensibilities and beliefs but also the question of the experiential basis for these sensibilities.

In perhaps his most famous work, *The Varieties of Religious Experience* (1902), James focused not on religion in general but upon more extreme cases of religious experience, which often appeared to be tied to supposedly unmediated forms of mystical experience.[52] For James, such moves were consistent with his espousal of radical empiricism and represented continuity with other parts of his thought. To the more historicist-minded of his critics this line of exploration has remained problematic both because it, like radical empiricism in general, appears to repudiate historicist interpretations of the mediated character of all experience and because it forgoes what might be more historicist explanations for religious experiences. Wayne

Proudfoot, the well-known critic of Schleiermacher's claims about religious experience, also takes James to task for this element of his thought, asserting that his appeal to this experience of the More is "intentionally ahistorical," failing to explore more historical explanations that might be available, such as the ones Emile Durkheim and Sigmund Freud would articulate soon after James's death.[53] Other critics such as Grace Jantzen have argued that James has privatized religion in an ahistorical manner that misses the communal basis and function of religious sentiments and beliefs.[54] Other thinkers, more supportive of James, have pointed to the hypothetical character of all James's claims, its continuity with more historicized elements of his thought, and his early and important assertion of the embodied character of experience. In another tack, Jamesian analysts such as Leigh Eric Schmidt have insisted that James's historicist critics have failed to provide a thoroughly historical exploration of James's and others' work concerning religious experience in the context of the late nineteenth and early twentieth centuries. When contextualized against the Civil War, the breakdown of traditional worldviews, the rapidly changing modern economic order, and the intense existential and communal questions that plagued this environment, claims about religious experience seem less strategies for denying historical realities than responses to them—in Schmidt's words, constructs "formed of lacking and loss," "made by seekers for seekers."[55]

James can thus be seen to occupy an ambiguous position in any tale about historicism. Few thinkers evidence a greater willingness to acknowledge the contingent and fallible character of human thought, the funded nature of human experience, and the open but risk-filled character of a finite universe that is our only home. But James also refused to keep human experience within the prison house of language and insisted that, on all levels, experience always outruns our conceptual understanding of it; we traffic with reality in ways not mediated by language, including trafficking with that More James chose to call God. For James, such claims did not entail a repudiation of historicist insights but a more holistic understanding of human historical existence, including bodily experience. To those who have followed James he stands both as a beacon of historicist thought and a challenge to its limits, offering a heritage that has been debated ever since.

John Dewey and an American Historicism

John Dewey (1859–1952) is among America's most significant intellectual figures and, importantly, his work details an American version of historicism and its implications for a wide range of issues and areas. Born and raised in Vermont, Dewey's early life reflected the values and ideas of New England congregationalism. Dewey studied first at the University of Vermont and then at the first secular graduate institution in America, Johns Hopkins University. From Johns Hopkins he went to the University of Michigan to teach and eventually to the University of Chicago as chair of the philosophy department at the early age of thirty-five. At Chicago Dewey increasingly became a philosopher who radically challenged classical understandings of philosophical reflection. In Chicago and later at Columbia and in New York City he authored not only philosophical works in logic, metaphysics, and ethics but also works in psychology, education, religion, and art. He was a professional philosopher while also being a public figure, speaking to wide audiences. He wrote technical works but was as well a frequent contributor to more popular and broadly distributed journals such as *The New Republic* and *The Nation*. He was involved in progressive political and reform movements such as the National Association for the Advancement of Colored People (NAACP), the American Civil Liberties Union, the League of Industrial Democracy, the New York Teachers Union, the American Association of University Professors, and Jane Addams's Hull House. He was, indeed, the quintessential public intellectual whose thought and social activism were intimately interconnected.

Dewey's historicist view of human thought and action continually highlighted the importance of context. The context of Dewey's own life and times played major roles in shaping his intellectual and public agendas. His life spanned almost a century of radical change in America and the world. Born on the eve of the American Civil War, Dewey came of age in the last decades of the nineteenth century in an America reconstructing its identity in the aftermath of this catastrophic conflict. The United States was also, during this period, undergoing rapid change on all fronts as it moved from a rural agricultural society to an urbanized and industrialized one characterized by manufacturing and a *laissez-faire* capitalistic economic system increasingly nationalized through such mechanisms as the expansions of railroads and the development of monopolies. These developments led as well to increased social strife as industrialists and workers were pitted against each other in the struggles emerging out of the new economic order.

Another element that shaped Dewey's American context was the changing population of the country. The last half of the nineteenth century was also a period when America underwent great demographics change as waves of new immigrants came to the American shores, now not from northern

Europe or Great Britain or, through the forced relocation of slavery, from Africa, but from southern and eastern Europe, Ireland, and Asia. The population of the United States exploded during these decades with much of that expansion fueled by new immigrant groups who both stretched the boundaries of American identity and were stressed as their own national, ethnic, and religious identities were altered in the new American context.[56] The late nineteenth century was thus both a time of rapid expansion, change, and growth but also, as Cornel West notes, a period of great misery caused by "economic deprivation, cultural dislocation, and personal disorientation."[57] Moreover, such ferment issued forth not only in the labor and social strife West comments upon but also in what Richard J. Bernstein calls "a strange mixture of evangelical social zeal, reformist rhetoric, populist sentiment, and fragmented utopian projects."[58]

Finally, it is important to note that the first half of the twentieth century was also a period of major shifts in the position of the United States on the global scene. It was a world in which America emerged as an international political, economic, and military power, in which global conflicts of World War I and World War II deeply affected the United States and determined its role in the world context, and in which new forms of political and economic systems, especially communism, challenged American democracy and capitalism. Technological developments, social movements related to African Americans, women, and immigrant communities, the Depression, and two world wars thus became the context within which Dewey sought to formulate and make relevant his philosophical theories and especially his efforts to nurture a culture of democracy that could be responsive to the changing world conditions.

Dewey's life, therefore, encompassed enormous change. Being a participant in and a product of these world-altering events contributed greatly both to how Dewey came to understand human thought, including its philosophical forms, and to how Dewey perceived his own responsibility to the world as an intellectual and an activist. A good starting point for understanding Dewey's version of historicism and its implications for all arenas of human thought and action is his rejection of the classical understanding of philosophy.

Dewey and the Reconstruction of Philosophy

John Dewey, in a manner that foreshadowed many of the present-day criticisms of classical Western philosophy, called first for reconstruction *in* philosophy and then, more radically, for the reconstruction *of* philosophy.[59]

While Dewey acknowledged radical differences in philosophical systems and in the varied proposals that mark different periods of time, he also thought that the Western tradition, including its modern renditions, was characterized by a quest for certainty, for timeless and immutable truths, along with a disdain for the historical, the changing, and those aspects of human life most closely associated with practice and doing.[60] Hence, accompanying the search for timeless and universal truth is a panorama of hierarchically arranged dualisms that include the elevation of theory over practice, the eternal over the temporal, and the spiritual over the material. Dewey challenged the interpretation of philosophy as the formulation of universal truth and repudiated the dualisms embedded in such a quest. In their stead he articulated a thoroughly historicized interpretation of philosophy and human inquiry as the finite and human attempt to grapple with the problematics of concrete human existence.

According to Dewey, much of the Western philosophical tradition had seen itself as dealing with the ultimate or the "really real," described variously as Nature, Being, the Universe, the Truth, or God. He stated that while there were differences, "Whatever names were used, they had one thing in common: they were used to designate something taken to be fixed, immutable, and therefore out of time. . . . Philosophical doctrines which disagreed about virtually everything else were at one in the assumption that their distinctive concern as philosophy was to search for the immutable and ultimate—that which *is*—without respect to the temporal or spatial."[61] And, concomitantly, the claims made about such ultimate realities also were thought to carry a timeless and immutable character.

For Dewey, the rise of modern science radically challenged the underlying assumptions about reality that funded these philosophical views. Natural science had abandoned "the assumption of fixity" and undermined all references to the immutable and extra-temporal.[62] Dewey suggested that, in the face of the challenges of changing conceptions about the world, philosophy and other forms of human thought such as theology had not simply forgone their traditional claims. Instead, a truce of sorts was made wherein science and its methods and claims were understood to deal with the natural and material world and philosophy and religion with the moral, the spiritual, and the distinctly human. In relation to the latter, the quest for certitude continued even as it was eschewed in relation to nature and those arenas of process and change. This division of authority allowed modern humans to pursue developments in science, technology, and politics while simultaneously affirming traditional values and, of special interest to Dewey, maintaining traditional sites of authority and power. Dewey thus argued that the continued clinging to ideas of timeless truth and, with them, to notions of special forms of thought and of persons with special access to these truths is not merely an abstract concern. Rather, it deeply relates to the interests of those who have traditionally held power because of these assumptions and, therefore, contributes to bolstering the status quo. "To the vested interests, maintenance of belief in the transcendence of space and time, and hence the derogation of what is 'merely' human, is an indispensable prerequisite of their retention of an authority which in practice is translated into power to regulate human affairs throughout—from top to bottom."[63] Consequently, for Dewey, claims to timeless truth and ultimate certitude are not abstract matters but deeply tied to the interests of those who wield them; they are matters of power and authority.

While Dewey believed that much of the modern period was characterized by these ongoing negotiations of interests and by a truce that delineated separate spheres of authority, he no longer believed that the truce held or was desirable for twentieth-century society.[64] As science, technology, and, for Dewey, new political movements enlarged their arenas of influence, traditional conceptions of reality and the authority of their safekeepers held less and less sway. Such assumptions of authority were maintained only by living bifurcated lives in which one set of beliefs about the world shaped everyday life and organization and another was held to determine the moral, spiritual, and distinctly human realms that were more and more isolated from real life. Rather than bemoaning these developments, Dewey saw in this situation the possibility to reinterpret philosophy and, as we will see, religion, and to see them not as in opposition to the workings and methods of science but as forms of historical human inquiry that might benefit from and contribute to concrete human existence.

In contrast to interpretations of philosophy as the search for certitude and unassailable truth, Dewey proposed an interpretation of philosophical inquiry as emergent out of the human need to deal with and adapt to our natural and cultural environments and, as such, a thoroughly historical, fallible, and eminently revisable endeavor. Dewey espoused an anthropology that stressed that humans are bio-social beings who are in continual interaction with their natural and historically developed worlds. From the earliest beginnings of human existence humans were forced to adapt to and respond to the conditions of these intermingled worlds. For Dewey, the insights of evolutionary science and historicism supported this version of human life as dynamically interactive and as developing and changing in relation to the contexts and conditions within which it is found. Human thought, including what came to be known as philosophy, develops not in abstraction from these concrete needs and problems but is from the beginning a response to the concrete problems of life and a contributor to their resolutions. That is, for Dewey, human thought has always been practical in nature. Even our ideas of the absolute, or the real, or of a timeless, unchanging deity are, according to Dewey, really attempts to resolve the problems of historical and natural life, to give it direction, avoid chaos, and enhance its possibilities.[65] They are, however, for Dewey, misguided efforts and doomed to fail.

In the place of the classical views of philosophy Dewey thus proposed a historicized and naturalized version. In this view philosophy and, indeed, all modes of human inquiry, would be interpreted as efforts to understand the human condition as it is situated in the natural and historical world and to clarify the possibilities for enhancing that existence and furthering the potentials for a more humane existence. Philosophy would now be seen as dealing with "the stresses and strains in the community life" with its task being to examine and understand the actual state of affairs at any given time and place in order to move human life "toward order and toward other conditions of a fuller life than man has yet enjoyed."[66] The questions with which this mode of reflection would now deal, to the disdain of those thinkers whose goal is some timeless truth, would "not concern Being and Knowledge 'in themselves' and at large, but the state of existence at specified times and places and the state of affection, plans, and purposes under concrete circumstances. They are not concerned with framing a general theory of reality, knowledge, and value once for all, but with finding how authentic beliefs about existence as they currently exist can operate fruitfully and efficaciously in connection with the practical problems that are urgent in actual life."[67] Gone are the illusions of final or absolute or ultimate truth and in their place are concerns for the enhancement of finite existence and the nourishment of humane possibilities. In crossing what Cornel West calls this Rubicon of historical consciousness a new terrain is entered.[68] This is a terrain in which human concerns, for Dewey, are now proximate, not ultimate; concrete, not abstract; and born not out of dualistic hierarchies that bifurcate human life, but from a sense of the interconnection and the interplay of thought and action, with both being the means for fuller human life.

Dewey emphasized this more locally focused and more human-scaled task by substituting the term *intelligence* for reason and calling his version of philosophy a pragmatic instrumentalism. But how should humans carry out this pragmatic task? Dewey believed that modern science points the way here. According to Dewey, the scientific method, broadly conceived, is the most efficacious procedure for engaging in critical reflection and for developing constructive proposals in any given context. By the scientific method Dewey meant a process of observation or analysis of conditions and contexts, the development and employment of theories interpreted as hypotheses, and experimentation to test outcomes and consequences. While this method has gained its fullest expression in the natural and physical sciences and in such areas as the development of technologies, it is also one that will be helpful within other arenas of human life, including those we associate with morality, aesthetics, and religion. To examine contexts and conditions, to offer theoretical interpretations understood as hypotheses, and to test the repercussions of our values and actions in relation to the consequences they engender is an approach that is appropriate not only for the laboratory but to the widest range of human life and community.[69]

Dewey was often accused of espousing a new form of scientism. Yet his understanding both of science and the scientific method belied such criticisms and suggested an interpretation of these in close alliance with his historicist insights. Several factors are important to note here. First, Dewey's understanding of science and, in particular, of the scientific method did not interpret these as means to some new certitude but as thoroughly historical and finite efforts at understanding. Claims developed out of the procedure of observation, theorizing, and experimentation are always open to criticism and revision. As conditions change, as values undergo revision, as the range of humane potential is enlarged or restricted, so too, will our human interpretations of them and our theories for improving them be open to question and alteration. It is precisely the revisability and critical engagement at the heart of this approach that made it compelling for Dewey.[70]

A second and extremely important aspect of this method is what Dewey termed its public character. Dewey had a profound repugnance toward claims of special knowledge, whether they be in the form of appeals to reason accessible only to the few or revelations. While he was an advocate of the importance of experts in any field, he regarded such expertise as positional, dependent upon the deployment of critical intelligence—a matter of knowledge and expertise publicly defended, not authority conveyed by power, birth, or position. The assumption that only some persons have special access to truth and that such access gives them the authority to impose their positions on all others was in tension with all of the more equalitarian and democratic values Dewey came to espouse. The tests for human claims need to be in the public arena, and they need to be according to criteria that can be publicly determined and publicly challenged.

John Dewey was perhaps the greatest champion of democratic ideals in the twentieth century. He looked out over the latter part of the nineteenth century and the first decades of the twentieth century and saw massive changes. Among the ones he continually remarked upon were those cited above of technology, immigration, and the mechanizing not only of industry but also of culture—what he termed "the mass production" of society.[71] Earlier forms of association and communal identity had been lost in the face of rapid change that occurred without social integration. According to Dewey, the "machine age in developing the Great Society has invaded and partially disintegrated the small communities of former times without generating a Great Community."[72] The public was, thus, in "eclipse." For Dewey, the need for a new community was immense. In contrast to earlier modern interpretations of humans as isolated individuals, Dewey argued for a social understanding of the human self in which distinctive individuality is the product of social relations and dependent upon human community and interaction. The potential for individual development and enhancement is predicated upon the character of the social realm and, in turn, such individual development contributes to the possibilities inherent in that larger community. This insight into the social character of human life was expressed in Dewey's claim that critical intelligence, focused on the problems of everyday life, requires democratic participation and responsibility in order to work. Democracy is linked not just to individual rights but, importantly, for Dewey, to social responsibility: "From the standpoint of the individual, it consists in having a responsible share according to capacity in forming and directing the activities of the groups to which one belongs and in participating according to the need in the values which the group sustains. From the standpoint of the groups, it demands liberation of the potentialities of members of a group in harmony with the interests and goods which are common."[73] But democracy does not point just to responsible and intelligent interaction *within* groups; in a social world humans belong to numerous groups and groups interact. Hence, democracy requires the intelligent integration of and communication between the elements of an ever-widening social arena whose boundaries are flexible and permeable.

Hence, for Dewey, commitment to the ideals of democracy flow out of his vision of historical and social human beings who are always embedded in both communal and natural contexts and whose potential for humane existence depends upon and contributes to these interrelated webs of existence. Democracy, for Dewey, "is the idea of community life itself."[74] The modern revolutionary calls for freedom apart from a sense of human sociality are empty and, even more, dangerous. In Dewey's words, "fraternity, liberty and equality isolated from communal life are hopeless abstractions. Their separate assertion leads to mushy sentimentalism or else to extravagant and fanatical violence which in the end defeats its aims."[75] The goal, then, for Dewey, is to recognize the natural and historical character of human existence, to forgo the illusions of absolute truth, and to turn our attention to the real problems of everyday life. In responding to those problems humans should cultivate a critical intelligence that is shorn of arrogance and oriented toward the public analysis and debate of human projects, ideals, and potentialities.

Dewey and Religion

John Dewey argued not only for the reconstruction of philosophy but also for a new understanding of religion and its human function. Although he was raised in the New England Congregationalist tradition he found himself increasingly disenchanted by organized religions. Personally, he distanced himself from the explicit practice of Christianity. At various points he engaged in discussions about religion but his most sustained statement about religion came in the Terry Lectures at Yale University, which were later published as *A Common Faith* in 1934.[76] This volume offered both a serious and sustained attack on certain forms of religion but also a constructive alternative that emerged out of Dewey's historicism and naturalism.

Dewey's critical take on religions parallels his criticism of philosophy. In particular, he asserted, revealing his own limited knowledge of religions outside of Western theism, that historical religious traditions are tied in an untenable manner to forms of supernaturalism. There are many differences characterizing historical religious traditions; indeed, for Dewey, the term *religion* is merely a heuristic abstraction for what are really only singular and multiple realities. According to Dewey, "concretely there is no such thing as religion in the singular. There is only a multitude of religions."[77] Still, despite this acknowledgment of the plurality and distinctive character of concrete traditions, Dewey went on to argue that they all share something in common: "They agree in one point: the necessity for a Supernatural Being and for immortality that is beyond the power of nature."[78] Such supernaturalism has characterized every level of historical religions:

(1) they assume a supernatural realm often populated by supernatural beings; (2) they assume that ideas and beliefs about such a realm are of a different order than those about historical and natural existence; (3) they are predicated upon special access to this realm whether it be through supernatural persons, texts, or experiences; and (4) most often, they have apparatuses of authority that determine which humans control the access to the supernatural and the beliefs and practices that flow from those sources.

All of these levels have been under assault in the modern era, according to Dewey. Just as the philosophical claims to absolute truth or timeless reality have been undermined, so too have religious assertions that are grounded in supernaturalist assumptions. Historical and scientific knowledge have discredited supernaturalism and, in turn, have destabilized the religions that are predicated upon it. Views of reality as divided between material, historical, and finite existence and a timeless, unchanging, eternal, and infinite realm have been dismissed by modern science. Assertions about texts as inspired or founders of traditions as divine have all been open to challenge. Dewey acknowledged that these beliefs and the traditions that espouse them have continued to exist. But he suggested that in fact these beliefs are out of tune with everything else modern persons believe and that, therefore, religions are increasingly displaced in modern life. Hence, for him, the social place and function of religion was "shifting."[79] The hold of supernaturalism had "oozed away" as the "interests and values unrelated to the offices of any church now so largely sway the desires and aims of even believers."[80]

Dewey argued that the proponents of supernatural-based religions and their critics both concur that religions are fundamentally linked to and identified by this recourse to the nonnatural and the nonhistorical. "There is," he stated, "one idea held in common by these two opposite groups: identification of the religious with the supernatural."[81] The guardians of supernaturalism and its apparatuses and the critics of religion draw, however, opposite conclusions from this assumption. The former reassert their authority and claim that the distinctiveness of religions protect them from the onslaught of modern historicism and science while the latter argue that being religious and being modern are fundamentally incompatible and, therefore, religions must be left behind as some atavistic phase of human development. Dewey agreed with the critics concerning the tension between supernaturalism and the humanistic and naturalistic assumptions that increasingly shape modern life. Moreover, he asserted that supernaturalism and its mechanisms inhibit the free flow of critical intelligence and therefore hamper the very kind of human activity that could enhance human

existence and bring about a better world.[82] Despite these trenchant criticisms, however, Dewey did not suggest that religion simply be jettisoned.
Instead, he argued for a radical reinterpretation of religion in terms of what
he called the religious dimension or factor in human existence, a dimension
that he believed is thoroughly compatible with critical intelligence and its
deployment in science and other human endeavors.

Dewey stated that he wanted to emancipate *the religious from religions*.[83]
Over against historical religious traditions grounded in supernaturalistic
assumptions, Dewey presented a naturalist version of the religious aspects of
experience. This dimension has to do with the human attempt to harmonize
the self with the rest of reality and, in particular, with the process by which
the human self is unified in the midst of a reality in continual flux. Dewey
proposed that such unification comes about as humans identify and project
ideals that, in turn, provide the normative direction for human action. For
Dewey, the religious attitude does not consist in loyalty to supernaturalistic
beliefs but in a natural piety, in "faith as the unification of the self through
allegiance to inclusive ideal ends, which imagination presents to us and to
which the human will responds as worthy of controlling our desires and
choices."[84] The religious, interpreted as the unification of the self in terms of
ideal ends, is not in opposition to human critical intelligence but is a dimension of it. It can, accordingly, be seen as denoting "attitudes that may be
taken toward every object and every proposed end or ideal."[85] Here religious
experience is not rare or isolated or *sui generis* but is part of everyday life; it
is that which has "the force of bringing about a better, deeper, and enduring
adjustment in life" by critically identifying those ideals to which we will be
devoted and that will give direction and meaning to human existence.[86]

Several elements should be noted about this interpretation of the religious. First, for Dewey, the religious is a thoroughly naturalistic and historicized factor in human existence. The ideals to which it points emerge out
of finite existence and are not imposed upon it from some supernaturalistic realm. The ideals that are identified and projected as values to which
humans should be devoted and which should direct our actions are natural
and historical ones; they are "goods actually experienced in the concrete
relations of family, neighborhood, citizenship, pursuit of art and science."[87]
While Schleiermacher also rejected the isolation of religious experience
from other human experiences, he nonetheless grounded that experience
in a dimension of reality not reducible to the finite and the historical. For
Dewey, no such dualism exists. Second, as a function of ordinary human
experience, there is no need for special access or for sites of authority that

control the religious dimensions of life. Hence, for Dewey, the emancipation of the religious from religion restores the religious not only to the realm of open and critical inquiry but also to the sphere of democratic ideals to which he was so committed. There is no "monopoly" in religious matters, and the guardians of the supernatural are relieved of their claims to exclusive authority.[88]

Third, Dewey appreciated how these ideals have emerged over time and acknowledged the inherited character of the accumulated accomplishments of humanity.[89] To a far greater extent than the German historicists and even of James, however, Dewey emphasized the role of the not-yet, of the future, and of the imagination as that human means of articulating ideals that continually move the human community forward. For him, ideals do not depend either upon external authority or upon being embodied in some past moment. They represent the imaginative reaching of the human community into an unfinished future that calls humans beyond any present or past accomplishment. They remain human and finite and they emerge out of what has occurred or is taking place. They are, however, continually moving human society toward the future and as such contribute to our historicized existence in a different way than does the recognition of the past and its importance. For Dewey, interestingly, the symbol *God* is related to this imaginative articulation of human ideals. God is not the name for a supernatural being or for some achieved reality but is the symbolic embodiment of human ideals; "it denotes the unity of all ideal ends arousing us to desire and actions."[90]

Thus, Dewey presented a naturalized and historicized version of human existence. Humans live within the matrix of nature and human history. Our efforts at knowing our world emerge out of the need to direct our action and to set goals for the human community in every time and place; they are the outgrowth of this finite need for meaning, order, and direction and do not entail any necessity or capacity to move toward a supposed transcendent or supernatural realm. Nor do religions, in fact, despite their pretensions, have to do with such a nonhistorical or nontemporal or nonspatial realm. The religious has to do with the ideals humans set forth and imagine as we traffic with and within historical and natural reality. Dualistic notions dividing reality into separate realms do not enhance human life or contribute to its continual transformation but hinder it. Only a naturalized interpretation of the religious can bridge the dualisms that stand in the way of intelligently and critically seeking more humane forms of existence. The issue for Dewey, as for historicists that would follow him, is whether such naturalized and historicized views of the religious are adequate and acceptable either for those who continue to cling to forms of supernaturalism or for those who seek to leave religions behind because they are assumed always to be supernaturalistic in character. Is a thoroughly historicized and naturalized religion possible? Can it find expression in the kind of communities Dewey thought so important to other dimensions of human life but seemed to avoid espousing in relation to the religious? What would such communities of faith, a natural faith in finite human options, look like in terms of belief and practice? These are the questions Dewey bequeathed his followers.

The Chicago School of Theology

It was not only philosophers and psychologists who took seriously the contextualization and historicizing of human experience. Theologians and other scholars of religion in America in the first half of the twentieth century also sought to draw out the implications of historicism both for their subject matter and for their understanding of their scholarly disciplines. Chief among such scholars were those of what has come to be known as the Early Chicago School of Theology at the University of Chicago Divinity School. Numerous scholars across the fields of inquiry represented at the Divinity School sought to carry out their scholarly investigations in light of modern science and modern historicist claims. Thinkers such as George Burman Foster (1858–1918), Edward Scribner Ames (1870–1958), and Albert Eustace Haydon (1880–1975) sought ways to engage religions critically, especially Christianity, in the changing circumstances of the twentieth century. Three names, however, stand out in the early Chicago School for their historicist orientation: Shailer Mathews (1863–1941), Gerald Birney Smith (1868–1929), and Shirley Jackson Case (1872–1947).

As we turn to the Early Chicago School thinkers, it is important to note that these scholars faced the same issues that other American thinkers did in that protean period between the end of the Civil War and the decades of the early twentieth century. Like Dewey, they too needed to come to terms with the shift of population centers from rural areas to vastly expanded urban centers, with the developments in the American economy that now stressed industrialization over agriculture, and with the arrival of new immigrants that were changing the texture of American life. These developments, however, had special repercussions in relation to American religious life, and they set the stage for very particular issues to which these thinkers, as scholars focused on American religion, would have to respond. Importantly, the shifts to cities, to industry, and to an influx of immigrants significantly altered the nature of American religion. Small-town America, in which Protestantism reigned and was continually reinforced, gave way to a more polyglot urban America in which the social supports for Protestant Christianity were less strong. Large numbers of immigrants came now not from northern Protestant Europe but from southern Catholic Europe and Catholic Ireland. Significant numbers of Jewish immigrants arrived, as did groups of orthodox Christians. While Christianity was still dominant, it no longer had the same Protestant tone and texture.

Other developments also challenged Christians, especially those representing the dominant Protestant groups. The intellectual developments in Europe reverberated across America as colleges and universities adopted the model of the modern university, now less tied to religious standards and goals. Science had enormous impact, especially as educated persons grappled with the claims of Darwinism and evolutionary science that undermined the most basic inheritances of the Christian tradition, including claims found in the Bible. For Christians, the claims of science coalesced with the growing challenges of higher biblical criticism to assert that traditional beliefs, especially about the Bible, were no longer acceptable. The result was an intellectual crisis in American Christianity.

Christian intellectuals and practitioners responded to these developments in a variety of ways. One large-scale response was the emergence of what came to be known as fundamentalism. Across many Protestant denominations, especially in Baptist and Presbyterian churches, Christians asserted such things as the inerrancy of the Bible and rejected the tenets of modern intellectual inquiry, including evolutionary science and biblical criticism. A fierce internal battle for the nature and direction of American Protestantism ensued, and the arena of conflict involved not only struggles for control of local churches and national denominations but also divinity schools and seminaries. The latter were both the strongholds of these conservative developments at places such as Princeton Theological Seminary and the sites of resistance and modernist alternatives in places like Chicago Divinity School. Thus, it is in the context not only of social, political, and economic changes that the Early Chicago School crafted its liberal and modern positions but also over against fundamentalist religious movements that rejected the very tenets the Chicago thinkers sought to embody and defend.

Shailer Mathews

Shailer Mathews was a scholar of rhetoric, the New Testament, historical and political theory, and sociological approaches to the study of religion.

He was dean at the University of Chicago from 1908 to 1933 as well as a leader in the Northern Baptist Convention and a strong opponent of the fundamentalist movements that characterized many Protestant denominations in the early twentieth century.

Mathews is especially interesting in his assertion that religious traditions, including Christianity, are sociohistorical realities, not realities that are isolated from the rest of social and historical life. In contrast to the interpretations of religion as some *sui generis* realm that requires methods peculiarly suited to religion, Shailer Mathews argued that religions are part of the interconnected movement of history. Thus, speaking of Christianity, he stated, "The history of Christianity is one phase of general history."[91] The Christian movement needs to be studied as part of human history, "not as something apart from the development of civilization but as one aspect thereof."[92] "One can," he argued, "understand the history of Christianity only as a social eddy within the main current of the stream of history."[93] And the methods for approaching such historical eddies are the sociohistorical ones that had emerged in the late modern period.

Shailer Mathews applied his historicist approach not just to Christianity as a broad historical movement, but in particular he asserted that doctrines and theological claims must be understood as historical responses to concrete social and historical conditions and situations.[94] Gone, for Mathews, is any sense of doctrines as articulations of timeless truth or as expressions of some transcendent revelation. Instead, doctrines and theologies are the claims of historical human beings grappling with the problems of their times and places in the idioms and conceptual frameworks of those contexts. Doctrines are not "independent systems of truth" but historical responses to changing circumstances.[95] Just as religious traditions cannot be separated from the wider sociohistorical contexts within which they arose and developed, neither can doctrines be understood apart from their location in the wider web of human history; there is no abstract history of doctrine in which ideas float freely but only a history of peoples struggling with real issues and problems and utilizing the tools at hand to understand and respond to them.[96] Thus, Mathews stated, "a theology is a function of the religious life of a given period and this in turn is the expression of a social order conditioned not only by elements of culture, like philosophy, literature, and science, but also by the creative economic and political forces which engage in the production of the social order itself."[97] Far from being a separate realm, religions engage, reflect, appropriate, and respond to the political and economic developments of their time. Moreover, the doctrines that become solidified and dominant do so less because they are truth guaranteed by God, revelation, or eternal reason but because they are espoused by those who hold political, social, and economic power in a particular time and place. "Heresy," Mathews notes, "is always the belief of a defeated party."[98] Therefore, if we are to understand religious claims we must do so as sociohistorical artifacts; they can never be understood or assessed for their validity in isolation from these thoroughly human elements.

Doctrines and theologies, as well as practices and rituals, thus arise in social contexts. To understand them we must understand those settings. In particular, Mathews was cognizant that religious persons inherit from their pasts doctrines and practices, theologies and rituals that arose in earlier times and were responses to different realities and needs. Hence, he asserted that not only do we need to historicize the doctrines to understand them but we must also stand ready to have a clear sense of present-day contexts, needs, and developments in order to evaluate the continuing validity or lack thereof of inherited ideas. Often, for Mathews, religious ideas or practices no longer functioned helpfully because they were the expression of outmoded and no longer acceptable ideas. In his work *The Growth of the Idea of God* Mathews pointed to the changing content of this idea as worldviews, notions of the nature of reality and society, change.[99] And in *Is God Emeritus?* he continued this line of argumentation, suggesting a radical reconstruction of the idea of God, now no longer reflective of societies controlled by monarchs or tyrants but ones structured by democracy and modern science.[100] In his own reconstruction Mathews called for understanding God as the personification of *personality-producing forces* in the universe, those cosmic activities and elements that had brought forth consciousness and were the grounds for its development. For Mathews, a transcendent, supernatural God modeled on a king or emperor was no longer religiously feasible for twentieth-century persons. Religious ideas, developed as means of grappling with the problems of everyday life, require continual assessment and reconstruction so that they can continue to function in a creative manner. When ideas are reified and continue to reflect assumptions rejected in other areas of life, they become problematic, hindering human development and undermining the positive function religions can play in the enhancement of humane existence. For Mathews, "no religious faith can be satisfactory that is out of harmony with what have been shown to be the facts of the universe."[101]

Mathews thus developed a sociohistorical approach to religions and especially to religious doctrines. He located them in the midst of the political, intellectual, cultural, and economic webs that are the ongoing context of human life and development. He separated them from assertions of supernatural origins and guarantees and called for the continual reconstruction of inherited religious ideas and practices in light of new challenges and emerging assumptions. In his own reconstructive efforts he sought to articulate new ideas that were reflective of and consonant with modern science and democratic movements and hence functional for a new century with new assumptions and new concerns.

Despite Mathews's strong historicist orientation it must be stated that he did refer occasionally to what he termed the "permanent values" of Christianity. Hence, while he seemed at almost every turn to reject an essentialist view of religious traditions in which some doctrines or practices remain despite changes through time, he also seemed to want a certain stability and continuity at the heart of the Christian tradition, though he was quite vague about what that might be. It remained for his colleague Gerald Birney Smith to repudiate even this remnant of an essentialist and dehistoricized approach to Christianity.

Gerald Birney Smith

Gerald Birney Smith is another prominent representative of the sociohistorical school at the University of Chicago during the early twentieth century. An ethicist and theologian, Smith was educated at Brown University, Union Theological Seminary, and Columbia University. He also traveled in Europe where he studied with such luminaries as Adolf von Harnack and Wilhelm Herrmann. Smith, however, increasingly became wary of the essentialist project of thinkers like Harnack and more and more identified with the historicist orientation of scholars such as Ernst Troeltsch. After joining the Chicago faculty in 1900 he also was greatly influenced by John Dewey and, eventually, William James and Henri Bergson.

G. B. Smith is significant for this project because of the thoroughgoing manner in which he thought through the major shifts he detected in his era and their implications for how religious traditions and theology should be understood. As is true for most of the thinkers dealt with in this chapter, Smith's major concerns focused on the developments in the modern Western world and their effect upon Christianity. Like Mathews and Dewey, the two major changes that Smith repeatedly pointed to were the emergence of the scientific method, within which he placed historicist developments, and the growth of democracy and democratic ideals. The combination of these two factors presented enormous challenges and new possibilities to members of religious communities and to those scholars who study religions.

Smith argued that prior to the modern period and, indeed, in the early stages of modernity itself both thought and social organization in the West were characterized by what he termed "aristocratic" forms of power in which elites controlled society and in which religious and other sorts of claims to truth were predicated upon appeals to authority, be they supernatural or some sort of notion of reason as transcendental.[102] In both of these guises, the goal was unchanging and timeless truth to which human thought and action were to conform. In Christian circles these claims to absoluteness were grounded in assumptions concerning revelation and such things as the divine authorship and inspiration of the Bible, while for rationalists reason provided access to certain truths that were unassailable. In both forms Smith saw a dogmatism that moves not inductively from the uncertainties and vicissitudes of concrete life to claims about reality but deductively from some assumed-to-be-constant point to the less-regarded realms of history and nature.

The assumptions that grounded such authoritarian and dogmatic approaches had, according to Smith, all come under severe challenge.[103] In particular, the scientific attitude and its accompanying scientific method had come to dominance and with them a new spirit that rejected the dogmatisms, both ecclesiastical and rationalistic, of the past. Now Smith, like Dewey, Mathews, and, as we will see, Case, had a very particular understanding of the scientific method. He did not see it as the means to a new certitude or any form of timeless truth. Instead, what Smith meant by the scientific method was an approach to human inquiry that is public, experimental, self-consciously critical, and empirically focused on concrete human and natural existence. Such human inquiry yields not unassailable claims but tentative, revisable, and context-specific assertions about human and natural existence and their betterment. For him, the new historicist orientation concerning human affairs embodied these characteristics and, hence, was a form of the new scientific spirit.[104]

When applied to human affairs, especially those arenas referred to as religious, a new understanding emerges. First, in keeping with evolutionary notions that living creatures are continually responding to and adapting to their environment, Smith interpreted human history as that ongoing process of adaptation to changing conditions. Importantly, human ideas and claims about reality are also part of the human adaptation process. As new challenges arise, new interpretations and ideas take shape as humans attempt to preserve and further enhance human life. Human thought and practices are, therefore, thoroughly practical in nature; they, like biological adaptations, consist in the adjustment of the organism and its environment. Far from being timeless or mirrors of some unchanging reality, human ideas, claims about reality, and normative visions for human practices all, as historical studies clearly demonstrate, undergo change as the conditions of life and contexts within which life takes place shift. Religions, by which Smith identified human efforts to name and pursue the highest human ideals and values, equally carry this character of historical responsiveness to concrete conditions and hence are also thoroughly finite and fallible.[105]

Smith, echoing Dewey, also saw a profound connection between this scientific/historicist orientation and emerging democratic sentiments and commitments. For him, the development of the scientific method and the rise of modern democracy are correlative, implying and necessitating one another.[106] According to Smith, "it may almost be said that the scientific attitude is an inevitable accompaniment of democracy. For if we are to set rules for our own guidance, we must cultivate the most exact possible methods for discovering the truth."[107] In particular, both the scientific attitude and democracy demand that we forgo appeals to authority and reject "predetermined conclusions" and inductively analyze the contexts and conditions under which present-day life occurs with the intention of improving and edifying it. Rather than asking whether current claims or values conform to ancient ones or to those enshrined in the past, contemporary persons or, as Smith called them, "free men" should forgo a "helpless dependence on antiquity," and ask instead what is most efficacious for their present needs and contexts.[108]

Such a position severely undermines the importance and, in relation to religion, the sacrality of past figures, positions, and practices. The American historicists, in a manner quite different than their European counterparts, took a much more critical attitude toward the past. Smith believed that the past provides a "stimulus and help" to the present.[109] It offers models of creative adaptation, revision, and change. What it does *not* do is present some truth to which the present should conform or be beholden. By seeing the past as a resource, the role and function of tradition is severely altered. "Tradition," for Smith, "thus becomes a servant of the present and not its despot."[110]

Over against the emphasis upon the past often found in European thinkers, Smith embodied an interest in the future that seems to be more characteristic of American thinkers. According to Smith, both democratic orientations and scientific attitudes are forward looking, not backward looking. Criticism, transformation, and revision are all seen as potentially creative and positive, not destructive or problematic. Criticism in this view is not what we should fear as being destructive but what we should openly court as the means by which the borders of our knowledge are expanded.[111] Democracy has at heart both the conviction that humans can improve the future and the commitment to engage continually in practices that will enhance that future. As such, "democracy is inevitably more interested in the possibilities of the future than in the sanctities of the past."[112] Those persons committed to democratic ideals consequently derive their standards not from the "mandates of the past" but from the emerging possibilities of an open future.[113] Smith did not offer any guarantee that the future would by necessity be better than the past; by no means is history necessarily progress in this view. But there is, for Smith, in the conjunction of the scientific and democratic orientations, a conviction that the future is open and the human task is creatively to construct its contours and possibilities.

When these assumptions and methods are applied to religions and especially to theological claims a number of things occur. First, they, like all other human ideas, practices, and forms of communal organization, are radically historicized. The old authoritarian appeals to revelation or supernatural origins or guarantees are eschewed and replaced by notions of the human character of religious ideas. Rather than embodying or being expressions of some sacred truth or reality, religious claims, doctrines, and practices are no different in kind or character than any other human product. Whether it be an artifact (the Bible), a person (Jesus), or a set of beliefs or ideas (the doctrine of the Trinity), all are to be treated in the same manner as other elements of human history. Second, Smith, along with his Chicago cohorts, stressed that religious claims and practices are emergent in, reflective of, and contribute to the social context within which they develop. In order to grasp the meaning of these ideas and practices the scholar of religion must engage in a thoroughgoing analysis and investigation of the context and social setting that give rise to them. Third, when religious ideas and practices are no longer understood to be the expression of some uniquely communicated or guaranteed truth but the product of the human engagement with its historical and natural environment in its quest for meaning, then the grounds for evaluating such claims are altered as well. Instead of approximation to the past or to some supposed timeless truth, now religious claims, like all human claims, are judged according to how well they function within their particular contexts and how well they contribute to confronting the challenges of the time and place in which they arose and functioned. It is these historically derived pragmatic standards to which religious movements, persons, texts, and practices, as well as reflection upon them, are now held. Thus, for Smith, "the value of a given theology consists in the success with which it furnishes a solution to the historical problems which it faced."[114]

Smith is especially significant to this study not only because he asserted the thoroughly historical character of all human thought and activity but also because he set forth what he understood to be the ramifications for theology of such a historicist orientation. In his essay "Task and Method of Systematic Theology" Smith asked what happens to theology and the theological task when not only the object of theological reflection, be that a text, a religious personage, or idea, but also the explicit work of the theologian are all historicized. His response was that theology now becomes a form of cultural and social analysis whose goal is to understand and be responsive to the challenges of present-day life. He articulated his view of theology by setting forth four steps or tasks facing contemporary theologians. First, the theologian must have a historical understanding of the religious tradition and its social and cultural locations in relation to which he or she carries out their work. The theologian must grasp the conditions that give rise to ideas and practices and that shape them as well. "The theologian will, therefore, endeavor to have a clear and accurate conception of the reasons for the rise and growth of fundamental ideas and institutions in the history of the religion which it is his especial task to interpret."[115] Moreover, religious traditions are not separate from other elements within their own culture or society. Nor do religious traditions or wider historical periods exist in splendid isolation from the wider world around them. Historical analysis leads us both into the particularities of place and time and into ever-widening explorations of an interconnected world. Gone forever is a history-of-ideas approach that examines the doctrinal inheritance of a religious community or its philosophical tradition apart from its social and historical setting.

Two further elements of this first task are especially important here. First, for Smith, this historical analysis does not assume that a tradition is characterized by some essential continuity. Rather, he was convinced that historical and social analysis display ongoing change. A historicist approach to the history of any tradition reveals no stable center, no unchanging body of doctrines or practices, nor even essential interpretations of originating religious figures. "There has not and never has been" any such stable essence in religious traditions but only ongoing permutations and a diversity of interpretations.[116] Smith's favorite example of this was the history of the idea of God that he believed demonstrated change, not continuity, at the heart of theistic traditions.[117]

Another element of the historical analysis moment of the theological task entails the recognition that we interpret the past for didactic reasons. Theologians explore what has already occurred not to identify some final truth or to proclaim one period more normative than the rest but to learn from what has already happened. In Smith's words, one studies history in order "to appeal to that past with critical intelligence."[118] Hence, the theologian studies the past because humans are inheritors of that history and are therefore shaped by it. But the theologian has no expectation that the past yields a truth that is absolute, an essence that is unchanging, or a norm to which contemporary persons must submit.

The second major task of the theologian is the analysis of the contemporary situation and especially the needs and challenges related to the religious quest for meaning and value.[119] Theologians must be able to carry out social and cultural analysis in order to understand the problems of their era. What are the problems that confront any present moment? What solutions are possible given the complex challenges that face the present? What resources, including those from the past, are available in the here and now? For Smith, the theologian is to analyze contemporary existence in order to discover "the sort of belief which men today can really *believe*, not how men may be brought to give assent to some belief formulated in the past."[120] If historical analysis instructs us about the conditions and solutions of the past then the analysis of the present sets forth interpretations of current problems. And it does so by locating religious needs within the ever-broadening contexts of society, of politics, of economics, and of culture.

The third task of theology flows from the first two. Both historical analysis and social and cultural analysis are carried out not for themselves but for more constructive purposes. According to Smith, "the analysis of present religious conditions and problems, therefore, is undertaken for the positive purpose of formulating religious convictions which shall answer certain pertinent questions of the human spirit in our day."[121] This constructive task is at the heart of the theological enterprise, not repetition of what went before, nor translation into new idioms of ancient truths. Instead, the task is the creative and, indeed, imaginative one of making new proposals for a new age. According to Smith, "If we know the real needs of men, the next undertaking is to meet those needs by organizing the available forces of the universe so as to provide the most satisfactory answer to the problems of life."[122] While relying on history to instruct us, the theologian must seek new and more appropriate ways forward, and to do so must utilize what Smith referred to as the theologian's "constructive imagination."[123]

A fourth task also faces the historicist theologian, which Smith referred to as the "apologetic defense" of theological claims.[124] There are several important elements to this branch of theology. Centrally, for Smith, to mount a defense of theological claims is not the same as being an uncritical advocate of a religious tradition, especially one that bases his or her assertions of validity on nonhistorical or nonempirical grounds. Instead, Smith argued that theologians, like other thinkers, must first investigate and then give public reasons for the claims they develop.[125] This means that while imaginative construction is an important dimension of theological work as theologians consider possibilities for the present and future, such constructive proposals must "be justified by the facts," be verified by experiments, must "fit with the conclusions of other sciences," and finally must be pragmatically verified in terms of their repercussions or fruits for real life in the world.[126] Theological ideas cannot claim a special status that protects them from public scrutiny. For Smith, these ideas must be willing to enter the sphere of public debate if they wish to have any credence for contemporary persons.

Two final dimensions of Smith's work stand out as important in the context of this book. The first is that Smith, following through on his understanding of the theological task as continually engaged in critical revision, strongly argued that the contemporary situation mandated a radical alteration of the Christian idea of God. A notion of God as a supernatural being omnipotently controlling the world is unacceptable, according to Smith, in a context that is shaped by new scientific interpretations of nature and human society and in a world committed to democratic ideals. Thus, he called for a twofold reinterpretation of God in which there occurs a "translation of categories of divinity into terms compatible with democratic ethics"[127] and in which God is understood not as a supernatural power over against the world but as an immanent force within finite reality.[128] Only a finite, naturalistic interpretation of the sacred could meet the requirements of the twentieth century. Smith went so far as to raise the question of whether Christianity might outgrow the idea of God completely.[129]

The other final element in Smith's work that is important to note is his self-conscious openness to other religious and secular traditions. Smith asserted that a central task is to explore the past for resources for the present. But he also argued that because all religious traditions are human and historical, in principle they can provide resources for one another.[130] This is not because they all claim the same thing but precisely because this variety of perspectives offers a multiplicity of tools for responding to the challenges that face humanity. Smith thus balanced his assertion of the particularity and time- and place-conditioned character of human religious traditions with the claim that such traditions are not isolated from one another but available for communication with and mutual enhancement of one another.

Smith is a remarkable representative of the Early Chicago School. His historicist commitments led him, in the early twentieth century, to argue for the conditioned character of all religious persons, artifacts, and claims, and to propose out of this insight a view of theology as imaginative construction that evaluates its claims publicly, pragmatically, and empirically in conversation with the views of other sciences and human discourses. Last, in a manner that was considerably before his time, Smith argued for open dialogue between religious traditions in order not only to enlarge our knowledge of the world but to enhance the resources humans have available to them to respond to the challenges that confront an ever-changing world situation. If no one has absolute truth, for Smith, then it is imperative that humans are open to and generous with their finite and fallible efforts to understand the world and humans' place within it.

Shirley Jackson Case

Shirley Jackson Case is the last of our Early Chicago School figures upon whom we will focus in this volume. Case, a Canadian Free Baptist, was educated at Yale University, primarily in New Testament Studies. He joined the University of Chicago's Divinity School faculty as a New Testament professor in 1908, went on to teach the history of early Christianity, and, from 1933 to 1938, to be dean of the Divinity School. In those roles he both exemplified the historical-social approach to religion so prevalent at Chicago during this era and also formulated the underlying assumptions that animated much of this orientation. In particular, Case sought to challenge what he termed the "normative hypothesis" that underlay many scholars of religions' approach to history and the past.

During the nineteenth and twentieth centuries there were a number of conflicting interpretations of the past and its status for the present. As we saw in chapter 1, many thinkers of the Franco-British Enlightenment proffered negative views of the past. Even when that aggressively negative stage of the Enlightenment had been moved beyond, there were new views that asserted that historical development is progressive and that later historical periods represent clear advancements over earlier eras. On the other hand, there were orientations, developed especially in the nineteenth century, that celebrated the past and often offered idealized notions of what went before. Shirley Jackson Case is important because he sought to develop a view of history that avoided *both* the dismissal of history and the problematic idealization of the past as authoritative.

Case, in particular, set himself over against those perspectives that overestimate the stature of the past. He thought most religious traditions interpret the "voice of antiquity" as the "voice of authority."[131] Religious traditions bolster their own claims to authority and power in any present era by claiming an intimate connection with a normative past. Hence, according to Case, "its officials have held their position by right of tradition, its ceremonies have derived their validity from ancestral practice and its teachings have been thought to embody a wisdom divinely authorized in by-gone times."[132] And while many religions have engaged in such modes of self-justification, these have been, Case argued, particularly prevalent in Christianity.

Behind the claims of a normative past lay certain assumptions that Case found problematic. First, he asserted that such views assume a "segmented" view of history in which eras, places, and times can be separated from each other, singling out sections to be elevated and idealized.[133] The notions of a sacred history separated from secular history or of pristine origins embody such ideas. Corollary to this segmented approach to history that idealizes certain parts of the past is, according to Case, a theory of "a decadent present."[134] Over against those notions in which history is progress, this approach sees history as a tale of loss and fall in which humanity is progressively separated from those elevated moments of primal truth or relationship with the divine. And finally, Case argued the assumption of an idealized past is further strengthened by adding in the idea of revelation; thus, antiquity and revelation combine to identify the past as the premier site of authority for Christianity. In this perspective the past has a status denied the present: "Its primary value lies in its normative significance. It is the one authoritative guide in all matters of religion. It is the ultimate court of appeal for one who would ascertain the proper content of Christian doctrine, and it is the infallible source for every preacher's message."[135]

For Case, modern historicist insights and the historical method have rendered this "normative hypothesis" thoroughly unacceptable. The past no longer presents itself as the site of some pure origins or "an age of slightly tarnished perfections."[136] The past instead simply designates earlier times, representing the beginnings of various human enterprises but lacking any distinctive character to set the past over against the present. History emerges in this view not as a series of segmented eras that can be separated from each other and assigned differing statuses. Instead, it is an ongoing process in which distinctive moments exist in a vast, interconnected web.

When history is interpreted in terms of process, for Case, several things follow. To begin with, and perhaps most importantly, Case argued that we must give up the "quest for a normative guidance."[137] The past, including times, texts, institutions, and persons, can no longer be assumed to have utterly unique significance. But this did not mean for Case that the past has no importance. Indeed, as historical creatures, humans are always dependent upon and influenced by history. Case asserted that history is not irrelevant, for "there is no aspect of our modern civilization in which the present is not deeply and widely rooted in the past."[138] If the quest for a normative past is wrongheaded so too, for Case, is the attempt to rid ourselves of our history. The modern attempt to deny the significance of the past is a "quixotic aspiration" doomed to failure.[139]

Case thus ruled out a normative past but also rejected the attempts to jettison history. In their stead he suggested, like other Chicago thinkers, that the past has a didactic role; its task is to provide stimulus to our contemporary understanding of the world and to generate new solutions to present-day problems. The appeal to the past then is a heuristic appeal. The past, therefore, provides "equipment for the journey" of human experience. Significance is linked to what "equipment" history provides, but the past determines neither the "itinerary" nor the "destination" for human history.[140]

Several other important elements are central to Case's approach to history. One relates to what is significant in the past. Not only did Case rule out the segmented view of history, but he also rejected approaches that highlight only great figures or certain texts or prominent institutions or supposedly unchanging dogmas. Moreover, he denied that traditions have essences in any of these forms that can be traced as unaltered from one generation to the next. History is a process in which every moment is characterized by its human quality. But having acknowledged this means, further, that historically minded thinkers must attend to the full scope of history in all its dimensions and manifestations. The interest in the past for historicists is consequently all-encompassing; it is related to how real people lived their lives, not to an abstract history of ideas or a bloodless portrayal of what was a complex and diverse living tradition. No one strand dominates the study of the past for Case but, rather, the historicist should attend to the full "stream of vital social experience."[141] Thus, vanished for Case is an assumed essentialism but also elitist approaches to the concrete history of religious persons.

Going along with Case's repudiation of an authoritative past was his equally strong assertion that history is not necessarily a tale of advancement. Historical process does entail ongoing change, but such change "does not necessarily imply that the historical process is always progress."[142] In a manner parallel to thinkers such as Gerald Birney Smith, who linked evolution to adaptation but not necessarily progress, so Case associated history with changing circumstances without assuming that such alterations are always for the good.

But if both the notions of the past as normative and history as progress are to be rejected, the question remains how historical developments are to be assessed and evaluated. When the appeal to history is heuristic, what standards or norms guide contemporary determination of those resources? Case responded to these questions in two ways. First, he stressed that the importance of ideas, figures, institutions, and practices lies in their pragmatic function, in the kinds of lives they make possible or hinder. Viewed from this perspective, "a moral precept, a ritual act, or a creedal affirmation derives its significance, not from the assumption of normativeness for the past, but from the pragmatic fact of functional worth in the vital experiences of the individuals and groups who first instituted and subsequently perpetuated the items in question."[143] Not only do we assess the value of the past in relation to its own context in such functional terms, but these also guide our evaluation of what should be retained in one's own or others' heritages. The past remains alive and a resource for the present in so far as it can contribute to the enhancement of present-day experience. Its viability for the present is hence linked to its pragmatic usefulness in facing the challenges of today. In Case's words, "the perpetuation of heritages from the past will derive justification solely from the measure of their functional value in the experiences of the continuing Christian society."[144] Finally, when pragmatic considerations are the guides for assessing what developments in the past compel loyalty or criticism in the present, then the clear location of the standards for assessing the past lie in the present. That is to say, the ongoing validity of beliefs or practices that emerged in other historical ages is gauged by present-day standards, not historical ones. It is the "imperious command of present duty" that directs contemporary decision making.[145]

This meant for Case that what is really important for contemporary thinkers, including theologians, are the creative and constructive tasks of interpreting human experience in the present and imagining new possibilities for human development in the future. For theology this means that the concerns related to preserving or disregarding religious heritage are secondary to the responsibility to create viable visions of reality for the present and future.[146] In particular, Case asserted that outmoded religious ideas and practices must be moved beyond and replaced with notions and ways of living more attuned to contemporary assumptions. A major example for Case, as it was for G. B. Smith, related to the idea of God. For Case, like Smith, the idea of God has had a long and varied history though it has often carried supernaturalistic overtones. In his context traditional forms of supernaturalism no longer were compelling and were at odds with other widespread assumptions about reality. In their place Case proposed a reconstruction of the idea of God, forgoing any remnants of supernaturalism and its traditional attendant ideas such as omnipotence.[147] A more acceptable notion of God would be naturalistic, identifying God both with the creative urge in nature and toward cultural advancement and the human quest for moral and spiritual values.[148] Creativity, as part of the processes of nature and human history, now becomes the touchstone for a naturalistic religiosity suited for the modern world.

Many of the Chicago thinkers applied their historicist assumptions not only to reconstructing the idea of God but also other areas, such as biblical interpretation and the burgeoning quest for the historical Jesus. Case was at the forefront of these efforts as well. He embodied his historicist commitments in his own biography of Jesus and in his writings on the status of the Bible. While Case's portrayal of Jesus as a Palestinian Jew who preached a prophetic vision of eschatological hope is interesting, for our purposes the historicist assumptions that drive Case's study are perhaps more important. In many senses Case's interpretations of Jesus provide a sort of case study of his historicist claims about the nature and status of the past, the constructive tasks of theology, and the historicist commitments to the present and future.

For Case, the first task of the historian engaged in the quest for Jesus is to offer as accurate a picture of Jesus' public career and times as possible. Hence, Case shared the commitment to objectivity of other historians, though, as we will see, this was somewhat muted by other assumptions. Second, Case distanced himself from other approaches to the historical Jesus by his clear rejection of what he termed "documentarianism."[149] In particular, Case, in accordance with his historicist assumptions, was underwhelmed by assertions that the canonical literature of Christianity should be given special status. The traditional linking of canonicity and supposed apostolic authorship with historicity is deeply flawed. The canon is a product of historical developments, including the manipulation of power; it was and has continued to be a "machinery of control."[150] As such, "neither the prestige of canonicity nor the hypothesis of apostolic authorship can insure the accuracy of any ancient biography of Jesus."[151] Thus, historians, according to Case, must challenge these assumptions of what he termed ecclesiastical custom and instead open themselves to the critical exploration of all the data available, including so-called apocryphal sources and other information available about the social world of Jesus' time and of the world of developing Christianity.

Having rejected any elevated status for canonical materials, Case went on to emphasize that these materials, canonical and extra-canonical alike, do not offer historical portrayals of Jesus or his times. Instead, he argued for a historicist interpretation of these sources. They are, to begin with, creative renderings of Jesus that emerged out of the early Christian movement, and as such they reflect its social world, its developing theologies, and the particular issues and problems to which they were responses. Jesus was configured and reconfigured not so much to offer an accurate picture but to name and respond to the realities of the various early Christian communities. Even the earliest portrayals of Jesus are creative reconstructions or fabrications. In that sense these materials tell too little and too much; they tell about the world of developing Christianity but less fully about the world of Jesus. Hence, for Case, a major role—perhaps *the* major role—they play is as helpful entrees into Christianity as it emerged and, from a historicist perspective, they need to be treated as such rather than as adequate sources for a biography of Jesus.

When Case sought to delineate what then might be possible in relation to Jesus, he argued that the task is twofold; it entails discriminating within the sources what can be legitimately related to the historical contexts of the emerging Christian communities and what might be reflective of the Palestinian context within which Jesus himself had lived. Repeatedly, Case argued that this "social point of view" is what is required. That means that the historian of Jesus must really be a historian of the social world of Palestine, utilizing whatever resources are available to understand that historical milieu. Therefore, for Case, historians cannot try to treat Jesus as somehow unique but must see him as a product of his times and of his own experience: "He was connected with a past which played its part in the process of his development, he was surrounded by definite historical circumstances, and he had his own personal inclinations, his own characteristics, his own intellectual life and his own spiritual experiences."[152] Jesus was hence produced by, part of, and a contributor to a very specific time and place. To search for modern ideas or a modern religious model or some timeless truth in the historical figure of Jesus is to search in vain.

Case's views of the historical Jesus resonated quite fully with his overall historicist outlook. He did think, perhaps in tension with those historicist assumptions, that Jesus embodied commitments to certain principles, most especially, love of God and neighbor, that could be relevant in other times and places. But Jesus' own interpretations of what such principles meant were thoroughly time-bound. What was appropriate in Palestine two thousand years ago might be inappropriate in the twentieth century. Case declared, Jesus might "have taught and acted otherwise had he been placed in these modern surroundings."[153] Therefore, contemporary theology and religious belief and practice cannot return to the past, even the past Jesus represented, to get clear guidance for the present. It is not only that it is difficult to identify in great detail who Jesus was but, more significantly, his life and thought did not provide a blueprint or authoritative guide for Case's own world. Instead, Case, embodying what was argued above, asserted that the task of present-day theologians is to analyze critically the present and its problems, to engage the past didactically in order to see what resources it might offer the present, and to propose the best vision for their times that is possible knowing that in the future others will surely supplant their imaginative visions just as they have those of Jesus' time and place.

Thus, Case, whether he was speaking about the nature of the past, the idea of God, or how Jesus is to be interpreted, always made clear that he was deeply aware of the tentative character of all ideas and practices, including, especially, religious ones. All of our claims, be they about God, Jesus, or human nature, are human-made pronouncements, and there is no guarantee of their ongoing validity. Case repeatedly cautioned his readers that a historicist perspective is a humble and tentative stance, reminding us always that "it is altogether too evident that today's truth may become tomorrow's error and that tomorrow's truth may be today's heresy."[154]

Mordecai Kaplan

Mordecai Kaplan (1881–1983), the founder of Reconstructionist Judaism, shared with the other thinkers in this chapter the profound changes that shaped the United States during the late nineteenth century and during the twentieth century. But he experienced these changes not as a member of the still-dominant, if ever less so, Protestant majority but as a Jewish immigrant from eastern Europe who was deeply immersed both in the traditions of eastern European Jewry and in the newfound possibilities of life in modern America. Trained in a Yeshiva and at Jewish Theological Seminary, where he would later teach for many years, Kaplan also studied at City College of New York and Columbia. It was out of the confluence of these varied experiences that Kaplan would craft his innovative interpretation of what it meant to be Jewish and American in the twentieth century.

For Kaplan, Jews and other religious persons of his day faced a grave crisis. They had inherited religious traditions steeped in supernatural assumptions about a God who transcends humanity completely and who is not, in Kaplan's words, "subject to any empirical law of nature."[155] Such supernatural assumptions are linked to other ideas as well, especially to notions of revelation that locate knowledge of God in sources that escape the dictates of ordinary knowledge. A supernatural God who reveals Godself through nonhistorical and miraculous sources entails several other implications. One implication often accompanying supernaturalistic assumptions is, Kaplan argued, an elevated sense of the past, a rendering of the past as different in kind from the present and as the site of revelation or as the originating point of a supernaturally constituted people.[156] In Kaplan's words, "the practical outcome to such an elevation of the past is that whatever has come down from it to our own day is, *ipso facto*, sacrosanct and binding. Tradition does not present itself merely as a medium of information about the past but speaks with the voice of authority commanding us to heed and obey whatever in the past was regarded as the will of God."[157] Going along with these assumptions, especially for Jews, are other elements, such as notions of a Chosen people who are supernaturally brought into being and who are the historical conveyors of God's will. And, Kaplan argued, a climate of authoritarianism also has developed that he saw as pervasive in supernaturally grounded religions. When our sources of knowledge are ahistorical and grounded in the miraculous suspension of the laws of nature, then special access is required and authorities are needed as purveyors of religious knowledge and guardians of religious truth.[158]

For Kaplan, this interlocking set of ideas—of a supernatural God, ahistorical sources, authoritarian approaches to religious truth, elevation of a tradition's past, and convictions of chosenness or superiority—had become problematic. While they may have been compelling in a premodern world they no longer embodied interpretations of reality that modern persons could easily espouse. Modern science has undermined the vision of reality in which a supernatural transcendent God makes sense; historicist insights into the character of all our claims have challenged the special pleading of authoritarian claims to miraculously grounded truth; the appeal to the past as some site of special revelation or a pristine tradition also collapses in the light of modern scholarship. The assertions of chosenness or superiority are undermined as their supernaturalistic foundations falter and as our knowledge of other ancient traditions expands. And all of these premodern notions stand in defiance of commitments to democracy and freedom. Thus, for Kaplan, "authoritarianism is incompatible with freedom of thought and with the diversity of practice to which such freedom must give rise."[159]

Kaplan proclaimed that these developments present modern religious persons with a dilemma of crisis proportions. He contended that many modern persons no longer find religious beliefs interesting or coherent. Others continue to espouse traditional claims, sometimes with the renewed vehemence of modern fundamentalism. But religiously espousing ideas that contradict or stand in tension with other basic assumptions about reality, Kaplan argued, causes the modern person to live a bifurcated life, accepting and living out modern convictions in relation to most aspects of his or her life while continuing to accept, in the arena of religion, what would be untenable assumptions concerning anything else. The result is, according to Kaplan, a life lived with "a split mentality."[160] Such a person "tries to live in two universes of thought and attitude, one natural and secular, the other supernatural and religious."[161]

Kaplan's life-work posed the question of whether this bifurcation can be overcome, whether there are ways to be modern and religious at the same time. His constructive efforts represent a sustained attack on what he termed the logic of supernaturalism, and in its place he proffered historicist, naturalist, and pragmatist alternatives to this logic. In *Judaism as a Civilization* (1934) Kaplan engaged in the dismantling of the supernaturalist logic by developing an interpretation of the Jewish people as a civilization that is thoroughly historical in nature.[162] Gone are any assumptions of the supernatural origins of the Jewish people. Instead, he proposed a dynamic, evolving view of Jewish culture in which religion plays a central role but does not exhaust the meaning of Jewish peoplehood. Instead, languages, history, art, and the wide variety of cultural practices all contribute to a living, diverse, and thoroughly human heritage. If the origins and the various stages of Jewish life are historical expressions like those of all other civilizations and cultures, then neither the past nor any particular moment or element from it, such as the Bible, carry any special status. In an eloquent statement in his work *Judaism without Supernaturalism* (1967), Kaplan argued, "We should accept the past as no more authoritative than the present. It should have the right to vote but not the right to veto."[163] Tradition should thus be taken seriously but not literally or uncritically.[164] When the past is shorn of its elevated status and our religious claims take on the character of other human claims denied special pleading or access to the truth, then the mechanisms of authoritarianism are also to be rejected. In their place Kaplan commended a new spirit of democratic participation in religious life and debate, a spirit that enhances the participation of religious persons in the public sphere of modern democratic America and contributes to the development of moral responsibility and freedom. Religion, in Kaplan's view, is now to be disassociated from supernaturalism and given a pragmatic interpretation as part of the effort to find orientation in the world and to seek salvation, a salvation no longer defined in terms of otherworldly realities but as the progressive enhancement and fulfillment of human potential for freedom and responsibility within the only world we know.[165]

At the center of Mordecai Kaplan's reconstructive efforts was his repudiation of supernatural conceptions of God and his reinterpretation of this notion in naturalist, or what he termed *transnaturalist,* terms.[166] As stated above, the idea of a supernatural God who transcends all finite reality had become problematic in light of modern notions of science and history and, for Kaplan, as the twentieth century unfolded, in light of the enormity of evil and violence of the period. While some would forgo notions of God altogether, opting for more materialist or reductive forms of naturalism, Kaplan argued for the reconstruction of the God-idea in terms that resonate with other contemporary assumptions about reality. Influenced by those who would come to be called process thinkers, such as Alfred North Whitehead, Henri Bergson, and Henry Nelson Wieman, as well as pragmatists and historicists such as John Dewey and William James, Kaplan proposed an idea of God not as a supernatural being outside of finite history and nature but as the creative power or process within finite reality that impels humankind as well as the rest of nature toward ever-greater development and fulfillment, including toward greater human responsibility and freedom: "Transnaturalist religion beholds God in the fulfillment of human nature and not in the suspension of the natural order."[167] At various points, not always consistently, Kaplan referred to God as the creative process that transforms chaos into order, or again as the aspect of reality that is the source of all moral and spiritual values.[168] "God," for Kaplan, "is the power that makes for salvation of man through the community which organizes its entire social order around the purpose of man's salvation."[169] As such, God is the natural source of all moral and spiritual values, and devotion to this creative process or source enhances humane existence.

Thus, for Kaplan, a naturalistic or transnaturalistic idea of God did not stand in contradiction with the scientific or historicist or democratic ideals of his era. It was an understanding of the God-idea as the human attempt to name and orient human life toward the creative processes and forces within reality out of which human existence emerged and which can be furthered and enhanced through human self-conscious commitment. Such a God-idea resonated, Kaplan thought, with the evolutionary science of his day but, equally important, contributed to the democratic ideals that he saw as central to modern, especially American, identity. This idea of God as creativity or creative process would not, Kaplan asserted, diminish Judaism as a civilization or as a religion but would revitalize it in the modern world—a Judaism no longer dependent on an outmoded supernaturalism but on a vital new sense of the world and humans' place within it.

Kaplan thus encouraged modern persons, especially Jews, to confront openly the intellectual challenges of their twentieth-century world. For him, science and historical studies had effectively undermined the supernaturalism, authoritarianism, and assumptions of divinely mandated uniqueness that had grounded much of the religious traditions bequeathed from the past; these ideas were without intellectual credence and were, as Kaplan stated, "gone with the wind."[170] As Kaplan sought to delineate the American and modern context within which modern Judaism needed to interpret itself, he highlighted two other factors that have remained important for subsequent historicists. First, he often noted that as our knowledge increases it is no longer possible for proponents of particular religious or cultural traditions to interpret negatively other traditions. The comparative study of religions and cultures challenges notions of unique and pure origins, singular ideas of the divine, and some sort of ethical superiority.[171] Historicist orientations thus relativize and equalize human traditions while at the same time they assert the individuality and "otherness" of particular human religious and cultural formations. This balance of similarity and otherness has become an ongoing issue for historicist-minded thinkers who both recognize the uniqueness of human traditions but deny that traditions arise and exist in isolation from one another or that they represent incommensurable ways of thinking and living.

One final element of Kaplan's legacy to historicism was his profound sense that human interpretations of reality, the divine, and human community are tied to matters of power and control. Ideas do not merely float free; they are always linked to the mechanisms of power. Like John Dewey, who was convinced not only of the intellectual bankruptcy of philosophy's quest for timeless truth but of the dangerous authoritarian political ramifications of such quests, Kaplan also saw in supernaturalism a profoundly anti-democratic dynamic that must be repudiated in the American context. This linking of ideas to power arrangements suggests that more than intellectual viability is at stake in our struggles over ideas and that democratic practices as well as democratic ideas are necessary if historicized, naturalized, and pragmatically viable perspectives are to survive in the contemporary world. In closing this chapter we will turn now to W. E. B. Du Bois, the great American thinker who utilized these claims both as grounds for a positive vision of American culture and as the means to challenge and confront the continual failure of American culture to understand the dynamics of unequal power and anti-democratic practices in relation to African Americans.

W. E. B. Du Bois

William Edward Burghardt Du Bois (1868–1963) is the last of the American thinkers to be considered in this chapter. Increasingly, such commentators on American pragmatism as Cornel West and Giles Gunn locate Du Bois as a significant contributor to this tradition of historicized and pragmatic thought. For our purposes, it is important to focus on Du Bois because his work raised issues that were missing or not fully attended to by his fellow American thinkers, issues that are central to prospects for a twenty-first century historicist theology.[172]

W. E .B. Du Bois was born and bred in New England, shaped by a Congregationalist religious upbringing in a largely white town of Great Barrington, Massachusetts. He received first a B.A. from Fisk University and then matriculated at Harvard University where he was deeply influenced by William James. After graduating with an undergraduate degree in philosophy, Du Bois remained at Harvard to study political science and history, receiving both an M.A and a Ph.D. He also spent several years at the University of Berlin studying sociology. From Harvard, Du Bois went to teach first at Wilberforce University and then for many years at Atlanta University. While a professor of economics and history at Atlanta University, he conducted his groundbreaking sociological studies of black American life that shaped not only future interpretations of the black American experience but also the field of sociology more generally and especially sociology of religion. Du Bois was, however, like Dewey, not content to be only an academic. He sought a role as a public intellectual and an activist for racial and social justice in twentieth-century America. From 1910 to 1934 he was editor of *The Crisis*, the publishing arm of the National Association for the Advancement of Colored People (NAACP), of which he was a founding member. In that role and as a prolific writer of essays and articles in popular publications, Du Bois sought to explore and respond to the situation of African Americans in the modern United States. Increasingly in his work and life Du Bois would insist on a more global perspective as he supported pan-Africanism and eventually communism as alternatives to the racist realities of the United States. He would return to Atlanta University to chair the sociology department from 1934 to 1944, but late in his life he traveled broadly and eventually moved to Ghana, where he became a citizen and died in 1963.

Virtually all of the thinkers dealt with in this chapter have tied the realization that human ideas, philosophies, religions, and social/political organizations are historical constructions with the further commitment to democracy and to the democratic participation in their evaluation and creative transformation. If humans are historical beings who create the social worlds within which they dwell, then, for persons such as Dewey and the Chicago theologians, it is imperative that the creation of these worlds not be the province of the powerful few but the result of input from the widest number of persons possible and done in light of the ramifications for all those affected by such visions of reality and the institutions that give expression to them. In a manner simply absent from the thinking of many German historicists, American thinkers linked the recognition of historicity to pragmatism and to the cultivation of democratic values and practices.

W. E. B. Du Bois was clearly part of this strand of American thought. But he was also clear that the language of democracy is hollow and hypocritical on the most fundamental level. Despite commitment to a progressive politics on the part of the thinkers associated with this American lineage, no American thinker before Du Bois offered a sustained analysis of the role race played in the American experience or of the profound conflict between the rhetoric of democracy and the reality of racism experienced by Americans of African descent. Mordecai Kaplan asked what it meant to be American and to be Jewish and sought ways to make these cohere. For Du Bois, racism thwarts any possibility of reconciling being black and

American for those of African descent, leaving blacks with a strange and disquieting experience of double consciousness and dual identity. In his groundbreaking study *The Souls of Black Folk,* Du Bois referred to life lived always within the Veil of Color, a "double life, with double thoughts, double duties, and double social classes."[173] Democracy in the United States, Du Bois asserted throughout his life, will be a lie until there exists a full understanding of the role of race and the ways in which racism inhibits democratic possibilities. In his work *Dusk of Dawn* he stated, "The democracy which the white world seeks to defend does not exist. It has been splendidly conceived and discussed, but not realized."[174] Without the inclusion of those least protected in society and those who least benefit from the modern world, then "democracy is a mockery and contains within itself the seeds of its own destruction."[175]

Importantly, for Du Bois, if recognizing the historical character of human existence requires a future-looking commitment to democratic participation in the creation of society, it must also embody the commitment to radical inclusion of the least powerful voices in society and to the testing of our institutions and political, social, and economic policies in light of their ramifications for the most marginalized in human societies. Du Bois saw that democracy also requires profound social and cultural criticism and that those aligned with historicism and pragmatism need also to be engaged in cultural critique.

Du Bois's significance for this study further includes his insistence that religion is a central site for understanding the black experience in America but also for interpreting the ways in which cultural construction generally takes place. Like the members of the Chicago School, Du Bois discerned the potential for transformative action within religious communities. The black church is, according to Du Bois, the center of black life, the source of social identity, and political power in the face of racist sentiments and policies.[176] At its best the church can and should be that place where "colored men and women of education and energy can work for the best things regardless of their belief or disbelief in unimportant dogmas and ancient and outworn creeds."[177] But also like the Chicago theologians, Du Bois thought that the world of religion continued to be a world of outmoded ideas and corrupt practices. As a cultural critic the task was also to be a critic of religion, pursuing its transformative potential but rejecting its failure to be responsive to the contemporary world.

Du Bois's criticism of both black churches and leaders and white religious communities with their simultaneous assertion of Christian beliefs and racist behaviors stemmed in good part from his insistence that religious traditions, beliefs, and institutions do not exist in some separate realm but are deeply intertwined with other social and political realities.[178] In a manner that presaged the current rejection of *sui generis* notions of religion, Du Bois argued for their social nature, insisting that they arose from these wider realities and that their functions must be understood in relation to the political, social, and economic contexts within which they arose and exist. In *The Souls of Black Folk,* he insisted that the role of the black church is foremost a social role, growing out of the realities of a racially divided America and responsive to the needs for social, political, and economic organization and the importance of transmitting cultural traditions both from America and Africa.[179] Moreover, white churches are not disentangled from political realities; their beliefs, practices, and functions are also tied to the social location of their members. With Du Bois, religion becomes the conduit for power, unintelligible apart from the place and role it plays in wider society.

Du Bois moved historicist and pragmatic thought in several other significant directions. Perhaps most importantly, he raised the prospect of a more global perspective. Personally he became more and more skeptical of the possibility of reconciling American and black identity. This led him eventually to Ghana where he claimed citizenship in the closing years of his life. But for our purposes, he broke the hold on nationalistic forms of identity that historicism and even American pragmatism had touted. Du Bois saw clearly that nations are deeply interconnected politically and economically. Moreover, he also had a profound understanding that the dispossessed of the earth share identities and conditions that transcend any national boundaries. For him, the entire economic foundation of the modern world is based on racial and class divisions. There is, he repeatedly noted, a deep connection between "race and wealth." Historicism, especially in its German form, had emphasized the particularity of national formations and national identities. Du Bois stressed particularity no less than did these German thinkers or the white American pragmatists and historicists. But for him, these particularities are not only tied to geography but also to race and to economic class. If the future is to hold the possibility for a democratic, just, and transformed world social order, then global economic and political conditions will need to change and "the progress of the white world must cease to rest upon the poverty and ignorance of its own proletariat and of the colored world."[180] For Du Bois, international movements such as communism and pan-Africanism and the beginnings of postcolonialism held promise as ways to transform a racist political and economic system deeply tied to Western forms of capitalism and imperialism. These suggested for him very particular historical identities but ones tied not to nations but to the transnational realities of the modern world.

With Du Bois, historicism and pragmatism entered a more politically sophisticated phase. He, in a good sociological manner, turned attention to the particularities of time and place, refusing easy generalities or assumptions of homogeneity. He, moreover, asserted that social and cultural identities, beliefs, practices, and institutions arise from, reflect, and contribute to an intricate web of political, social, and economic realities. Religious beliefs and practices result from and give expressions to these realities as well. Religion is thus linked not to a private realm of experience or an ahistorical realm of revelation or supernatural beings; it arises from the stuff of everyday life. Its function, value, and prospects are tied to its place and role within the web of concrete existence—a web of unequal power and yet also a web laden with the potential for a transformed world.

Conclusion

Historicism in the United States during its formative period took many forms and articulated a number of varied themes. In particular, historicism was linked by many thinkers with pragmatism and naturalism and deeply intertwined with the American commitment to democratic processes and institutions. The ramifications of such developments for theology were significant, as the work of the early Chicago School of Theology demonstrated. Religious traditions were increasingly interpreted as sociohistorical formations, emergent from finite human circumstances without divine origins or supernatural guarantees. Religions issued forth not from some *sui generis* experience or transcendent revelation but from the concrete needs of human beings to gain orientation in life, to identify ideals and values that might endow human life with meaning and direction. Theology, hence, also became fully human and, like all human efforts, was to be considered conditional and tentative, judged not according to timeless truth or supernatural standards but against the concrete forms of life such visions made possible.

The crises that confronted German historicism did not challenge the historicism of the American thinkers to the same extent or in the same ways. The conflict between a lingering supernaturalism and historicism, a sense of history's potential and the burden of the past, and the profound implications of a global war now lost all coalesced to undermine the promise of German historicism and to see it yield to other forms of thought including, in theology, neoorthodoxy. But historicism faced its own challenges on the American scene, and with it, pragmatism especially. In philosophy an interest in analytical thought moved to the fore, and in theology, while fundamentalism was defeated in many theological schools, neoorthodoxy would be for many a compelling perspective in light of the world wars, the Depression, racial strife, and eventually a nuclear threat. Even at the University of Chicago the sociohistoricism of the early Chicago School was replaced by the new liberal metaphysics of process thinkers Henry Nelson Wieman and Charles Hartshorne. Still, as philosopher Richard Bernstein has noted in relation to pragmatism, the challenge of historicism, naturalism, and pragmatism did not disappear but took new forms as the twentieth century advanced and, as the concluding chapter of this work will delineate, they now present us in the early twenty-first century with new ways of conceiving the theological task. To those new forms of theology we now turn.

4

Toward a Contemporary Historicism

Historicism at Mid-Century

The preceding chapters demonstrated that historicism emerged as a vital, diverse, and widespread set of developments in the nineteenth and early twentieth centuries. These trajectories found expression in many levels of thought, permeating disciplines and interpretive frameworks and providing methods of analysis and norms of evaluation. In German popular and intellectual thought historicist sentiments dominated the nineteenth century, and in the United States they found profound and extensive expression in the work of the Chicago School and the positions pragmatists articulated for a significant period of the opening decades of the twentieth century. In particular, historicism had significant impact upon how religious traditions were viewed and on how religious beliefs and practices and theological claims came to be conceived. But, while extensive, historicism was not singular in form nor did all of its adherents share the same assumptions or goals. As the two preceding chapters illustrate, there were, in fact, many historicisms, including metaphysical, ontological, anthropological, theological, and epistemological ones that at times clashed in significant ways. Moreover, there were profound differences in the historicisms that took shape in the context of an emerging German nation-state and those that developed in an American context committed to democracy and oriented toward an open future rather than a revered past.

Despite the proliferation of these influential trajectories, standard accounts of both European historicism and American historicism point to the decline and eclipse of historicism as the twentieth century progressed. In Germany, the crisis of historicism led to history being interpreted as a burden and to fundamental attacks on the lingering metaphysical and theological elements of much historicism. In theology, neoorthodoxy supplanted, at least for a time, the theological liberalism of Schleiermacher and his heirs that had in part depended upon historicist impulses. In the United States, the pragmatic form of historicism in philosophy was displaced by analytic philosophy and positivism. In theology, contrasting trajectories developed that, on the one hand, mirrored neoorthodoxy and the work of Karl Barth and, on the other hand, embodied new forms of metaphysics, centered in innovative categories of process but without the strong historicist understanding of the nature and status of their claims that had characterized important strands of American thought earlier in the century. In the standard interpretations of historicism it is only in the last several decades that historicism has reemerged to be contended with once more.

In many ways it is the case that historicism was exhausted as the decades of the twentieth century unfolded. But, as Richard J. Bernstein argues about pragmatism in eclipse in the mid-twentieth century, it would be a mistake to fail to recognize that historicism continued to shape much of the thought of the twentieth century and to provide the impetus for the developments that now confront us.[1] That is, historicism was, in some profound ways, "forgotten but not gone." One place that we can see these ongoing historicist impulses is in the work of American theologians at mid-century. A premier illustration of the continuing grappling with historicist concerns can be found in the work of American theologian H. Richard Niebuhr, and it is to an examination of his transitional work that we now turn.

H. Richard Niebuhr

H. Richard Niebuhr (1894–1962) was one of the most significant theologians to work in America during the twentieth century. Importantly for this study, his work formed a bridge connecting American theology with what was taking place in Continental theology, especially in the form of neoorthodoxy and the theology of Karl Barth. He also attempted to hold together insights that emerged from the nineteenth century and early twentieth century concerning the fallible and contingent status of human claims with ideas of God associated most often with the Reformed Christianity that neoorthodoxy attempted to revitalize. Thus, Niebuhr linked a strong sense of human historicity with the Barthian concern for divine sovereignty, a cultural, social, and historical relativism with a profound sense of divine transcendence.

H. Richard Niebuhr received his graduate education at Washington University and Yale University. After teaching at Eden Theological Seminary and serving as president at Elmhurst College, Niebuhr went on to hold a faculty position at Yale Divinity School for over thirty years. While at Yale, Niebuhr emerged as one of America's most significant theological voices, writing on a wide variety of topics, including ethics, theology, the social analysis of Christian denominationalism in America, and theological education. Repeatedly in his work he treated religious traditions and communities not as isolated phenomena but as social, cultural, and political realities that could only be understood contextually and concretely. In *The Social Sources of Denominationalism* (1929) Niebuhr sought to trace the ways in which factors as wide-ranging as economics, regional proclivities, and racial perspectives influenced Christian institutions.[2] And in two later books, *The Church against the World* (1935, with Wilhelm Pauck and F. P. Miller)[3] and *The Kingdom of God in America* (1937),[4] Niebuhr sought to examine how religions, in turn, influenced cultural life in particular contexts. In all of his works, Niebuhr interpreted religions as dynamic processes, not stable entities, and he sought to locate them in the complex matrices of culture and society from which they emerged and that they reflected but also profoundly shaped.

There are several important elements within Niebuhr's thought that are particularly significant for this study. Throughout his work Niebuhr developed a complex of ideas that embodied historicist commitments while also introducing other themes that, for him, cohered with historicism and its implied relativizing of all things human but which more contemporary historicists have subsequently challenged, especially his idea of God. We will turn first to Niebuhr's historicist orientation.

In many ways, it was Niebuhr who, at mid-century, was the clearest articulator in America of the issues of historicism, relativism, pluralism, and the agential character of human historical existence. Influenced by a wide range of earlier thinkers from Kant to Schleiermacher, Søren Kierkegaard to Karl Barth, Ernst Troeltsch to the American philosopher Josiah Royce, Niebuhr developed an innovative and critical challenge to theology in the twentieth century. To begin with, Niebuhr, in various works, argued for the historical and, equally importantly, the social character of human existence. In his volume *The Responsible Self* Niebuhr set forth a view of human existence as centrally historical and temporal in nature.[5] By temporal, Niebuhr meant that humans always come from the past and are shaped by their pasts; the human self is dependent upon its history. But equally humans live toward the future in purposiveness and anticipation, anxiety or hope. How humans act in any present, how they respond to their current situation, is tied to the particularities of their remembered pasts and their anticipation of a not-yet future.

Niebuhr also stressed that how we remember the past and anticipate a not-yet future are shaped by patterns and interpretations of history and nature that we carry with us both on a social and personal level. According to Niebuhr, the human time-filled self comes to the present "not with timeless ideas, recollected in Platonic recall of the soul's participation in the eternal; not with timeless laws of never-changing nature or of a pure reason, unhistorical reason, does the self come to its present encounters. It comes rather with images and patterns of interpretations, with attitudes of trust and suspicion, accumulated in its biographical and historical past."[6] Humans are, for this reason, not humans in general but specific historical beings that encounter, interpret, and respond to reality out of the traditions of interpretations they inherit and toward open futures whose unfinished character also shapes and gives direction to human experience. In his volume *The Meaning of Revelation* (1941) Niebuhr stressed this historicity as well, stating that "man . . . is not only in time but time is in man. Moreover, and more significantly, the time that is in man is not abstract but particular and concrete; it is not a general category of time but rather the time of a definite society with distinct language, economic and political relations, religious faith and social organization."[7] According to Niebuhr, historicity is, therefore, never abstract or nonspecific but always concrete and particular, bearing distinctive markings and colorations.

Niebuhr gave expression to this historicity in other ways as well. One way was to stress the perspectival character of all human experience. His theological way of articulating this was to claim that all humans, religious and nonreligious alike, are *faithful* persons. In *Radical Monotheism and Western Culture* (1943) Niebuhr once more analyzed the historical character of human life and its ramifications.[8] In this work he stressed that humans always live out of faith. By faith Niebuhr was not referring to intellectual assent to propositions or exclusively to beliefs or commitments that are found in religious communities. Instead, by faith Niebuhr meant fundamental stances toward centers of value and loyalty that provide orientation and direction for historical persons in their concrete settings. Human historical existence requires interpretation and orientation. As was demonstrated in the previous chapter, earlier American thinkers proposed that such direction is gained in relation to the identification and articulation of ideals. Niebuhr, for his part, argued that humans gain direction and value in life by interpreting existence through the lens of loyalty to and trust in centers of value that are larger than themselves. There are, according to Niebuhr, no humans who live without such interpretive perspectives that direct human action, endow existence with meaning and value, and orient human persons in the midst of an ever-changing environment. In Niebuhr's words, "no man lives without living for some purpose, for the glorification of some God, for the advancement of some cause."[9]

Niebuhr combined this insight into the interpretive character of human life with its value-laden and, indeed, normative thrust with his insistence, noted above, that humans always carry out such interpretation, such formation of faith, from particular time- and place-bound locations. These normative interpretations are, accordingly, always perspectival, conditioned by context and history. There are no value-free or so-called objective understandings of reality but only historically located and conditioned ones. For Niebuhr, then, in a very real way, interpretations of reality and of humanity's place within the larger world are all confessional; that is, they reflect the assumptions and commitments of their particular context, not timeless or absolute truth. As such, they are contingent, fallible, relative to context, and open to criticism.

For Niebuhr, various dangers resulted from the failure to acknowledge adequately the relativity, contingency, and fallibility of human claims. On the one hand, that some modern persons apparently recognize that interpretations of reality are historical has led us to a form of skepticism and the failure to take responsibility for our human claims and values: our awareness "that all our historical philosophical ideas, religious dogmas and moral imperatives are historically conditioned" tempts us to what Niebuhr called "a new agnosticism."[10] On the other hand, Niebuhr recognized a perhaps greater peril, the failure to acknowledge the relativity of our claims and to assert for them an absoluteness to which no human claim is entitled. From Niebuhr's perspective this was the great danger of his age, the danger of idolatry, "the absolutizing of the relative."[11] This is a danger that confronts religious assertions and secular ideologies alike. It is present in the misplaced love and loyalty to political and economic systems and in religious loyalty to historical figures such as Jesus or to institutions such as the Christian church. It is always lurking in the human tendency to take what is partial and incomplete and proclaim it final and above the vicissitudes of history. All of Niebuhr's work stood as a challenge to the idolatries of his age, expressing his resistance to claims of absoluteness and certitude.

When Niebuhr articulated what this means for theology he asserted repeatedly that religious persons and theologians have no peculiar vantage point that removes them from the contingencies of history. Religious beliefs and practices are, like all others, the products of time and place, with the same historical character as other human claims. Theology, perhaps more than other human enterprises, needs to acknowledge its contingency, lack of finality, and implication in the social order. Niebuhr's concern with the absolutizing of relative forms of meaning and value was most explicitly evident in his book *Radical Monotheism and Western Culture* (1960). In this work Niebuhr explored the ways in which humans organize their personal and social lives through the articulation of those centers of trust and loyalty mentioned above. He discerned three types of such organizing centers or faith: polytheism, henotheism, and radical monotheism. The first, polytheism, is a form of faith that has many objects or centers of trust and devotion. The result of such disparate and fragmented loyalties is, on both the individual and the societal levels, a lack of integration and a proliferation of diffused and scattered purposes and competing values. Internal incoherence and an inability to direct actions according to singular or common visions follow when the organizing centers of personal and social life are many, not one. For Niebuhr, the human self, in order to be a coherent and integrated agent, must have a center of trust and loyalty that is integrated and singular as well. Polytheism leads to chaos and confusion, not responsible selfhood and agency.[12]

The second form of faith Niebuhr examined is what he termed henotheism or social faith. According to Niebuhr, henotheism, in contrast to polytheism with its fragmented, multiple, and competing centers of value, has one object of trust and loyalty. However, this one object is still a finite, limited object. It is one, but one center of value among many.[13] Niebuhr suggested that such a form of henotheistic faith can be observed in the devotion to smaller social units of family, sectarian community, and church or religious tradition. Or again, he saw henotheism dangerously manifested in the all-encompassing loyalty to nation, racial group, culture, or even civilization or humanity as a whole.[14] All these are still closed associations, calling for loyalty to the group, without external or built-in self-critical mechanisms. In Niebuhr's words, in contexts characterized by henotheistic loyalties, the power of the social group is immense: "When men's ultimate orientation is in their society, when it is their value-center and cause, when social mores can make anything right and anything wrong, then indeed conscience is the internalized voice of society or of its representatives."[15] Henotheism provides a unified center of focus and devotion for the self, in contrast to multiple centers, but these singular centers are all, for him, idols.

Thus, for Niebuhr, both more local centers of orientation and commitment as well as more encompassing but still finite ones present dangers of self-absolutizing, narrow self-referencing, and lack of critical consciousness. They also, he argued, always fail humans in their quest for meaning and orientation in life. Not only are they socially divisive and personally fragmenting; they all eventually fall apart and are revealed not as absolute but as finite, partial, and limited and, most importantly, as objects unworthy of our complete devotion. In Niebuhr's words, "the causes for which we live all die. The great social movements pass and are supplanted by others. The ideals we fashion are revealed by time to be relative. The empires and cities to which we are devoted decay. At the end nothing is left to defend us against the void of meaninglessness."[16]

Over against these fragile and fallible objects of faith Niebuhr reintroduced what he took to be the center of his Reformed Christianity—a third form of faith, radical monotheism. Radical monotheism calls for faith not in finite centers of value and orientation, in human causes or local states of loyalty. Instead, it is a faith in that void that is left when all more narrow loyalties fail, a void that somehow, for Niebuhr, is experienced not as an abyss or enemy but as a friend that simultaneously calls into question all human tendencies to idolatry yet endows finite existence with immeasurable significance.[17] This object of faith Niebuhr called the One Beyond the Many, signifying its radical transcendence and nonidentity with any finite form of existence. "It is the source of all things and the end of all. It surrounds our life as the great abyss into which all things plunge and as the source whence they come."[18] It is the power that shatters all human pretensions *and* the one that gives life meaning and orientation; it is both relativizer and sanctifier. It is that which calls into question all finite pretensions at ultimacy while at the same time demanding that humans see all reality as worthy of love and commitment. Importantly, for Niebuhr, devotion to the One Beyond the Many moves humans continually beyond the borders of their more local loyalties, including loyalty to humanity, toward a great encompassing loyalty to all that is. It pushes toward a radically self-critical orientation in life that results in a loyalty not merely to self or to nation, to religious tradition or to racial group, but to reality itself.[19]

H. Richard Niebuhr was a significant transition figure in twentieth-century thought. He sought to foreground the historical and hence relative and contingent character of human life and of all human claims. He stressed that human existence is marked by its conditioned and located character and thus is always "confessional" in nature. But his version of human historicity is not a narrow or parochial one. *Confessional* never meant for him self-referential or self-enclosed. Indeed, when linked with his notion of radical monotheism, humans simultaneously are located *and* called beyond any narrow borders; they are always both citizens of particular times and places and citizens of the universe. They are located in particular traditions but loyal to and hence open to all that is. For Niebuhr, therefore, the recognition of historicity and the acknowledgment of divine sovereignty went together. And the result of such linking of human historicity and divine transcendence is a located cosmopolitanism, a historical life that "opens out infinitely into ever new possibilities."[20]

Nineteenth-century thinkers often, as we saw in chapter 2, invoked a traditional notion of God in order to harmonize the multiplicity of perspectives and to overcome the danger of the anarchy of values that historicism reveals and, indeed, seems to cultivate. Niebuhr, for his part, invoked a divine sovereign in the face of what he interpreted as the dangerous absolutizing of finite, parochial perspectives. Idolatry, not pluralism, was the problem he saw as central to his war-torn century. In each case the dangers were real but the solution was in tension with the very historicism and its implications to which the ideas of God sought to respond. While both German historicists and thinkers such as H. Richard Niebuhr historicized their human ideas of God, leaving them open to revision, they continued to assume that the reality those ideas sought to name is beyond history, utterly transcendent of all finite reality. Whether as harmonizer or as relativizer, these notions of God point to a God above and over against history. Such partial solutions failed in the nineteenth century as the crisis of historicism grew, and for many at the end of the twentieth century, they would again appear inadequate. How historicism played out in the last decades of the twentieth century and confronts us today is the topic to which we now turn.

Theology and Historicism at the End of the Twentieth Century

The closing decades of the twentieth century witnessed developments in theology and other disciplines that both built on earlier historicisms and also intensified the challenges to which historicism had given birth. The attempts by neoorthodox theologians to hold together, through the mechanism of radical revelation, their sense of human relativity and ideas of a thoroughly transcendent God were increasingly treated with skepticism as late twentieth-century theologians began to intensify their questioning of how historical,

finite creatures bound to the realms of finite history could ever gain knowledge of this utterly transcendent and nonhistorical reality. The Barthian
appeals to a radical revelation unlike all forms of human knowledge and even
the more historicized positions of H. Richard Niebuhr began more and more
to take on the aura of special pleading. The most dramatic repudiation of the
lingering ahistorical dimensions of theology came in the form of the death-
of-God movement that rejected, on both theoretical and ethical grounds, traditional conceptions of a God utterly transcendent of history, declaring this
idea intellectually incoherent and morally reprehensible.[21] What remained
for the proponents of the death-of-God movement was either a divinization
of history or a historical realm shorn of all pretensions of the sacred.

Other movements and developments also called into question the
twentieth-century attempts to hold some forms of traditional theology and
historical consciousness in tandem. In particular, movements associated
with social change utilized the insights of historicism to attack the alliance
of much traditional theology with dominant and oppressive elements in
Western culture. Thus, Latin American, black, and feminist theologians all
asserted the historical relativity of traditional forms of theology that had
been utilized to explain and justify the oppressive conditions under which
much of humanity suffers. Increasingly, these critical analyses insisted on
linking historical ideas, practices, and institutions, including religious and
theological ones, with the unequal distribution of power. For them, the recognition of historicity did not imply a benign situatedness but an unholy
alliance of, especially, religion and an often-unjust status quo. The historicist insights into the connections between claims to truth and power came
to the fore in many of the most vital and explosive theological trajectories of
the last quarter of the century. Whether in the form of Gustavo Gutiérrez's
assertions that Christian theology was often intimately tied to the subjuga-
tion of the powerless and poor, or James Cone's correlation of much of classical Christian theology with white racism and supremacy, or Mary Daly's
radical assault on the male character of Christian theology, many theologians representing heretofore absent voices utilized the insights into the
historical, conditioned, and fallible nature of human claims to undermine
dominant forms of religious and theological thought and practice just as
their counterparts in other disciplines would challenge secular versions of
dominant ideologies.[22] For those committed to emancipatory movements,
religious beliefs and practices and, along with them, theological claims were
no longer expressions of timeless truth but historically conceived strategies
in the manipulation and deployment of power. Theology now, in the words

of religion scholar Lonnie Kliever, became a "shattered spectrum," marked not just by the particularities of location and context but by contestation and struggles over power.[23]

Theological and political movements for liberation would become a permanent part of the theological landscape of the late twentieth century with new groups continually joining the theological debate, including more voices from parts of the two-thirds world and perspectives emergent out of movements for sexual liberation, especially of gays, lesbians, and transsexual persons.[24] As historian Peter Novick would say of similar developments within the discipline of history, the universalisms of the past gave way to "newer particularistic sensibilities," engendering calls for each group to construct its own history or, in our case, theology.[25] Such perspectives embodied both theologies of criticism and protest that attacked what were interpreted as the oppressive agendas associated with dominant perspectives and constructive alternatives to the varied forms of theology that had heretofore dominated the theological scene. The recognition of the time- and context-bound and power-infused character of theology led to the critical rejection of much traditional or orthodox theology and to the proliferation of new theological possibilities. Accompanying these developments was a profound sense of the contested nature of theological discourse.

Soon, however, many of these liberatory discourses were in turn challenged both by succeeding generations within these movements and by external critics. One such challenge pointed to the often ahistorical elements that continued to plague the positions of these critical thinkers who utilized the recognition of historicity to undermine their opponents but frequently continued to incorporate ahistorical appeals to revelation or experience to validate their own positions. For example, black historicist theologian Simon Maimela contended that much black theology suffers from serious internal contradictions and that other black theologians such as James Cone employ historical consciousness to attack white theology but predicate the normativity of their own claims on nonhistorical assumptions about scriptures, God, and revelation. In Maimela's words, "although wanting to enjoy the benefits of modern historical consciousness—on the basis of which they are enabled effectively to confront and expose the complicity of white theology in the legitimation of white socioeconomic interests—black theologians appear unwilling to accept the full consequences of modern historical consciousness for black theology."[26] Other examples can be found in the challenges to feminist theology by women of color, especially womanist thinkers, and more historicist-minded white theologians in their claims that white feminists, while criticizing men, make universal assertions about all women that fail to analyze critically the ways in which they, as white and often privileged members of cultural elites, are implicated in systems of oppression.[27] Issues of Christian imperialism and heterosexual dominance also were named as examples of the failure to interrogate thoroughly context and power relations. The location of the theologian, in all its particularity, thus became a defining element in understanding and evaluating claims to theological validity even if those who utilized it to criticize others often failed to maintain the relativizing and historicizing implications of the turn to particularity in relation to their own claims.

The demise of neoorthodoxy in the 1970s and the concurrent multiplication of critical perspectives in theology during the 1970s and 1980s pushed the discipline, especially in the United States, into a period of intense introspection about the nature and tasks of theological reflection in an age when traditional sources for theological claims all seemed to be eroded.[28] The cumulative developments from the nineteenth century until the late twentieth century systematically undermined appeals to revelation, reason, and experience as grounds for sure and certain truth. Questions concerning what kinds of theology are possible in light of such erosion, the relation of those theologies to particular histories and to present-day political and social interests, what status such theological claims might have, and what norms might be invoked for evaluating them all became matters of intense debate. Seemingly endless discussions concerning theological method preoccupied the work of increasing numbers of theologians.

These developments and debates were very significant for theology, especially in the United States. In the closing decades of the twentieth century, however, other shifts occurred across a broad spectrum of academic disciplines and more popular cultural locales that signaled new directions for many intellectual trajectories, including theology. "Postmodernism" is the general term that has come to designate this complex, multivariate, and sometimes conflicting set of perspectives.[29] Like historicism, many diverse intellectual and cultural trajectories are signified by the postmodern designation, and various thinkers articulate distinctive versions of what *postmodern* means to further their agendas. For the purposes of this volume, the question is how these various postmodernisms are related to historicism.

Approaches to Postmodernism

Many postmodern thinkers have focused their critical work on challenging that phase of modernity associated with the Enlightenment, its assumptions about universal reason, and its assertion of sure foundations for truth and the possibility of absolute and unchanging claims to truth. In these approaches, postmodern means post-Enlightenment. The relation of these forms of postmodernism to the second phase of modernity, historicist modernity, is not always clear. Often postmodern assaults on modernity assume all of modernity is characterized by the ideals and assumptions of the Enlightenment, and hence they exhibit a remarkable amnesia by ignoring the second, historicist phase that the modern period pursued.[30] In so doing these perspectives have both missed the resources a close examination of the nineteenth and early twentieth century would yield as well as sometimes recapitulated the problems to which historicism failed to respond adequately. At other times, historicism is acknowledged but is reduced to its nineteenth-century German mode and is dismissed as a form of lingering metaphysics or "theology," a term that, for many postmodern thinkers, indicates the persistence of those forms of supernaturalism, metaphysics, universal claims to truth, and strategies of special pleading that faltered in the crisis of historicism in the early twentieth century. Perspectives characterized by such forgetfulness or dismissal are not, however, the only ones on the current postmodern scene. In contrast to these positions a number of contemporary thinkers see postmodernism as either an outgrowth of the more radical implications of earlier historicisms or, alternatively, contemporary historicism is interpreted as one mode of a larger, more diffused postmodern shift.[31] This chapter will turn now to examine several theological trajectories that have, in recent decades, grappled with the implications of these current shifts while embodying different approaches to the challenges of our postmodern moment.

In theology, postmodernism has taken a number of forms and, in its varied forms, has expressed all of the above stated relations to historicism. In one mode, deconstructionism, it has focused its critical attention most intently on the Enlightenment and has engaged most positively those continental thinkers who distanced themselves from the forms of metaphysics that characterized much of Western thought, including both its rationalist modes and those forms focused more centrally on history. The historicism of the nineteenth century has often been dismissed as just another form of Western metaphysics, especially as it was expressed in the thought of philosophers of history such as Hegel. In this perspective of contemporary thought the historicist and pragmatist trajectories found in America in the early twentieth century are virtually absent from consideration. Hence, thinkers such as Mark C. Taylor have critiqued not only the Enlightenment but also the Hegelian metaphysical forms of historicism, articulating in their stead an "a/theology" that proclaims in a sweeping manner that God is dead, the human self has disappeared, the Book is closed, and history is at an end.[32] For Taylor and others that share his perspective, the long "logocentric" tradition of Western philosophical and theological thought that failed to acknowledge the contingency, arbitrariness, and particularity or irreducible otherness of finite existence is interpreted as exhausted, to be replaced by "writing," "markings," "mazing," and "erring."[33] In their repudiation of universalism, ahistorical reason, and certain forms of speculative metaphysics, positions such as Taylor's share a critical resonance with many types of historicism. However, this perspective exhibits an ahistorical bent of its own. It places enormous emphasis upon the agential, constructive side of human historicity with little acknowledgment or analysis of how the historicized subject is constituted by relations to others, by context and past history. Its overwhelming stress upon discontinuities, instability, and always-deferred meaning often appears to neglect the importance of tradition, context, and the dynamics of power at play in its own erring ways. Importantly, while deconstructionists have put away grand schemas, they have often failed to render transparent their own entanglements in history and context and thereby have obscured the social and political function of their own work. Hence, while resonating with many of the critical stances that emerged from historicism, deconstructionist perspectives most often fail to utilize historicist insights to interrogate their own positions or to trace the very real relations that constitute historical reality in all its concreteness.

David Tracy and Revisionist Theology

Other theological trajectories have not only repudiated the Enlightenment pretensions of objectivity and certitude but have simultaneously argued for the importance of history and context, building upon, rather than neglecting, the insights developed by historicists over the last century. Two such approaches are revisionist and postliberal theology. Revisionist theology is most often associated with the work of David Tracy. Tracy's work represents, in many ways, the struggle of liberal theologians to maintain a number of the concerns that have animated the liberal trajectory of the theology from Schleiermacher to the present while also confronting the implications of historicism and, now, the challenges of postmodernism. Tracy's early work is characterized by the recognition of the marginalization of theology in the public realm and the necessity to set forth an understanding of theology's nature and task in the present-day world. Tracy's attempt to carry out this task was first fully articulated in his work *Blessed Rage for Order* (1975), in which he critically examines five methodological models for contemporary theology, including what he terms orthodox, neoorthodox, liberal, and radical approaches to theology.[34] Over against these he argues for his own approach, designated as revisionist theology. In particular, Tracy urges that Christian theology requires, at its most basic levels, reflection upon common human experience.[35] Such interpretation of human experience, moreover, needs to stand up to the public criteria according to such categories of meaningfulness, internal coherence, or meaning and truth. Tracy set out, thus, to formulate a foundational theology that offers public forms of argumentation beyond the confines of particular traditions concerning human experience in general. At this stage in Tracy's work, he continued the modern liberal quest for public criteria and for a more comprehensive view of human experience across the boundaries of individual traditions.

In relation to both his concern for public criteria and his articulation of more universalistic-sounding notions of human experience, critics assailed Tracy as continuing outmoded forms of modernity, especially those associated with Enlightenment rationalism and with the theological liberalism initiated by Schleiermacher. Tracy has been, in particular, a central target of postliberals who have interpreted his early understanding of experience in more universal terms as unacceptable in light of the recognition of historical particularity and of the primacy of culture in shaping experience. For this reason theologian George Lindbeck has placed Tracy in the historical lineage of liberal theology, or what he terms experiential–expressivist theology, that stretches from Schleiermacher in the nineteenth century to revisionists in the contemporary era.[36] These liberal forms of theology, Lindbeck contends, are predicated on ahistorical, essentializing, and universalizing assumptions that are no longer tenable. Moreover, the concern for public criteria or norms for assessing claims to truth is also problematic in postliberal approaches, which, as we will see, argue that the recognition of historicity and the cultural location of all thought and experience preclude public or transtraditioned criteria and instead point to more confessional modes of theological reflection.

While Tracy's postliberal critics have focused on his early foundational concerns, Tracy's later work has, in fact, included many dimensions that have expanded his positions beyond these early interests and have incorporated more historicist sensibilities and clearer responses to the challenges of postmodernism. In particular, he has extended the hermeneutical discussions he began in *Blessed Rage for Order*, engaging the debates that arose first in the nineteenth century and have continued to animate many theological and philosophical discussions as more historicist-oriented thinkers have engaged the questions of how particular historical presents relate to their traditions. In *The Analogical Imagination* (1981) Tracy emphasized the interpretive character of human existence and, with it, the importance of history and the past.[37] He sought to articulate a model of creative interaction between past and present and to reflect upon the possibility for interpretation in contexts characterized not by homogeneity or commonality but, rather, pluralism. In particular, Tracy articulated a correlational view of theology in which, in any historical present, humans give expression to the particular issues and questions of their time and then correlate those dilemmas with the answers developed within their distinctive historical traditions, especially the answers that are found in what traditions, including religious traditions, have designated the classics of their traditions. Such classics (or, as Tracy calls them, "expressions of the human spirit") provide resources for the present in that they display an "instinct for the essential" and are characterized by both a permanence and excess of meaning.[38] Religious classics, for their part, seek to respond to the most fundamental concerns of humans for meaning and value and seek to disclose some truth about reality as a whole.[39] Creative engagement with these cultural and religious classics, however, does not result, for Tracy, in the rote repetition of older solutions but in new possibilities emerging from the encounter of current questions and past answers.

If Tracy's foundational theology has been questioned, so too has his view of theology as correlational been critiqued, especially by postmodernists and historicists. In particular, Tracy has been challenged as offering too benign an interpretation of history, too much of a hermeneutics of consent and retrieval. Critics of this approach have called for a more critical hermeneutics, a hermeneutics of suspicion that interrogates how classics are constituted, by whom and on whose behalf, as well as questions the usefulness of the past in light of contemporary commitments and values. Tracy, in response to these challenges, has come to offer a much more nuanced interpretation of the relation of past and present, stressing in more recent works the ambiguous character of all human history, including what have come to be seen as classics, be they texts or persons or religious traditions. Historical traditions offer great resources—"the good, the true, the beautiful, and the holy are present in our history."[40] But also present in all human heritages are evil, loss, ignorance, and simply the presence of competing goods that cannot be reconciled. Nothing, now, for Tracy, is innocent or wholly positive.

"There is," as Tracy has put it in his work *Plurality and Ambiguity* (1987), "no innocent interpretation, no innocent interpreter, no innocent text."[41]

Tracy, influenced by the challenges of postmodernism, has moved not only toward a version of historicism that has highlighted the ambiguity of history but his work has come to emphasize more forcefully the lack of stability in history, the sheer plurality and contentious multiplicity of human historical heritages. History is not singular, driven by a telos, moving in any predetermined direction. Instead, it is chaotic, driven by unpredictable dynamics of power without any guaranteed end. In opposition to narratives of Western history that emphasize continuity and development, Tracy's version of historicism now is a tale of contingencies, interruptions, and continual struggles for power and resources. In his words, "Western history is, through and through, an interruptive narrative with no single theme and no controlling plot."[42] For Tracy, this recognition of what he terms plurality and ambiguity does not entail the repudiation of history's significance for human existence. What it does do is complicate that relationship between individuals and communities and their heritages. Tracy still refers to classics but they are now multiple, ambiguous, and always the subject of ongoing struggle about what and who will claim this designation. To wit, now for Tracy, there is no final and uncontested consensus in any historical tradition about what or who are classics or what their function should be. Tracy's approach rules out any easy conformity of present to past, any naïve elevation of historical texts, persons, or periods as above the historical fray. Instead, multiple approaches are called for, including appreciation and appropriation, suspicion and criticism, and finally even resistance to the destructive and problematic dimensions of historical traditions, including, most especially, religious ones.

If Tracy has rendered history ambiguous he has also radically historicized the norms for deciding how to interpret and judge those ambiguous inheritances. In contrast to the postliberal trajectory in theology that will argue for norms internal to cultural or religious traditions, Tracy has not fully given up his early concern for public criteria. Instead, he has greatly historicized his understanding of these criteria and given them a decidedly pragmatic tone. While universal, timeless, or absolute claims can no longer be assumed to be possible for Tracy, humans, at any given time and place, can critically engage their ideas, their actions, and their commitments in terms of their relative adequacy.[43] We can claim "our theories and our conversations" for what they have always been: "limited, fragile, necessary exercises in reaching relatively adequate knowledge of language and history alike."[44] Such relative adequacy is always determined in light of historically derived criteria that are open to revision and, increasingly for Tracy, in light of the concrete repercussions of our interpretations for the real lives of real persons; historicist insights and the accompanying recognition of ambiguity have, for Tracy, thus resulted in a turn to what he sees as a Jamesian pragmatism focused on concrete gains and losses.[45] Finally, for Tracy, this historicizing and pragmatizing of criteria need not be interpreted as an insular or parochial activity of a self-enclosed tradition. Tracy continues to assume that historicity and particularity do not imply isolation or incommensurability, but instead they point to the necessity of historically informed conversations within and across cultures and traditions. Recognizing the historical Other as other does not rule out understanding but indicates the necessity of the hard work of historical communication.[46]

David Tracy's work is important because he takes prior historicist insights so seriously while critically reworking them in light of contemporary assertions concerning plurality, ambiguity, and the contested and contesting dynamics of historical existence. In this sense he has proposed one of the more compelling and attention-worthy forms of historicist theologies being developed on the current scene. Still, despite his historicist adjustments and clarifications of his positions in light of criticism from, especially, postliberals and in response to postmodern challenges, there are ways in which Tracy's work still is open to historicist challenge. He continues to utilize the language of classics, thus narrowing the range of historical material contemporary thinkers engage. Moreover, the language of classics, despite its complexification, suggests that historical traditions have stable essences even if these are contested. When coupled with a continuing prioritizing of the hermeneutical form of theology, the focus of theology is strongly turned toward the past, not the present and future, and interpretation of that past becomes the central task of theology rather than one moment in a more constructive enterprise. If deconstructionists devalue serious engagement with history, Tracy appears to keep our attention too fully focused on the past. Hence, Tracy both embodies a lively option for historicist theology today but also leaves lingering questions about the extent of his historicist commitments.

George Lindbeck and Postliberalism

Another central theological movement that has emerged out of continuing historicist concerns and especially in conversation with the contemporary postmodern developments is postliberalism. George Lindbeck has been the architect of this perspective in theology, and his work *The Nature of*

Doctrine (1984) is not only the originating document of the movement but remains its most influential expression.[47] In this volume Lindbeck, like Tracy, articulates a view of human existence, but his interpretation leads him in significantly different directions than those pursued by Tracy. According to Lindbeck, humans are thoroughly historical creatures who live, think, act, and experience within and out of particular historical locales with specific histories, languages, symbol systems, and so forth. There is no universal human experience but only historically and culturally specific forms of human life circumscribed by temporal and physical location. Over against those forms of modern thought, including that of both Schleiermacher and, according to Lindbeck, David Tracy, that assume some prereflective or decontextualized or universal experience as the foundation for their positions, Lindbeck has posited what he calls a cultural-linguistic view of human life in which language, culture, and tradition all precede experience, give it content, and determine its limits and possibilities. Building on assumptions of historicity, contemporary challenges to universalism, and the current recognition of the centrality of culture and language for human experience, Lindbeck has developed a cultural-linguistic model that "stresses the degree to which human experience is shaped, molded, and in a sense constituted by cultural and linguistic forms."[48] In this view, experience does not precede culture and language that then express that experience but, in fact, culture and language are the *sine qua non* without which human experience could not take place or be known at all.

Lindbeck has developed his cultural-linguistic approach in several distinctive ways. He has utilized the assumptions of the importance of history, language, and culture to set forth a view of religions as cultural linguistic formations within which human existence gains meaning and direction. Following the work of modern anthropologists such as Clifford Geertz, he has argued that religions are "comprehensive interpretive schemes, usually embodied in myths and narratives and heavily ritualized, which structure human experience and understanding of the self and world."[49] What makes an interpretive worldview religious is not that it emerges out of some prelinguistic or prereflective experience of a cosmic divine reality or some common human religious experience, but that it is an encompassing framework for "organizing all of life, including both behavior and beliefs."[50] As such, it "shapes the entirety of life and thought."[51] Religions and other cultural systems, rather than giving expression to nonculturally situated experience, in fact, for Lindbeck, constitute the forms experience can take in any given time and locale.

In *The Nature of Doctrine* Lindbeck went on to offer a very specific analysis of these comprehensive systems by interpreting them as akin to languages, characterized by specific vocabularies and regulated by distinctive grammatical rules. There are several important elements in this Lindbeckian association of cultural systems with language. First, for Lindbeck, such systems, especially comprehensive religious ones, provide the "medium in which one moves."[52] Therefore, it is imperative, according to Lindbeck, that humans become what he terms culturally or linguistically competent in such systems so that they might avail themselves of the resources that are necessary for experience and thought.[53] The task for historical creatures is, therefore, to interiorize and become ever more adept at utilizing the store of historical resources that have developed in their particular context. In order to live full historical lives humans must both continually expand their particular vocabularies and utilize such resources according to the dictates of a tradition's grammar (or, as Lindbeck called them, "the rules of the game").[54] The richer such competency, "the more subtle, varied, and differentiated can be our experience."[55]

Second, and of central importance to postliberalism, Lindbeck proceeded to offer a view of grammar as those rules or defining directives of a tradition located in its founding narratives. These provide the norms for the correct use of a worldview's language, symbols, stories, and values. When he applied these assumptions to Christianity as a religious system he concluded that the grammar of faith is to be found in what he termed "the self-identical story" found in the Bible.[56] In his words, "in the case of Christianity, the framework is supplied by the biblical narratives interrelated in certain specified ways (e.g., by Christ as the center)."[57] Significantly, for Lindbeck, the grammar of faith located in the Bible is not altogether self-evident. Rather, the Bible must be read christologically and through a trinitarian hermeneutic supplied by the early church in order to perceive the grammar in an appropriate way within Christianity.[58] Thus, Lindbeck's theory, when played out in relation to Christianity, combines a view of Christianity focused on the Bible, understood as the narratively portrayed story of God's relation to the world, and interpreted through a christological and trinitarian unifying hermeneutic.

Lindbeck's theory of religions as language systems with vocabularies and grammars has other components as well. On the one hand, he recognized the plurality of Christian forms, the multiplicity of vocabulary, and the various possible combinations language can have. As in any language, many things can be said, novel insights may gain expression, and even radical departures from previous ways of viewing and naming the world may emerge. On the other hand, however, utilizing his model of religions as languages shaped by grammars, Lindbeck has suggested that the grammar at the heart of these systems is a stable set of rules, an essential core that does not undergo trans-formation or alteration over time. Much changes throughout a tradition's (such as Christianity) history but, for Lindbeck, stability and continuity are at the center of the Christian historical lineage. Furthermore, the bibli-cal narrative, seen through the hermeneutical christological and trinitarian lens, is the normative center in relation to which all subsequent theological claims and religious beliefs and practices must be evaluated and judged. To be legitimately Christian, to use the Christian language in a grammatically correct manner, any new formulation or practice must adhere to the "same directives that were involved in their first formulation."[59] Conformity to a supposedly stable Christian essence is thus the goal both for theology and for Christian thought and practice on the ground.

Theology in Lindbeck's system does not entail, as it did for, especially, early Tracy, any broad concern with human existence. Lindbeck's basal assumptions of radical human historicity and, hence, particularity, rule out more general claims beyond the recognition of such historicity and its implications. Nor in Lindbeck's view is theology a public enterprise that seeks visions of reality acceptable and defensible across different cultural and religious traditions. Instead, theology becomes primarily a descriptive and confessional endeavor that seeks "to give a normative explication of the meaning a religion has for its adherents."[60] It is thus intratextual, an inter-nal practice of a community with clear boundaries and internal structures, setting itself off from other cultural or religious formations. Lindbeck thus has stated, "Intratextual theology redescribes reality within the scriptural framework rather than translating Scripture into extrascriptural categories. It is the text, so to speak, that absorbs the world, rather than the world the text."[61] When theology becomes primarily an intrasystematic affair, then its primary criterion consists in faithfulness or conformity to the originat-ing tenets of the tradition and its reference is almost exclusively to the particular community and its history. While persons within one tradition may join forces with those in another, it is on the basis of unsystematic and occasional conversations around specific shared concerns, not on any commonality of vision, history, or values.[62] Literally, human beings speak different languages.

Lindbeck has forged a powerful and far-reaching interpretation of human historicity and its implications for understanding religions and theology. He has stressed the traditioned character of human existence and the indispensability of historical inheritance for purposeful and meaningful existence. Like the earliest historicists, Lindbeck has rejected any notion of "humans in general," insisting that human existence is always historical existence, lived out within and made possible by the rich fabric of particular cultural and religious heritages; there is no human experience uninflected by place and time, language and culture, prior beliefs and practices. Consequently, Lindbeck sets himself in opposition to those lingering universalistic tendencies in the line of liberal theology stretching from Schleiermacher to the early Tracy. In their stead, Lindbeck and other postliberals have substituted a new version of confessional, intra-traditioned theology that is predicated upon a rejection of public argumentation or accountability and assumes the stability and normativity of an authoritative biblical core.

By critically interrogating the nonhistoricist dimensions of modern theology, postliberalism has articulated an important form of historicism in contemporary theological reflection and has emerged as a powerful voice, especially for those thinkers most interested in recovering the centrality of tradition, in particular the founding narratives of varied traditions.[63] Like Tracy's revisionist approach to theology, however, this version of a historicized theology has also been strenuously criticized.

While Lindbeck has been criticized from a number of perspectives, the concerns of this volume relate, as they did with Tracy, to his understanding of historicism. In relation to his version of human historical existence and the implication of such historicity for interpreting the theological task, several interrelated issues come to the fore. Lindbeck assumes, in a manner more reminiscent of early historicists than of current postmodern interpretations, that humans firmly reside within singular historical traditions, characterized by firm boundaries delineating insiders and outsiders, and structured by stable and unchanging cores that can be used to regulate the beliefs and practices of a tradition's adherents. Criticisms can be raised about all three of these components.

First, in our twenty-first century world it has become clearer and clearer that now it is, and perhaps it always was, the case that humans live within multiple historical trajectories, organizing and interpreting their lives out of plural sets of influences, not singular still points to which all other values, commitments, and convictions are subordinated. Contemporary life is far more of a balancing act in which present-day persons are continually weaving together multiple, conflicting, and fragmented sources and claims. We are not singularly traditioned but multitraditioned.

Second, Lindbeck and postliberals have emphasized not only the singularity of traditions but often the impermeability of their boundaries. Hence, often traditions, as languages foreign to each other, seem incommensurable, existing in splendid isolation from each other. Thus, postliberals can imagine and encourage ecumenical discussions within traditions but have little to propose for how persons residing in different traditions might engage one another. This concern for uniqueness and difference clearly emerges out of Lindbeck's desire to avoid any false universalism or easy assertion of commonality; in an important way in Lindbeck the Other gets to be really Other. However, the postliberal sense of distinctive traditions fails to account for the porousness of boundaries and the syncretistic nature of cultures and religious traditions. Cultures and religious traditions emerge out of multiple strands of influence, and their boundaries continue to be both contested and negotiated throughout their historical development. In the words of anthropologist James Clifford, "this ambiguous, multivocal world makes it increasingly hard to conceive of human diversity as inscribed in bounded, independent cultures. Difference is an effect of inventive syncretism."[64] In this view of historical persons and cultures as multivocal and syncretistic, the postliberal claims of singularity and intratextuality seem like assertions made for the purposes of control. Purity, isolation, and clearly drawn boundaries are the province of ideological gatekeepers and mapmakers; they are not the characteristics of living historical traditions.

More historicist concerns arise when we turn to Lindbeck's interpretation of theology. Here a very nondynamic and even antihistoricist set of assumptions emerges. Lindbeck asserts that at the core of traditions lie unchanging and stable cores and that subsequent religious beliefs and practices and theological reflections should conform to these and be disciplined by them. Such appeal to a stable essence seems in tension with the dynamism of many of Lindbeck's other claims and finally appears to be made more in the service of bolstering a renewed authoritarian form of theology than in following the implications of his most historicist insights. Historically oriented scholarship, be it emergent from anthropology, archaeology, or such textually focused fields as biblical studies, reveals contentious multiplicity in traditions' origins rather than singularity or stability. Moreover, origins, be they narratives, persons, doctrines, or texts, are part of traditions, not moments somehow outside of the flow of history; they are moments within, not above, history. Origins are, thus, just like the rest of living history, plural not singular, fragmented not unified, emergent out of, not divorced from, their own histories and contexts.

Furthermore, while participants within traditions continually articulate norms for belief and practice, there are few indications that those norms consist of unchanging rules upon which all agree. It is not the case, to invoke Lindbeck's analogy of language, that vocabularies change while grammar is given in the beginning *de novo* and remains unchanged throughout history. Grammars emerge over time and, like the other components of language, can be challenged and altered. And when we examine dynamic, living traditions in all the breadth of their beliefs and practices, all such pretense of stability, continuity, and uniformity are challenged. Kathryn Tanner, reworking the Wittgensteinian views—so often invoked by postliberals— concerning the importance of language and of experience as always located within webs of language, and elaborating discussions in current cultural theory of the fragmented and unstable character of norms and criteria, states that, contra the claims of postliberals, "nothing fixes these communal norms in place. They are susceptible to change in the historical course of decisions by the human actors involved. Appeal to communal norms will not guarantee, then, as postliberals want it to, stability underneath the changing forms of history."[65] In this more historicist rendered view, there is no self-same Christian story given in the beginning and unchanging over time. Instead, Christianity is an internally pluralist tradition, emergent out of multiple sources, intermingled with other cultural and religious trajectories and exhibiting both continuities and changes. There is, in fact, not one Christianity with an invariant core, but many Christianities competing for the loyalties of contemporary persons and altering themselves in the face of present-day exigencies.

Each of the theological perspectives we have been examining in this section incorporates central historicist insights. Liberation theologies, deconstructivist approaches, revisionist theology, and postliberalism all assume the historical character of human existence and seek to develop positions that take such historicity seriously. As such, they continue, sometimes explicitly and sometimes with little self-consciousness, the historicist debates begun over a century ago. Such positions have not been, however, simply reiterations of either nineteenth-century historicisms or of the more pragmatically inclined American historicisms of the early twentieth century. They all exhibit, though in quite diverse ways, an acute recognition of the challenges of postmodernism and, to some degree or other, represent postmodern adjustments and even challenges to certain dimensions of earlier historicism. Thus, they give expression to what might be termed a postmodern historicism. As such, they each offer the current theological scene lively possibilities for interpreting the nature and task of theology. Still, as our critical analysis has disclosed, each of these perspectives continues to combine historicist insights with decidedly nonhistoricist or at times even antihistoricist elements. They, like many earlier versions of historicism, finally appear fainthearted, unable to carry through the implications of their own central convictions.

Toward a Pragmatic Historicism

There is another historicist form of theology emerging that attempts to articulate historicist insights while avoiding the nonhistoricist shortfalls of the positions we have just examined. That trajectory I have designated pragmatic historicism.[66] As a way of drawing this study to a conclusion, I will set forth the outlines of this trajectory as well as highlight the challenges it leaves unresolved. Pragmatic historicism will be seen to articulate again many of the insights of earlier historicisms; it has been shaped by not only the work of nineteenth-century historicists but, in the version developed here, especially the positions of the early Chicago School and the first American pragmatists. Yet this form of historicism also deviates from what has gone before. Its proponents intend both to extend and to challenge the historicisms of the past, creatively reworking its formulation and pushing historicism's implications in more radical directions.

As an opening caveat, it should be stated that I have associated pragmatic historicism with a variety of thinkers who have engaged historicism, including Gordon Kaufman, Sallie McFague, Cornel West, Rebecca Chopp, Delwin Brown, Linell Cady, Victor Anderson, and myself. Just as there are a diversity of revisionist theologies and postliberalisms, however, there is no one position termed pragmatic historicism and none of the above thinkers, with the exception of myself, will agree with all that follows.

Close to the heart of historicist theology is the profound recognition that to be human is to be thoroughly embedded within history. The question since the late eighteenth century has been, What does such historicity mean and what does it imply about our ideas, our experiences, and our practices, and especially about those human modes of existence we associate with religions? This book has traced the long and complex attempts to answer these questions, stretching from the late eighteenth century up to our present day. At this juncture I will reiterate some general comments about historicity, query once more what such historicity implies for our understanding of past and present, and explore the implication of historicity for the status of human claims, especially those we designate theological.

Historical Particularity and Contextualization

To be historical means that humans exist within the complex and interrelated matrices of natural and humanly constructed history. Humans always exist somewhere, in particular locales demarcated by distinctive languages, political and economic systems, geographies, myths and worldviews, rites and practices, forms of embodiment and social organization. Humans are human in specific and distinctive ways; there are no humans in general, only humans finely drawn in all their concreteness and particularity.

Several important assumptions are embedded in this claim of historical particularity. The first points to the centrality of context and to the intertwining of relations and influences within specific locales and times. One way to express this is to state that humans as historical are also preeminently social or, put otherwise, are contextually constituted. They exist not in isolation but within the midst of interconnecting influences that constitute them in specific ways and to which they, as historical agents, contribute in turn. Humans are conditioned and constituted by the webs of relations within which they reside; they also contribute to those both intentionally and through the unself-conscious effects of their actions. Linguistic resources, economic realities, political conditions, the social formation of such things as gender, race, and class, and the organization of such things as labor, leisure, and reproduction all set the limitations and provide the creative resources in relation to which individuals and groups gain their identity, experience the world, and determine their practices. Understanding the particularity of any individual or community requires the subtle examination of these intricate contextual webs of influence and how these are deployed and operative.

Two significant dimensions of contextualization have come to the fore in much contemporary theory, including in the thought of pragmatic historicists. To begin with, the importance of power, first articulated by persons such as Marx, has become an ongoing theme in the analysis of any historical contexts. Power, as not only a coercive deployment of mechanisms of control but also power in terms of the ongoing creativity of humans in the midst of contextual constraints, has gained the attention of a wide spectrum of theorists ranging from Marxists to liberationists and postcolonialists to feminists and cultural theorists influenced by thinkers such as Michel

Foucault and Raymond Williams.[67] Refinement of understandings of power, its distribution and circulation, has been the concern especially of those thinkers committed to the task of disclosing mechanisms of oppression and creating counteremancipatory discourses, practices, and institutions. Across a wide range of intellectual disciplines and numerous political and social orientations has come the assertion that the recognition of contextuality requires the interrogation of such contexts in relation to the unequal distribution of power as well as the uncovering of creative and transformative ideas and practices in the midst of oppressive situations. Importantly, such contemporary analyses of power have sought to hold together both notions of power as coercion and as the ongoing capacity of human beings to be historical agents, productive of new meanings and values. Vanished from these views are *both* the easy celebration of particularity that animated the first historicists as well as forms of historical determinism that overplayed the power of context and history at the expense of human agency and creativity.

Another related recognition is that while humans reside in particular temporal and spatial locales, these contexts do not, as some historicists seem to apply, exist in isolation from one another.[68] Many contemporary intellectual disciplines, from the physical sciences to the study of politics and economics, have asserted that humans live within an interconnected world in which what occurs in one place or in one time reverberates across time and space. What is important here is that the recognition of historicity, with all its emphasis upon particularity and uniqueness, does not imply isolation but, rather, interconnectedness. Indeed, it is the ever-widening web of natural and historical relations that produces the very particularity and uniqueness of experience to which historicity points. Historical particularity does not entail a lack of reciprocal interaction between historical entities but, rather, complex and varied relations in ever-greater scope. To trade on a current dynamic, historicism implies, on a number of levels, a kind of global system of economics, politics, cultural exchange, and environmental interdependence in which, on every level, particularity and interconnection go hand in hand.

A number of theologians associated with the perspective being outlined here, including especially Sallie McFague and Gordon Kaufman, have extended, in a manner distinctive from that of many earlier historicists, this historicist insight of complex interaction to include not only human-made historical reality but also a historicized natural world. Many historicists in the past and those historicist thinkers today who link historicism overwhelmingly or exclusively to language and culture have often neglected nature or interpreted it in nonhistoricist terms. In contrast, thinkers such as Kaufman and McFague, while certainly emphasizing the importance of language and culture to human existence, have argued that humans exist within historical webs of relationship and mutual influence that include not only other humans but also nature. Moreover, nature is no longer treated as without a history but as historical itself. Hence, Kaufman refers to humans as biosocial creatures, products of a vast evolutionary process who depend upon and, in turn, influence the cosmic ecosystem of which all particular realities are a part and upon which every individual entity, human and nonhuman alike, depends for its survival and development.[69] And McFague asserts that all living and nonliving entities are the product of the same evolutionary history; "we are," she poetically states, "cousins to the stars, to the rocks and oceans and to all living creatures."[70] Thus, importantly, in this version of contemporary historicism, history and nature are not viewed as antithetical, and the bifurcation of history and nature that character-ized so much of both Enlightenment modernity and early historicism are now deemed as untenable. In the place of this long-standing bifurcation of history and nature, thinkers such as William Dean have called for, in a manner similar to Kaufman and McFague, an interpretation of our cosmic context as a participatory universe in which human history is naturalized and nature is understood as historical.[71]

Contemporary historicism, in this mode, thus turns our attention to local contexts, but such contexts are vastly complexified in this view. Con-text refers not only to particular or parochial locales with firm borders but the ever-expanding network of global relations out of which human historical particularity emerges. Such a network of relations includes not only the human-made dimensions of existence but also the natural and the cosmic setting of living and nonliving reality within which humans exist.[72] Pragmatic historicism, therefore, stresses particularity without isola-tion, individuality, and uniqueness of time and place without assumptions of disconnection. And, perhaps most importantly, it extends the network of relations within which humans reside to include nature as a central com-ponent of such context.

Understanding the Past and Tradition

If pragmatic historicism complicates our understanding of historical exis-tence when we view it synchronically or horizontally in any given present, it equally complexifies our understanding of the significance of the past.

It should be recalled, as detailed in chapter 2, that historicism emerged in significant part as a reaction against the Enlightenment dismissal of history and tradition. As we saw, many Enlightenment thinkers sought to "wipe the slate clean," to begin anew outside the constraints of particular traditions. Modern, enlightened persons were to ground their claims in a universal reason common to all humans and to organize their institutions and direct their actions according to the dictates of such rationally derived truth. In contrast, early historicists rejected these ahistorical interpretations of reason and human existence and instead proclaimed the particularity of localized forms of historical existence that emerged out of and reflected specific historical lineages. Hence, individual languages, cultural worldviews and practices, and historical experiences were no longer to be ignored or dismissed but were seen as the key for understanding any individual or group.

Almost all thinkers of historicist inclination have espoused this rehabilitation of tradition. However, how the past, how historical lineages are to be construed has been a matter of great debate in historicist circles, as this book has demonstrated. In the most general terms historicists agree that human beings live out of the heritages their histories have bequeathed to them; language, culture, interpretations of reality, practices, institutions, and so forth do not spring *de nova,* or from nothing, but emerge in particular times and places and change and are altered through complex histories of development. Any particular moment is always in some way the reworking, repetition, transformation, or creative departure from what has come before, and what has come before is also part of the ongoing flow of history.

As historical beings, humans live out of the resources of those that have lived before. No community or individual, therefore, stands alone. Many contemporary historicists, including those termed pragmatic historicists, have begun, however, to articulate a distinctive interpretation of human historical heritages with significant ramifications for how we view the relation of any present to the past. First, increasingly historicists have stressed that while historical traditions or lineages are specific, with unique characteristics, they are not thereby singular or unified. As the analysis of postliberalism suggested, the idea that historical traditions can be reduced to one story or some essence that remains unchanging over time, even as it is instantiated in different times and places, is severely challenged today. Historical traditions, be they national, cultural, or religious, are all internally plural, consisting in multiple elements interacting with one another. They are not composed of invariant cores, modified with extraneous but nonessential variations.

Every tradition is in reality many traditions, conglomerations of distinctive and even heterogeneous elements, sets of interpretations and practices that cannot be reduced to any persistent factor that determines a tradition's unique identity. Hence, this version of historicism, while maintaining the importance of the past, eschews any essentialist readings of human historical lineages. Historical traditions are internally pluralistic, encompassing multiple, even conflicting, factors, resisting reduction to singular meanings, They are truly many, not one; distinctive configurations, not variations on unchanging themes.

Accompanying this insight into the internally pluralistic character of traditions is the assertion that historical traditions have boundaries or characteristics that delineate them from other historical trajectories, but these borders are porous and ever changing. Just as contemporary historical sites are specific while being part of wider webs of influence, so too are all past configurations. Traditions, while particular, have always interacted with other traditions, responding to them as threats or resources, incorporating elements from one tradition into another, transforming themselves in the give and take of historical exchange. No cultural, national, or religious configuration of meaning and practice exists or has ever existed in some lofty self-enclosed purity or isolation from the wider historical and natural world in which it emerged and developed. Sri Lankan theologian Aloysius Pieris refers to this process of encounter and exchange among religious traditions as a symbiosis of religions in which a tradition "discovers and renames itself in its specificity in responses to other approaches."[73] This exchange and continual redefinition is how negotiation of identity takes place in a pluralistic world; it is the process by which both smaller and commonplace adjustments occur, but also, according to Pieris, it is the means through which profound alteration of character results from encounter, dialogue, struggle, and confrontation. Historical traditions, those lineages of past development, are hence distinctive but permeable; they have boundaries, but such boundaries are ever undergoing negotiation and change with time, place, and circumstance.

The kind of historicism articulated here thus stresses the internal plurality of traditions and the shifting and porous character of all borders demarcating one tradition from another. In particular, this perspective proposes a view of historical particularity without essentialism or isolationism. In contrast to current theological orientations, such as postliberalism, that argue that religious traditions have stable and invariant cores and distinguishing borders marking them off from other historical traditions, pragmatic historicism concurs with thinkers such as anthropologist James Clifford when he, referring to the dynamic, changing character of cultures, states, "There is no going back, no essence to redeem."[74]

The Polythetic Approach to Tradition

But if historical traditions lack essences and have shifting boundaries, how are we to distinguish one from another, how are we to identify those elements within any historical strand of existence that give that thread of human thought, practice, and organization its defining character? What makes, as the nineteenth century asked, a German different than a French person, or a Buddhist different from a Christian? Pragmatic historicism, as it is developed here, does not conclude that the rejection of notions of stable cores and fixed borders entails that all traditions are really alike or that individual traditions lack all distinguishing characteristics. Instead, this perspective suggests that the distinctive characteristics of human traditions of thought and practice are always historical and, as such, can only be known by tracing the particular, always internally diverse and plural, ways in which such traditions have taken shape over time and in different locales. Such a procedure would surely indicate specific, concrete elements that delineate, say, America in the twentieth century from India in the eighteenth. However, this approach would not presume that traditions are defined by distinguishing characteristics present in all their configurations; not only might America and India in different centuries be quite dissimilar from one another but so, too, might be Christian Rome in the fifth century and Christian Rome in the twenty-first century.[75] Moreover, while this perspective challenges notions of straightforward continuity *within* traditions, it does not rule out all similarity or overlap across traditions. Close analyses may well disclose that in significant ways members of one cultural or religious trajectory might more closely resemble or resonate with persons of other traditions than with some members of their own historical lineage. Hence, pragmatic historicism assumes that traditions exhibit both continuities and discontinuities within themselves but that these cannot be known abstractly or ahead of time, but can only be traced retrospectively. Moreover, this position assumes, because of the porous nature of all historical configurations and because of the interconnected web of historical reality, that traditions continually engage in transformative encounter and exchange and thus not only modify each other but also may exhibit crucial overlap.

The work of historian of religion Jonathan Z. Smith articulates a particularly helpful way to understand these dynamics of distinctiveness and similarity, continuity and discontinuity. In his important article entitled

"Fences and Neighbors: Some Contours of Early Judaism" Smith examines the character of early Judaism and the difficulty of establishing clear
distinguishing characteristics of its identity when internal diversity and
overlap with other traditions are so evident to the historical investigator.[76]
In order to develop a helpful theoretical approach to these matters, Smith
turns to the debates in biological sciences about how to classify biological
groups. He explores first the use of taxonomies referring to those theories
and practices that seek to identify "a single item of discrimination, the
sine qua non—that without which a taxon would not be itself but some
other."[77] Taxonomic approaches thus seek "shared common features" in
order to ascertain identity. When utilized in relation to cultural or religious
traditions, this approach focuses on the quest for unchanging and ever-
present essences. For our purposes, postliberalism exhibits in many ways
such a taxonomic approach when it assumes that the so-called grammar of
a tradition is invariant and provides the distinguishing characteristics of a
religious or cultural tradition.

Smith also explores what he calls evolutionary approaches to classification,
asserting that these approaches take time more seriously and do not focus so
steadfastly on common cores or unchanging features. Instead, the emphasis
is on origins and lineage—it is where a tradition came from, how it traces
its ancestry to its beginnings, that determines what is descriptively and nor-
matively within any tradition. Here again, postliberalism's concern for the
founding narratives, what Smith terms the historical primordium, of a tradition as the site of the originating grammar of traditions finds resonance.[78]

Both of these approaches—taxonomic and evolutionary—yield interesting information whether one is a biologist or a scholar of religion. But, for
Smith, neither is finally adequate to biological reality or to complex and
mutable human historical existence. Instead, Smith turns to a third mode of
classification that he terms a polythetic approach. This mode of classification does not decide *a priori* what factors are most important in determining
identity. These characteristics will only be disclosed through thick description and analysis. Hence, a polythetic approach is an *a posteriori* method
of analysis. But even more importantly, according to Smith, a polythetic
approach assumes a nonreducible plurality of features constitutes the complex identity of any group or class or tradition. Concrete groups are thus
characterized not by a few essential features exhibited by all of its members
but by a much larger body of properties "with each property to be possessed
by a 'large number' of individuals in the class, but no single property to be
possessed by every single member of the class."[79] Smith's polythetic manner

of classifying and identifying groups, classes, or traditions resonates well with what pragmatic historicists have been suggesting. It proposes that groups exhibit a plurality of distinguishing factors, all of which will be exhibited by differing members of a group at some time. However, none will be present everywhere nor will all be present in any given individual, subgroup, or temporal moment. Furthermore, the factors can be arranged in a wide variety of ways according to changing and differing priorities or needs. Not only is there a plurality of identifying elements in any historical tradition, but how they are arranged in relation to other elements, both within and outside the tradition, what factors are emphasized or marginalized, what values or norms or past experiences rise to prominence in any given moment while others fade or are forgotten—all shape and determine at any particular time and place the distinctive identity of a tradition.

Smith's polythetic approach demonstrates how someone can be Jewish or Christian or Buddhist and yet share little or, indeed—at the extremes of any historical configuration—nothing in common with others claiming that designation but might share a good deal with others in contiguous groups. In Smith's words, "If a class contained a large population, it would be possible to arrange them according to the properties they possess in common in such a way that each individual would most clearly resemble its nearest neighbor and least closely resemble its furthest."[80] And in some configurations the closest neighbor, for example, to a Jew might be a Christian rather than another Jew, or an African Christian might be closer to a practitioner of traditional African religions than to a North American Anglican. At the various ends of a spectrum, both synchronically and diachronically, there might be little overlap. Moreover, the organization of properties, the spectrum, also is always undergoing change in unpredictable ways. A polythetic mode of classification allows us thus to attend to a wide variety of continuities without making any one characteristic or set of elements the sole determining factor for inclusion in a group. Moreover, it allows for an analysis that recognizes discontinuities and differences within the group without assuming deviance or lack of identity—the distinguishing mark for one kind of Christian might be unimportant for another group of Christians. And finally, this mode of classification also gives us the means for understanding how traditions and individuals might share characteristics without being collapsed into one another.

The approach Jonathan Smith details is helpful in that it continually pushes us back to the thick matrices of lived history and away from abstractions and generalizations. It directs our attention to the widest range of historical realities in all their diversity and resists the exclusion of certain features through definition or appeal to nonhistorical authoritarian norms. Traditions are simply all they have ever been; they are the conglomeration of their diversities, contesting possibilities, continuities, and radical departures into new possibilities.

This approach does not rule out a particular group of Buddhists or Christians, at any given time and place, arguing that a particular value, practice, or belief is better than another. What it does rule out is the historical sleight of hand that authorizes such judgments by virtue of claiming that they represent or cohere with a supposedly uncontested essence of a tradition. Instead, it suggests that such judgments are always the decisions of particular historical persons and communities and that they need to be justified on other grounds than appeal to unchanging essences or recourse to supposedly pure origins.

Multitraditionedness

Contemporary historicism thus stresses plurality and diversity within traditions and a variety of relations between and across traditions. But another claim is emerging that complexifies these matters even more. Historicism, from its earliest formations, has maintained the concreteness and particularity of human experience, thought, and practice. It has done that most often by emphasizing human existence as located within particular contexts and constituted by specific historical lineages of thought and practice. Thus, the first German historicists sought to trace the contours of German national identity to, as we noted, blood, myth, and soil. So, too, did American historicists point, despite their antiessentialist stances, to a distinctive American experience and history. And theological historicists have often focused on specific religious traditions and communities as the primary sites of identity. Often, in these approaches, it has been assumed that there has been a defining or overarching context within which identity is gained, experience is shaped, and history is given. Increasingly, however, over against these more circumscribed notions of tradition and locatedness, there has emerged a growing sense of what might be termed multitraditionedness. There are a variety of ways to conceive of the multitraditioned character of life. First, we can point to the ways in which members of a tradition are influenced by events, ideas, and practices outside of the boundaries of their own tradition. As noted above, this is one of the ways traditions and individuals within traditions develop and change. Second, individuals sometimes migrate from one tradition to another. They have "seriatim" forms of identity. They change citizenship, convert to new religions, or claim differing political affiliations. They certainly carry with them their pasts, but still individual humans, indeed sometimes groups, undergo profound alteration of identity and loyalties. And, third, and perhaps most challenging to Western conceptions of historical particularity, many persons understand themselves as immersed within and defined by more than one religious or cultural tradition, racial or national identity, ideological or political set of commitments at once. They are Buddhist and Shinto, Catholic and practioners of the Mayan Cosmo-vision, carriers of multiple passports, biracial persons who refuse to check off one box, and inheritors of multiple cultures; they are internally many, and in the face of their reality, traditional historicism seems too narrow and inflexible.

Anthropologist Clifford Geertz, whose theories so many historicists have utilized to bolster their sense of human particularity within cultural frameworks, has recently pushed his own thought in new directions that acknowledge more clearly the plural forms human identities take in our globally diverse but interconnected world. He argues that we need new "ways of thinking that are responsive to particularities, to individualities, oddities, discontinuities, contrasts, and singularities, responsive to what Charles Taylor has called 'deep diversities,' a plurality of ways of belonging and being."[81] "There are," Geertz states, "nearly as many ways in which such identities, fleeting and enduring, sweeping and intimate, cosmopolitan or closed in, amiable or bloody minded, are put together as there are materials with which to put them together and reasons for doing so."[82] Geertz's sense of multiplicity, diversity, and even fragmentation is echoed across multiple contemporary intellectual disciplines. Not only are historical traditions and cultural frameworks internally diverse but so also are the identities of persons who reside within, across, and sometimes at the junctures of those formations; human identities are, according to James Clifford, "conjunctural," products of the constructive and creative intermingling of varied influences, historical and contemporary, from differing strands of interpretation.[83] H. Richard Niebuhr's sense of a stable self within a stable tradition oriented by loyalty to one center of value seems far from the reality of what Geertz calls "a world in pieces."[84] What such fragmentariness implies for identity, on a personal or communal level, for cultural or national or religious cohesiveness, is not clear. Questions abound in this world characterized by such profound multiplicity: What is a self if not a unity or, as Geertz queries, "What is a culture if not a consensus?"[85] The answers to these questions are themselves multiple and not yet clear. What is certain is that historicism, if it is to reflect and respond to our current world, requires an understanding of our historicity that can acknowledge and account for this situation rather than ignore it or impose upon it forms of coercive coherence and pseudo modes of unity.

Epistemological Implications

The version of historicism being set forth here thus continues to sound the themes of particularity, contextuality, and the traditioned character of human experience that were heard in much of nineteenth- and early twentieth-century historicism. But, in contrast to earlier forms of historicism, it refracts these themes through the lenses of plurality, diversity, fragmentariness, instability, and the dynamics of power. Moreover, it places human historicity in a wider natural context, now also historically rendered, in which human historicity is viewed as localized and situated but also as part of a complex web of global interactions and exchanges, negotiations and contestations. Thus, both on an anthropological level and on the level of more generalized reflection about the wider reality within which humans reside, historicist assumptions provide the central interpretive categories. The implications of this version of historicism are, as for its predecessors and contemporary alternatives, profound. Among the most significant ramifications of contemporary historicism are, as they have been since historicism's beginnings, its epistemological implications.

From its inception historicism has had epistemological reverberations on every level, from the sources of human knowledge to the status of human claims. From Hamman and Herder onward, historicists have argued for the historicity of all human existence and experience and hence for the localized, contextualized, and relative nature of all sources in relation to which every form of human knowledge is constituted. Accompanying this claim is the recognition that all of our linguistic and conceptual forms of thought, our assertions of knowledge and truth about such historical reality, are also situated and conditioned by their perspective. As at least some, if not all, of the earliest historicists noted, reason depends upon and is always expressed through the medium of language, and all languages are historical. Over against the universal tendencies of the Enlightenment, historicists have emphasized that knowledge is contingent, relative to its time and place, shaped by its history, infused by interests, and interpretive in character. Although early historicists often distinguished between the human and natural sciences, suggesting a different understanding of scientific claims to truth, increasingly historicists have emphasized the historical

character of scientific claims and, as we noted above, have offered a historicist rendering of the natural world, thus further blurring the distinction
between physical and human sciences, at least in epistemological terms. For
current-day historicists, humans have no unmediated access to the world or
any nonhistorical, nonperspectival way to compare an uninterpreted reality with humans' construal of it in order to determine which version has it
right. Historicism thus continues to imply the repudiation of timeless and
absolute truth.

Historicist Theology

This repudiation of nonhistoricized versions of human knowledge has
taken a variety of forms on the contemporary theological scene. As was
noted above, postliberals have grappled with the historicity of human
knowledge by asserting that truth is an "intrasystematic" concern, a matter
to be decided within contextualized systems of language and experience
rather than in terms of any supposedly universally agreed-upon canons
of truth. And revisionists such as David Tracy have come to emphasize
the changing nature of classics and the plurality and ambiguity of all of
our human sources in relation to which we interpret life. The historicism
being articulated here, however, intensifies these epistemological questions.
This version of historicism not only jettisons appeals to ahistorical reason
or to unconditioned experience as the basis for claims to knowledge and
truth. It equally problematizes those more recent appeals, such as those
made by postliberals that, while clothing their positions in historicist guise,
anchor their normative claims in appeals to nonhistorical cores, grammars,
essences, or norms. Rejecting the postliberal view that historical traditions
or systems, be they cultural, religious, or political, offer clear or stable sets
of internal criteria for evaluating claims to truth or adequacy, pragmatic
historicism has instead offered a more full-bodied historicist interpretation
of historical traditions characterized not by normative centers but by ongoing dynamics of contestation and negotiation.

When human traditions of thought and practice are more thoroughly
historicized—when appeals to ahistorical reason, experience, tradition, or
revelation are all ruled out—then questions of how adjudication among
competing interpretations of reality, normative proposals about beliefs and
practices, and propositions concerning social and institutional organization
take on a new character. The historicism being espoused here echoes the
Early Chicago School and the first American pragmatists as well as their contemporary reinterpreters by arguing that historicism, when fully articulated,

points in the direction of pragmatism and the pragmatic adjudication of claims to truth and adequacy. In particular, it suggests that human ideas and practices, forms of thought and ways of acting and being, emerge out of and are expressions of the human need to organize, give direction to, and endow human life with meaning and value. They are preeminently practical; human claims to knowledge and truth do not mirror some unchanging reality or reiterate in local idiom originating truths or primal experiences. Rather, they are the historically devised tools by which humans navigate life, interpret it, build on prior historical experiences and interpretations, and determine future directions for humans to pursue. Humans have no ultimate source of evidence for helping us determine what we should in any moment take as true or right or beautiful but only contingent, fallible, humanly devised criteria or, as philosopher Richard Rorty suggests, "temporary resting places" to guide our judgments.[86] Nor in this view do we have singular and uncontested sources for determining what it means to be Christian or American. There is no way outside of our humanly created languages, cultures, institutions, and practices. Because this is the case, pragmatic historicists ask not whose vision of reality conforms to some ahistorical realm of truth or some still point in history or some primordial but inaccessible experience. Instead, pragmatic historicists ask, What are the repercussions of thinking, acting, organizing life in one way or another? What kinds of life are made possible by living out of one vision of reality rather than another? Who benefits from one set of practices or way of organizing our social lives and institutions? What is historically inhibited and what is nurtured and supported? How does one set of beliefs or practices cohere with another, and what are the ramifications of such cohesion or dissonance? On the most basic levels, what persons, values, and possibilities get to survive and flourish, and who dies, what possibilities are lost, and which values disappear? These are the kinds of questions toward which pragmatic historicism points us.

Historicists of this school of thought concur with postliberals and revisionists that prior historical interpretations, texts, persons, doctrines, experiences, and practices all provide raw materials in relation to which contemporary persons construct their ways of thinking and being. Humans, as James noted in the early part of the twentieth century, build their present-day worlds out of the heirlooms of the past. Truth or knowledge in the present does not imply some total discontinuity with the past. Indeed, it is out of the creative engagement with what went before, in light of new circumstances that new and novel possibilities arise. But while the past is always an ingredient in the present, this past does not provide uncontested norms for thought or guidelines for action in any present. The past, exhibiting the same characteristics of contingency and fallibility (and with these plurality, diversity, and contestability) as does the present, cannot provide the present the normative sorts of direction that postliberals seek. Instead, the normative site for decisions in a historicist perspective is the present. Tracing our ideas, locating our experiences in the thick matrices of our histories, and examining the genealogies of our norms and criteria for judgment all help us know from where we have come. They do not, however, determine what is justified, transformative, aesthetically appealing, or ethically compelling in the present; historical lineage does not confer self-evident present-day legitimacy.[87] The past will contribute to those decisions, but it should not determine them.

This kind of historicism, thus, locates the site of normative judgments, be those about cultural, political, religious, or economic matters, firmly in the present. Moreover, it suggests that when the practical nature of human ideas, institutions, and practices are acknowledged and when the site of ongoing responsibility for those humanly devised decisions and activities is located in ever-changing presents, then the central norms and criteria for assessment and judgment are pragmatic ones concentrated on the concrete repercussions of beliefs and practices for human life and community. Historicism, in this approach, is thus firmly linked to a pragmatism in which questions of human and natural flourishing in a contingent world move to the fore, displacing concerns about coherence with the past, correspondence to timeless truth, or adequacy to some supposed depth of human subjectivity.

This approach accordingly suggests that all human claims and practices are historical and hence contingent and fallible, that the site of judgment or assessment about these human products is the present, and that the norms or criteria for engaging humans' ongoing efforts to negotiate life are primarily pragmatic in form. This perspective also insists that no sphere of human thought or practice escapes such historicity. Humans exist solely and only within the web of contingent relations; humans live in what British thinker Don Cupitt refers to as an "outsideless" world.[88] The historicity of human existence, ideas, and practices extends, as this volume has repeatedly argued, to those arenas humans have termed religions and to those human constructions that have been labeled theologies. As this chapter has detailed, many contemporary theologians, including liberationists, deconstructionists, postliberals, and revisionists, have attempted to rethink the categories of religion and their understanding of theology. In particular, there has been a decided move toward interpreting these as historical as well and as continuous with other human efforts to give life meaning and direction. Older notions of religions as *sui generis*, as different in kind from all other human spheres, have broadly given way within the study of religion and theology to interpretations of religions as cultural phenomena displaying similar characteristics to other historical formations. Scholars of religion have thus increasingly repudiated those strategies, including modern ones, that somehow have located religious beliefs, institutions, and practices outside of history.[89] It has been the contention of this chapter, however, that many of these efforts, especially on the part of theologians, have failed to carry out the implications of historicism fully but have continued to embody untenable assumptions about religions and have surreptitiously reintroduced ahistorical or even antihistorical assumptions into their perspectives. Pragmatic historicists have asked what a fuller historicism might imply both for how we understand religions and how we might interpret theological reflection.

The question of how to define what contemporary thinkers mean by religion is a contentious one and is far from resolution. It is possible to trace the developments that moved from interpreting religion as being grounded in nonhistorical elements, be those revelation or the depths of human subjectivity or arising from some superhuman or supernatural origins, to attempts to interpret the vast array of human beliefs and practices in terms of more mundane and natural explanations, such as the historical need to give meaning and direction to life. Moreover, there has been a decided move away from defining religions as all of one piece, embodying common essences whose differences are the result of secondary cultural factors. Instead, religions, as this chapter has demonstrated, are now interpreted, like all other human phenomena, as historical and hence truly diverse and nonreducible to singular essences or cores. Religions have been firmly relocated within history and within the broader matrices of human culture. But, beyond the move from religion in general to religions in particular and to the situating of these religious phenomena within cultures, there is little agreement.

A number of theological historicists, including, interestingly, both postliberal George Lindbeck and pragmatist Gordon Kaufman, have appropriated the work of historicist-minded anthropologists such as Clifford Geertz as they have set forth contemporary interpretations of religions. Both Lindbeck and Kaufman view religions as overarching or encompassing frameworks within which humans interpret existence, name reality, and delineate humanity's place within the wider cosmos.[90] Such overarching worldviews are thoroughly human, developed over time and in different places. What characterizes such systems as religion is that they are all-encompassing and comprehensive, not that they are nonhistorical, have extrahuman origins, or are populated with supernatural beings. These views clearly blur the distance between what once was termed the secular/sacred split or the distinction between religious and nonreligious interpretive systems. Religions and comprehensive worldviews become interchangeable, and the strategies that set religions off from the rest of social and cultural realities become less tenable.

Recent Developments

The move to worldviews or comprehensive orientations has been an important move in the study of religion and especially for theology. There have been developments, however, on the current scene that push in new directions and also, in significant ways, problematize these moves. One development that is having important repercussions has been the shift within numerous intellectual disciplines away from the ideational dimensions of cultures and traditions. Increasingly there has been a move to interpreting these human historical formations in more materialistic terms and in reference to the nonlinguistic dimensions of culture and tradition. Accompanying this shift from an exclusive focus on language, ideas, beliefs, and ideologies has been a growing interest in popular forms of culture and a decided shift away from elites and the cultural production of dominant segments of societies and traditions. For scholars interested in religions, this has meant a move away from the overwhelming preoccupation with texts and beliefs that has characterized much of the study of religions in the West and toward a fuller engagement with the negotiation of meaning and value carried out by ordinary people and the nonideational forms such negotiation takes in practice.[91]

But current cultural theory and historicist-informed reflection have not only pointed scholars to the thick and complicated matrices of history and culture. They have also, as we saw in the analysis of postliberalism above, problematized easy notions that cultures or traditions are unified or that individuals reside and gain their identities within singular historical traditions or social or cultural formations. This de-essentializing and de-unifying of traditions and cultures and this profound sense that individual identities are fabricated out of multiple sources and are often fragmented suggest that the idea of worldviews or religions as comprehensive systems of meaning and value may be inadequate in our historicist moment. At the very least it indicates that there is no Christianity or Buddhism or Islam in some singular mode but only Christianities, Buddhisms, and Islams in the plural. Such problematizing of the idea of religions, cultures, and historical traditions as unified wholes points to the ongoing need to exorcise the ahistorical elements that linger in our theories and categories and the necessity of seeing these notions as did James in the early twentieth century—as hypotheses in need of continual revision and as heuristic devices that help us interpret life but that require ongoing reformulation.

No broadly compelling redefinition has emerged for the category of religion or religions, though many notions, across multiple disciplines, are pointing to the splintered character of our historical worlds, to "existence among fragments," as James Clifford puts it.[92] The category of religion or religions remains thus a contested mechanism, a helpful but limited device for helping us identify and analyze complexes of meanings, beliefs, rituals, and practices by which humans negotiate their historical existence. The final question, then, remains for us, What do all these shifts suggest for how theologians should understand themselves and their work today?

When religious traditions, beliefs, and practices are all historicized and located within the thick matrices of culture and place and within complex historical lineages, theology takes on a new sense as well. One way to get at these shifts is to say what theology is *not*. Theology is no longer, for historicists, concerned with the identification or expression of timeless or absolute truth, be that ascertained through revelation or reason. Nor is theology the expression of some nonhistorical experience or the depths of human subjectivity. Instead, theology is one form of human historical and cultural discourse among other human intellectual endeavors.

Kathryn Tanner, a contemporary theologian deeply immersed in postmodern cultural theory, has suggested that theology is concerned with the "meaning dimensions" of historical and cultural practices.[93] In some ways theology has always been concerned with the meaning dimension of religious traditions and their practices. But the form of historicism articulated here suggests a particular interpretation of this theological task. It suggests, in particular, that theology is a second-order discourse whose attention is directed at the beliefs and practices of historical communities. As such, it might best be characterized as a form of cultural analysis and criticism that is distinguished from other cultural discourses by virtue of its concern with those human formations we are designating religions or similar cultural configurations that give meaning and direction to human existence.

Interpreting theology as cultural analysis and criticism moves theological reflection away from pretensions of timeless truth and away from the assumption that in theology humans traffic with some nonhistorical realm. Theologians, no more or less than all other human thinkers, deal with human history and finite nature. Theology as cultural analysis and criticism points us back to the concrete communities and traditions of belief and practice.

When we say theology is focused on the meaning dimension of such concrete historical communities and their practices and beliefs, several further caveats come to the fore. First, while clearly ideas, doctrines, systems of interpretation, and symbols all become the object of theological consideration, such elements of religious traditions are neither dehistoricized nor set apart from the wider cultural and historical contexts in which they took shape and continue to function. Disembodied abstraction gives way to viewing religious beliefs, symbols, and practices as cultural and historical artifacts that cannot be fully understood without reference to the contexts, with all of their dimensions, including power, that produced them and within which they function.

Such interpretation of human beliefs and practices as cultural products suggests as well that theologians must interpret them and criticize them in relation to more than systems of abstract ideas. The move, alluded to above, toward practice and toward nonelite forms of culture is enormously suggestive for theology in this mode. It pushes theologians not only to engage the traditions of elite theologies developed by powerful religious or intellectual leaders but also to consider the beliefs and practices of ordinary people. Rather than seeing the former as "real theology" and the later as insignificant or a shadow theology requiring little engagement, this view points theologians to the close consideration of theologies that operate on the ground, that are embodied in community practices and take form outside the confines of those who determine orthodoxy. When traditions are more than ideational systems of the elite and powerful and when they are internally diverse and contesting, then theologians are oriented toward the breadth of possibilities within traditions.

This perspective orients theologians back to lived beliefs and practices and to the full spectrum of diverse possibilities that inhabit religious traditions. But pragmatic historicism also suggests another move that is significant on the current scene. Pragmatic historicism has not only acknowledged the historicity of religious beliefs and practices and of the theological reflection upon them; it has also argued that such particularity and situatedness do not emerge out of or result in insularity and self-enclosed purity. Particularity is the corollary of interrelatedness, not its antithesis. There are boundaries between traditions, but they are porous and permeable, always being negotiated and undergoing shifts. When the contingency of our ideas and practices are linked to the potential for mutual influence, challenge, and creative reconstruction, then theologians are pointed not only to the individual traditions within which they might dwell or in relation to which they carry out their task but to an ever-broadening conversation across traditions and at their intersections. Such conversation suggests that not only is theology concerned with the past, identifying, analyzing, and criticizing the possibilities that have emerged within any tradition, but theology is also engaged both within and beyond particular traditions in creative construction of new possibilities for the future. Gordon Kaufman has given expression to this dimension of pragmatic historicism when he has asserted that truth is emergent, not given; truth, as the early pragmatists asserted, is to be made, not just discovered.[94] Both within and across traditions the question is not just what have humans been but what creative possibilities exist for meeting the needs of the present and moving humans toward more life-giving futures. When humans acknowledge the contingency and fallibility of all of our ideas, even our loftiest ones, then the visions of other traditions become not just threats or challenges but potential conversation partners. The goal that emerges is not to defeat the other or to prove that one tradition is superior to all others but to engage in open and ongoing interchange in which all are transformed and in which new possibilities emerge both within and beyond the confines of the historical traditions humans have inherited.

Such dialogue, whether within the competing strands of a tradition or across the boundaries of traditions or at their intersections, is not easy. It is predicated both upon the recognition of difference and the particularity of traditions and upon the refusal to interpret such distinctiveness as an excuse for parochialism and isolation. It recognizes that fruitful interchange demands hard work that assumes neither that all humans are somehow, under all our historically and culturally accrued particularities, the same nor that our differences rule out understanding, mutual influence, and criticism. What these differences of belief and practice require is humility, openness to criticism, creativity, and a commitment to the disciplined practice of challenge, exchange, and reconstruction.

The historicism endorsed here thus returns us to what Linell Cady has called the morass of lived religion in all its diversity and contentiousness.[95]

It proposes that the theological task is concerned with the engagement of complex traditions in all their messiness. Such critical engagement is not for the purpose of discerning some timeless truth. Nor is it to determine some pristine origin to which contemporary persons should conform. Nor is it, through the surreptitious introduction of nonhistorical norms, to determine who is orthodox and who is deviant or heretical. Its task is to engage the widest range of materials in order to make fallible, contingent, and revisable judgments about the viability of our resources for life lived in the present and for the construction of new and life-nourishing symbols, beliefs, and practices for the future. This form of historicism, like its earlier American modes, identifies itself, thus, with a pragmatism in which all human ideas and practices, including religious ones, are for the practical purposes of providing orientation in life, naming and symbolizing what we take to be of significance in existence, and determining those values and ideals to which we will, in any historical moment, commit our lives.

Pragmatic historicism, therefore, suggests that theologians must not only identify and trace the variety of options present in and across religious and secular traditions for endowing life with significance. This mode of historicism also has a normative intent and a constructive obligation. Pragmatic historicists must also engage in the critical analysis of our historical resources and in the ongoing work of revision of older beliefs and practices and the construction of new ones in light of present needs and a not-yet future.

The Democratization of Theology

When conformity to the past or ascertainment of unchanging truth are no longer norms for evaluation of theological reflection, then, according to this perspective, pragmatic norms emerge as the central consideration for critical and constructive theological reflection. What pragmatic historicism does not do is provide any settled content to these pragmatic norms. In general, pragmatism has invoked notions of human flourishing and, more recently, the flourishing of all existence, including nature. Thus, theologians such as Gordon Kaufman have asserted that we must critically evaluate all theological claims and religious beliefs and practices in light of what kind of human life they encourage or inhibit.[96] Pragmatists such as Cornel West, Rebecca Chopp, and myself, aligned with groups that have been oppressed, have insisted that such concern for human flourishing be especially attentive to these individuals and communities denied the resources and power for lives of meaning and value.[97] In Chopp's words, theology should be about the task of "negotiating practices to sanctify life," including especially the lives of those who suffer the most from human decisions.[98] Moreover, theologians sympathetic to this perspective have also turned their attention to nature, proposing a fuller form of historicism not reduced to language or culture. Broadening that sphere of validation, William Dean has argued that we must test our ideas not only against the "bar" of history but also against the bar of nature, and Sallie McFague has argued for the integrity of nature as an arena that not only is the context of human flourishing but also is valuable in its own right apart from its uses for humanity.[99] What is thus proposed here is a pragmatic approach to analysis and evaluation of ideas and practices, symbols and systems of interpretation, in which the specific content of such pragmatic norms would change according to the complex circumstances in which humans reside.

Pragmatic historicists do not, therefore, contend that the general norm of human or creaturely flourishing has the same content in all times and places. Indeed, the varieties of religious and nonreligious modes of being in the world are testimonies to the changing responses to the human need to understand and interpret life. To evaluate such efforts always means grounding our critical engagement in the specificities of the ever-widening contextual web that is history. However, while pragmatic historicism resists asserting some set of unchanging criteria for evaluating what constitutes human and natural flourishing in all settings, it is suggestive about what would go into such judgments; that is, pragmatic historicism suggests certain procedures that enhance the ongoing processes of evaluation of human ideas and practices. This procedural pragmatism acknowledges that human ideas and practices fulfill a wide array of diverse needs and purposes. While all are tools for navigating through life, they aid humans in quite different ways. Poetry, science, religion, legal argumentation, art, and sports all provide their distinctive ways of shaping and contributing to human ways of being, and hence they must be evaluated according to their distinctive purposes.

This approach also reflects the current debates about the nature and scope of what we call religions. During the last several hundred years, as this book has demonstrated, older notions of absolute truth, be they grounded in revelation or reason, have eroded. The modern turn to experience as providing a touchstone has been greatly complexified as experience's historicized character has become clearer. More recently the appeal to stable essences and pristine origins has been challenged. And now the seemingly more historicized paradigms of religions as encompassing interpretive systems of meaning and value have been shaken in terms of their assumption that what makes something a religion is its comprehensiveness; humans appear to gain identity, name reality, and pursue commitments that are not so neatly formulated within the confines of singular, be they historical, systems of belief and practice. Such contestation about what the category of religion refers to does not mean that theologians have no work to carry out. Just like other scholars of religion, theologians are engaged in these debates and contributing to the revision and refinement of these central ideas in light of that new information. The lack of consensus in these matters points both to the difficulty of our task and to the changing character of our undertaking.

In particular, the difficulties that confront theologians as they engage in both evaluative analysis and in more constructive efforts point, for pragmatic historicists, to the importance of the theological process. When we have no recourse to some transcendent truth or the depths of human subjectivity or founding narratives that are uninflected by their time and place, then we are confronted with the responsibility for making judgments in the present and justifying them in terms of our fallible human values and insights. And when we acknowledge and embrace such responsibility, pragmatic historicists suggest that certain dialogical commitments follow. In particular, pragmatic historicists have argued for the democratizing of theology.

The democratization of theology implies several elements. First, the mode of historicized theology embraced in this volume points to the importance of both popular religion and of nontextual expressions of belief and practice. Theologians need to engage communities on the ground as well as to explore the heritage of elite thought, and they need to recognize that beliefs are not the only site through which humans construct meaning and embody commitments. Theology in the mode of pragmatic historicism identifies thus with efforts to engage material culture and popular religions. Second, pragmatic historicism insists on the significance of those at the margins of traditions and at the intersections of cultural and religious formations. When historicist insights are taken seriously, orthodoxy does not imply some hold on the truth but often the dynamics of power and control. In a more democratized theological conversation, the full and equal participation of those persons and perspectives that have been denied voices in the theological arena and especially those who stand to be harmed most by their exclusion demand a prioritized hearing. Such a full and just exchange of views is only possible when issues of unjust distribution of power are first addressed. Democratic participation is severely limited by dynamics of oppression. In this sense, theology, as pragmatic historicism, is a form of liberation theology. Third, theology in this perspective takes seriously the insight that, as fallible and contingent, the resources of no one tradition can ever be fully adequate to the constantly changing needs of an interconnected world. Pragmatic historicists recognize that it is only as humans engage less in power struggles and more in the process of just and equal conversation that the prospects for all in the web of existence will be enhanced. Thus, theology in this mode resists insularity and narrow confessionalism and turns itself toward the hard task of interreligious and intercultural engagement. Theology is, for pragmatic historicists, always dialogical and comparative. Fourth, in the modern world often religions, especially Christianity, became identified with the private dimensions of life and, as Wayne Proudfoot has stated, sought protective strategies in the face of an encroaching and often hostile modernity.[100] Religion was confined to one sphere, science to another. In the view espoused here, in which all human discourses are historicized, including religious and scientific discourses, there is new reason to engage in conversation across disciplinary lines without fear or defensiveness. Theology in this perspective is open to the claims and insights of both the social and natural sciences and seeks to contribute to contemporary interdisciplinary debates.

This interpretation of theology as pragmatic historicism finally means that theology in this mode is a public form of theology. Often, as with postliberalism, the recognition of the historicity and the traditioned character of human claims has led to forms of confessionalism, to lively intrareligious dialogue and debate but a repudiation of more public engagement. Pragmatic historicists have reached quite different conclusions. When religious traditions are historical like all other cultural formations, when they are internally diverse, when their boundaries are porous and permeable, and when humans reside in multiple homes, then it is both possible to engage in more public conversations and it is important to make the case for our visions and values to those outside our immediate locales. Here *public* has two meanings. It points, to begin with, to the importance of testing our theological claims in terms of their significance to ever-broadening realms of existence. In an interconnected world the task is not only to ask what a belief or practice means for a local community but also for all those who are affected by such decisions and commitments. Thus, pragmatic historicism is public in the sense of being broad and inclusive in its concerns. But this mode of theology is public in another manner as well. It also claims that when the historicity of religious ideas and practices and the human character of all reflection upon religions are acknowledged then it is also imperative to make the case for theological claims in public contexts, especially in terms of the pragmatic ramifications of our beliefs and practices. Public here does not refer to some neutral sphere where everyone shares the same values, histories, or even languages. Instead, it refers to the ever-widening web of historical particularities, the vast web of local worlds, and recognizes that communication and debate within such spheres is a complicated and difficult process of ongoing explanation, translation, recognition of deep differences, and the creation of new forms of consensus. Public theology, for pragmatic historicists, does not assume shared values or commitments as the starting point of public conversations, but it does assert the possibility of understanding, clarity around differences, and the potential for new modes of solidarity emergent out of respectful and serious engagement.

When these procedures or practices that enhance theological conversation are activated, the evaluation and justification of theological claims in terms of their pragmatic repercussions can be undertaken. The questions asked of theological claims and the analysis of religious beliefs and practices theology engages in will not be the same in all circumstances. But what pragmatism does assert should be the case is that we do not ask what is life enhancing or what is life denying in some general or abstract way. Pragmatic historicism compels us to ask these questions concretely and particularly; it insists that the norm of human flourishing is about real humans, not some humans in general or in the abstract. It demands that we ask whose life is enhanced, who is denied the possibility of controlling their bodies and their choices, who retains power, or who is oppressed by one set of beliefs and practices instead of liberated by another. For pragmatism, justification of beliefs and practices is never just a matter of abstract coherence or resonance with past systems. It is preeminently a matter of real lives, real bodies, real cultures, and, in the long run, of the real viability or lack thereof of historical existence itself.

Conclusion

This volume has followed the long history of historicism and has explored the ramifications of the recognition of historicity for understanding religions and especially for interpreting the nature and status of theology. It has critically engaged contemporary versions of theological historicism and has advocated one particular mode—pragmatic historicism. It leads, as did earlier historicisms, to a view of religions without absolutes and of theology without certitude. It urges a resistance both to the desire to escape history and the lure of a confessionalism and parochialism that inscribe new forms of historicized absolutism within religious traditions.

Pragmatic historicism acknowledges human historicity and its implications for all of our human efforts to understand life and to endow existence with meaning and value. It extends the recognition of fallibility, contingency, and partiality to our most cherished beliefs and practices. It affirms that we live mediated lives, always encountering reality through the particularities of bodies, cultures, languages, geographies, and histories. To embrace such finitude and historicity does not lead to despair or to seeking safety in the narrow confines of a self-enclosed world. It leads instead to the possibility of a risk-taking, life-embracing existence among our fellow humans and all those who share our fragile world, grounded in who we have been and open to the possibility of new and more vital ways of being.

Notes

1. Modernity and the Emergence of Historicism

1. Jeffrey Stout, *The Flight from Authority: Religion, Morality, and the Quest for Autonomy* (Notre Dame, Ind.: University of Notre Dame Press, 1981), 41.

2. Stephen Toulmin, *Cosmopolis: The Hidden Agenda of Modernity* (New York: The Free Press, 1990), x.

3. Ibid., 16–17.

4. Stout, *Flight from Authority,* 13.

5. René Descartes, *The Philosophical Works of Descartes,* trans. Elizabeth S. Haldane and G. T. Ross, 2 vols. (Cambridge: Cambridge University Press, 1969), 1:149.

6. Quoted in Richard J. Bernstein, *Beyond Objectivism and Relativism: Science, Hermeneutics and Praxis* (Philadelphia: University of Pennsylvania Press, 1985), 16.

7. Ibid., 18.

8. Toulmin, *Cosmopolis,* 104.

9. Stout, *Flight from Authority,* 108.

10. See *Freedom and Religion in the Nineteenth Century,* The Making of Modern Freedom, ed. Richard Helmstadter (Stanford: Stanford University Press, 1997).

11. See Wayne Proudfoot, *Religious Experience* (Berkeley: University of California Press, 1985), 388; and Linell E. Cady, "Resisting the Postmodern Turn," in *Theology at the End of Modernity; Essays in Honor of Gordon D. Kaufman,* ed. Sheila Greeve Davaney (Philadelphia: Trinity Press International, 1991), 85.

12. See David Chidester, *Savage Systems: Colonialism and Comparative Religion in Southern Africa,* Studies in Religion and Culture (Charlottesville: University of Virginia Press, 1996).

13. See Cornel West, *Prophesy Deliverance! An Afro American Revolutionary Christianity* (Philadelphia: Westminster Press, 1982), for an explanation of both the emancipatory and less than liberating dimensions of modernity, especially chap. 2. See also the following for recent contributions to the debates concerning the problematic role Western thought has played in relation to non-Western religions and cultures: Talal Asad, *Genealogies of Religion: Discipline and Reasons of Power in Christianity and Islam* (Baltimore: Johns Hopkins University Press, 1993); Richard King, *Orientalism and Religion: Postcolonial Theory, India and "the Mystic East"* (New York: Routledge, 1999);

Charles H. Long, *Significations: Signs, Symbols, and Images in the Interpretation of Religion* (Philadelphia: Fortress Press, 1986).

14. See Immanuel Kant, *Critique of Practical Reason* (1788), trans. Lewis White Beck (Indianapolis: Bobbs-Merrill, 1956); and *Religion within the Limits of Reason Alone* (1793), ed. Theodore M. Greene and Hoyt H. Hudson (New York: Harper & Row, 1960).

15. J. Samuel Preus, *Explaining Religion: Criticism and Theory from Bodin to Freud* (New Haven: Yale University Press, 1987), x–xi.

16. Quoted in ibid., 3.

17. See ibid., 84–103. See also David Hume, *Dialogues Concerning Natural Religion* (1779), ed. Norman Kemp Smith (Indianapolis: Bobbs-Merrill, 1947); and *The Natural History of Religion* (1757), ed. H. E. Root (Stanford: Stanford University Press, 1957).

18. Quoted in Frank M. Turner, "Science and Religious Freedom," in Helmstadter, ed., *Freedom and Religion in the Nineteenth Century*, 59. While many scholars see secularism as the opposite of religious belief, increasingly contemporary scholars are reanalyzing the relation of Christianity and secularization and suggesting not their opposition but their profound entanglements. See Talal Asad, *Formations of the Secular: Christianity, Islam, Modernity*, Cultural Memory in the Present (Stanford: Stanford University Press, 2003), and S. N. Balagangadhara, *"The Heathen in His Blindness...": Asia, the West, and the Dynamic of Religion*, Studies in the History of Religions (Leiden: Brill, 1994).

19. Stout, *Flight from Authority*, 67.

20. Ibid.

21. See *The Spirituality of the German Awakening*, Classics of Western Spirituality, ed. and trans. David Crowner and Gerald Christianson (New York: Paulist Press, 2003); F. Ernest Stoeffler, *German Pietism During the Eighteenth Century*, Studies in the History of Religions (Leiden: Brill, 1973).

22. See Peter Hanns Reill, *The German Enlightenment and the Rise of Historicism* (Berkeley: University of California Press, 1975).

23. Ibid., 7–8.

24. Ibid., 8.

25. Ibid., 45.

26. Ibid., 82. See also Albert Schweitzer, *The Quest of the Historical Jesus* (1906, 1913), ed. John Bowden (London: SCM Press/Minneapolis: Fortress Press, 2000), for a history of scholarship related to the historical Jesus from Reimarus to the early twentieth century. Also for a selection of primary sources, see Gregory W. Dawes, ed. *The Historical Jesus Quest: Landmarks in the Search for the Jesus of History* (Louisville: Westminster John Knox Press, 2000).

27. An example of this can be seen in the work of Immanuel Kant, wherein Jesus is transformed into the model of the moral man; see especially *Religion within the Limits of Reason Alone*.

28. See Hermann Samuel Reimarus, *The Intention of Jesus and His Teaching*, trans. Charles H. Talbert (Philadelphia: Fortress, 1970).

29. Hans W. Frei, *The Eclipse of Biblical Narrative: A Study in Eighteenth and Nineteenth Century Hermeneutics* (New Haven: Yale University Press, 1980).

30. Ibid., 2.

31. Ibid.

32. Ibid., 3.

33. See especially Immanuel Kant, *The Critique of Pure Reason,* trans. Norman Kemp Smith (New York: St. Martin's Press, 1929).

34. Bruce Lincoln, *Theorizing Myth: Narrative, Ideology, and Scholarship* (Chicago: University of Chicago Press, 1999), 52.

35. For a readily available selection of Herder's work on history and historicism, including from *Yet Another Philosophy of History,* see Johann Gottfried Herder, *Against Pure Reason: Writings on Religion, Language, and History,* Fortress Texts in Modern Theology, trans., ed., and with an introduction by Marcia Bunge (Minneapolis: Fortress Press, 1993).

36. Ibid., 43.

37. Ibid., 40.

38. Georg G. Iggers, *The German Conception of History: The National Tradition of Historical Thought from Herder to the Present* (Middletown, Conn.: Wesleyan University Press, 1968), 30.

39. Herder, *Against Pure Reason,* 43.

40. Ibid., 38.

41. Ibid., 44.

42. Iggers, *German Conception of History,* 30.

43. Ibid., 35.

44. Herder, *Against Pure Reason,* 45.

45. Iggers, *German Conception of History,* 38, 41.

46. Ibid., 37.

47. Ibid., 41.

2. Nineteenth-Century German Historicism

1. James J. Sheehan, "Foreword," in *German Essays on History: Hegel, Ranke, Spengler, and Others,* The German Library, ed. Rolf Saltzer (New York: Continuum, 1991), ix.

2. Susan A. Crane, *Collecting and Historical Consciousness in Early Nineteenth-Century Germany* (Ithaca, N.Y.: Cornel University Press, 2000), esp. the introduction.

3. Hayden White, "On History and Historicism," Translator's Introduction to Carlo Antoni, *From History to Sociology: The Transition in German Historical Thinking* (Detroit: Wayne State University Press, 1959), xv–xxviii.

4. Van A. Harvey, *The Historian and the Believer: The Morality of Historical Knowledge and Christian Belief,* 2nd ed. (Chicago: University of Illinois Press, 1996), 4.

5. Georg G. Iggers, *The German Conception of History: The National Tradition of Historical Thought from Herder to the Present* (Middletown, Conn.: Wesleyan University Press, 1968), 3–4.

6. Ibid., 7.

7. Ibid., 4, 7.

8. Ibid., 8.

9. Carl Page, *Philosophical Historicism and the Betrayal of First Philosophy* (University Park: Pennsylvania State University Press, 1995), 25. See also Terrance N. Tice

and Thomas P. Slavens, *Research Guide to Philosophy,* Sources of Information in the Humanities (Chicago: American Library Association, 1983), 428–29.

10. Iggers, *German Conception of History,* 11.

11. Ibid., 10.

12. White, "On History and Historicism," xx–xxii.

13. Harvey, *Historian and the Believer,* 4.

14. Throughout his life, Humboldt emphasized the limits of reason and the significance of creativity and nature. See Wilhelm von Humboldt, *Humanist without Portfolio: An Anthology of the Writings of Wilhelm von Humboldt,* trans. with an introduction by Marianne Cowan (Detroit: Wayne State University Press, 1963), esp. 29–123. Also see Iggers, *German Conception of History,* 56–57.

15. Humboldt's emphasis upon creativity can be seen in what J. W. Burrow calls his "laissez-faire" version of an ideal social world that stresses moral and cultural experimentation. See J. W. Burrow, "Introduction," in Wilhelm von Humboldt, *The Limits of State Action,* ed. J. W. Burrow (Cambridge: Cambridge University Press, 1969), xxxvi. See also Iggers, *German Conception of History,* 57.

16. See especially Humboldt, *The Limits of State Action,* chap. 7. See also Iggers, *German Conception of History,* 59.

17. See Charles R. Bambach, *Heidegger, Dilthey, and the Crisis of Historicism* (Ithaca, N.Y.: Cornell University Press, 1995), 43n53, for the claim that Humboldt, like Ranke and Droysen, develops a view of history as meaningful predicated on the "precarious balance between ethical-spiritual forces and the world of human volition."

18. Iggers, *German Conception of History,* 58.

19. Iggers claims Humboldt is the first nineteenth-century thinker to offer a historicist theory of knowledge that sought to combine the irrational dimensions of history with "faith in an ultimate meaning in the flux of human events"; ibid., 59.

20. Leonard Krieger, *Ranke: The Meaning of History* (Chicago: University of Chicago Press, 1977), 4.

21. Ranke, in the introduction to his *History of the Latin and Teutonic Nations,* states "history has had assigned to it the office of judging the past and of instructing the present for the benefit of the future ages. To such high offices the present work does not presume; it seeks only to show what actually happened [*wie es eigentlich gewesen ist*]" in Leopold von Ranke, *The Secret of World History: Selected Writings on the Art and Science of History,* ed. and trans. Roger Wines (New York: Fordham University Press, 1981), 58. See also Krieger, 4–5.

22. Iggers, *German Conception of History,* 76.

23. Ibid., 63–64.

24. Quoted in Kreiger, 5.

25. Ranke, introduction to *History of the Reformation in Germany,* in *Secret of World History,* 72.

26. Kreiger, *Ranke,* 5. See also "History and Philosophy," in *Secret of World History,* 102.

27. Leopold von Ranke, in Saltzer, "On the Epochs of Modern History," ed., *German Essays on History,* 85. See also Iggers, *German Conception of History,* 65–66, on fissures at the University of Berlin about the nature of historical reality.

28. Ranke, in Saltzer, *German Essays on History,* 84.

29. Ibid., 84.

30. Iggers, *German Conception of History,* 72, 80.

31. Ibid., 82; for Ranke's reflections on the state and its "Spirit," see Ranke, *The Secret of World History,* parts IV–VI.

32. Krieger, *Ranke,* chap. 2.

33. Bambach, *Heidegger, Dilthey, and the Crisis of Historicism,* 58, 189, 269.

34. Iggers, *German Conception of History,* 69.

35. See Johann Gustav Droysen, *Outline of the Principles of History,* trans. E. Benjamin Andrews (New York: Howard Fertig, 1967).

36. Iggers, *German Conception of History,* 111. See esp. Droysen, "Nature and History," in *Outline of the Principles of History,* 90–105.

37. Iggers, *German Conception of History,* 105.

38. Friedrich Meinecke, *Historicism: The Rise of a New Historical Outlook,* trans. J. E. Anderson (London: Routledge and Kegan Paul, 1972).

39. Ibid., lvii. Here Meinecke ranks historicism with the Reformation as Germany's great achievement. Meinecke goes on to state that natural law, especially when reinforced by appeals to revelation, had been the "Polestar in the midst of all the storms of the world's history." It was this "absolute anchorage" that historicism undermined.

40. Quoted in Carl Henrich, "Introduction," in ibid., xvii.

41. Iggers, *German Conception of History,* 217.

42. Ibid., 205.

43. Ibid., 207–8. See Friedrich Meinecke, *Machiavellism: The Doctrine of Raison d'Elat and Its Place in Modern History* (New Haven: Yale University Press, 1957).

44. Friedrich Schleiermacher, *On Religion: Speeches to Its Cultured Despisers,* trans. John Oman (New York: Harper & Row, 1958).

45. Ibid., 16.

46. Ibid., 39.

47. B. A. Gerrish, "Friedrich Schleiermacher," in *Nineteenth Century Religious Thought in the West,* vol. 2, ed. Ninian Smart, John Clayton, Steven Katz, and Patrick Sherry (Cambridge: Cambridge University Press, 1985), 135.

48. Ibid., 136.

49. Friedrich Schleiermacher, *The Christian Faith,* ed. H. R. Mackintosh and J. S. Steward (Philadelphia: Fortress Press, 1976) 12–18, proposition 4.

50. Ibid., 16–17.

51. Ibid., 18.

52. Ibid., 26, proposition 6.

53. Schleiermacher, *On Religion,* 148.

54. Ibid., 149.

55. Ibid.

56. Ibid.

57. Ibid., 7, 51.

58. Ibid., 214, Also see Schleiermacher, *Christian Faith,* 30.

59. Ibid., 76.

60. Jack Forstman, *A Romantic Triangle: Schleiermacher and Early German Romanticism* (Missoula, Mont.: Scholars Press, 1977), 109–10.

61. Schleiermacher, *Christian Faith,* 88.

62. Ibid., 89–90. See also Forstman, *A Romantic Triangle,* 104, and Gerrish, "Friedrich Schleiermacher," 134.

63. Richard R. Niebuhr, "Schleiermacher, Friedrich Daniel Ernst," in *The Encyclopedia of Philosophy,* vol. 7 (New York: Macmillan and The Free Press, 1967), 318.

64. See Charles Taylor, *Hegel* (Cambridge: Cambridge University Press, 1977). See esp. chaps. 1–2.

65. See G. W. F. Hegel, *Phenomenology of Spirit,* trans. A. V. Miller (Oxford: Clarendon Press, 1977), and G. W. F. Hegel, *Lectures on the Philosophy of World History: Introduction,* trans. H. B. Nisbet (Cambridge: Cambridge University Press, 1975).

66. Taylor, *Hegel,* 87.

67. Hegel, *Lectures on the Philosophy of World History,* 64.

68. Ibid., 89.

69. Ibid., 63.

70. Ibid., 105.

71. Ibid., 104.

72. Ibid., 19.

73. Ibid., 74.

74. Ludwig Feuerbach, *The Essence of Christianity*, trans. George Eliot (New York: Harper & Row, 1957).

75. Ibid., see esp. the "Preface to the Second Edition."

76. Ibid., 1.

77. Ibid., esp. chap. 2.

78. See Ludwig Feuerbach, *Lectures on the Essence of Religion,* trans. Ralph Manheim (New York: Harper and Row, 1967). See also Van. A. Harvey, *Feuerbach and the Interpretation of Religion,* Cambridge Studies in Religion and Critical Thought (Cambridge: Cambridge University Press, 1995).

79. Feuerbach, *The Essence of Christianity,* 73.

80. Ibid., 26.

81. See esp. Karl Marx, "Economic and Philosophical Manuscripts," in Erich Fromm, *Marx's Concept of Man,* with translation from Marx's *Economic and Philosophical Manuscripts*, trans. T. B. Bottomore (New York: Frederick Ungar, 1983 [1961, 1966]), 129.

82. Fromm, *Marx's Concept of Man,* 26.

83. Karl Marx, "Contribution to the Critique of Hegel's Philosophy of Right," in Karl Marx and Friedrich Engels, *On Religion* (Chico, Calif.: Scholars Press, 1964), 42.

84. See Raymond Williams, *Marxism and Literature* (Oxford: Oxford University Press, 1977); and Cary Nelson and Lawrence Grossberg, eds., *Marxism and the Interpretation of Culture* (Chicago: University of Illinois Press, 1988).

85. Perhaps no contemporary discipline has engaged in more widespread self-criticism in relation to historicizing trends than has anthropology. For a selection concerning changing views of culture, see esp. James Clifford, *The Predicament of Culture: Twentieth-Century Ethnography, Literature, and Art* (Cambridge: Harvard University Press, 1988); and George E. Marcus and Michael M. J. Fischer, *Anthropology as Cultural Critique: An Experimental Moment in the Human Sciences* (Chicago: University of Chicago Press, 1986).

86. John Drury, ed., *Critics of the Bible 1724–1873,* Cambridge English Prose Texts (Cambridge: Cambridge University Press, 1989), 11.

87. R. E. Clements, "The Study of the Old Testament," in *Nineteenth Century Religious Thought in the West,* vol. 3, eds. Ninian Smart, John Clayton, Steven T. Katz, and Patrick Sherry (Cambridge: Cambridge University Press, 1985), 131.

88. See Gregory W. Dawes, ed., *The Historical Jesus Quest: Landmarks in the Search for the Jesus of History* (Louisville: Westminster John Knox Press, 1999), for a good selection of nineteenth-century examples of the so-called First Quest.

89. Albert Schweitzer, *The Quest of the Historical Jesus,* ed. John Bowden with foreword by Dennis Nineham (London: SCM Press/Minneapolis; Fortress Press, 2000), 68.

90. Dennis Nineham, "Foreword to Albert Schweitzer," in ibid., xii.

91. Wilhelm Dilthey, *Pattern and Meaning in History: Thoughts on History and Society,* ed. H. P. Richman (New York: Harper & Brothers, 1962), 107.

92. Bambach, *Heidegger, Dilthey, and the Crisis of Historicism,* 161.

93. Dilthey, quoted in ibid., 134.

94. Dilthey, *The Essence of Philosophy,* trans. Stephen A. Emery and William T. Emery (Chapel Hill: University of North Carolina Press, 1954), 63.

95. Ibid., 66.

96. Dilthey, *Pattern and Meaning,* 73.

97. White, "On History and Historicism," xv.

98. Dilthey, *Pattern and Meaning,* 77.

99. David Couzens Hoy, *The Critical Circle: Literature, History, and Philosophical Hermeneutics* (Berkeley: University of California Press, 1982), 11.

100. Claire Colebrook, *New Literary Histories: New Historicism and Contemporary Criticism* (New York: Manchester University Press, 1997), 22.

101. See Hans-Georg Gadamer, *Truth and Method,* 2nd rev. ed., trans. J. Weinsheimer and D. G. Marshall (New York: Crossroad, 1989); and *Philosophical Hermeneutics,* ed. and trans. David E. Linge (Berkeley: University of California Press, 1976).

102. Dilthey, *Essence of Philosophy,* 66.

103. Ibid., 66.

104. Iggers, *German Conception of History,* 134.

105. Bambach, *Heidegger, Dilthey, and the Crisis of Historicism,* 165.

106. Ibid., 148.

107. John Cobb, Jr., *Beyond Dialogue: Toward a Mutual Transformation of Christianity and Buddhism* (Philadelphia: Fortress Press, 1982), 13.

108. Mark Chapman, *Ernst Troeltsch and Liberal Theology: Religion and Cultural Synthesis in Wilhelmine Germany,* Christian Theology in Context (Oxford: Oxford University Press, 2001), 33.

109. Ibid., 30–52.

110. Ibid.

111. Ernst Troeltsch, "Historical and Dogmatic Method in Theology," in *Religion in History,* Fortress Texts in Modern Theology, trans. James Luther Adams and Walter F. Bense (Minneapolis: Fortress Press, 1991), 12.

112. Ibid.

113. Ibid., 11.

114. Ibid., 16.

115. Ibid., 13.

116. Ibid., 17.

117. Ibid.

118. Ibid.

119. Ibid., 13.

120. Ibid., 17.

121. Ibid.

122. See ibid., 22, for Troeltsch's description of dogmatic theology's appeal to non-historical authorities.

123. Ibid., 18.

124. Ibid.

125. Ibid., 19.

126. Ernst Troeltsch, *The Absoluteness of Christianity and the History of Religions,* trans. David Reid (Richmond, Va.: John Knox Press, 1971).

127. Ibid., 45.

128. Ibid., 46–47.

129. Ibid., 47.

130. Ibid., 46.

131. Ibid., 49.

132. Ibid., 64–66.

133. Ibid., 70.

134. Ibid., 78. Here Troeltsch is commenting on a position developed by David Friedrich Strauss and concurring with it.

135. Ibid., 113.

136. Chapman, *Ernst Troeltsch and Liberal Theology*, esp. chap. 6.

137. Troeltsch, *The Absoluteness of Christianity,* 96.

138. Ibid., 96–97.

139. Ernst Troeltsch, "The Place of Christianity among the World Religions," in *Christianity and Other Religions,* eds. John Hick and Brian Hebblethwaite (Philadelphia: Fortress Press, 1980), 11–51.

3. Historicism in America

1. William James, *Pragmatism* (New York: Dover Publications, 1995), 9.

2. Ibid., 8.

3. Ibid.

4. Ibid.

5. William James, *A Pluralistic Universe*, The Works of William James (Cambridge: Harvard University Press, 1977), 27.

6. Ibid., 28.

7. Ibid.

8. William James, *The Meaning of Truth* (Mineoloa, N.Y.: Dover Publications, 2002), 195; see pp. 69–72.

9. Ibid., 58.

10. James, *Pragmatism,* 24.

11. Ibid., 95.

12. Ibid., 98.

13. Ibid.

14. Ibid.

15. Ibid., 93.

16. Ibid., 26.

17. See in particular Richard J. Bernstein's essay, "What Is the Difference That Makes a Difference? Gadamer, Habermas, and Rorty," in *PSA 1982,* vol. 2: Proceedings of the 1982 Biennial Meeting of the Philosophy of Science Association, ed. P. D. Asquith and T. Nichles (East Lansing, Mich.: Philosophy of Science Association, 1983) for a contemporary application of a Jamesian view of the importance of consequences for adjudicating among competing theories.

18. James, *Pragmatism,* 18.

19. Ibid., 20.

20. Ibid., 21.

21. Ibid., 22.

22. Ibid., 23.

23. Ibid., 78.

24. Ibid., 77.

25. Ibid., 92.

26. Ibid., 86.

27. Ibid.

28. Ibid., 87, 92.

29. See esp. Richard Rorty, *Consequences of Pragmatism: Essays 1972–1980* (Minneapolis: University of Minnesota Press, 1982), and *Contingency, Irony, and Solidarity* (Cambridge: Cambridge University Press, 1989).

30. See James, *Pragmatism,* 1–16, for an explication of these two systems.

31. See Richard J. Bernstein, "Introduction," in James, *A Pluralistic Universe,* xix.

32. James, *Pluralistic Universe,* 117.

33. Ibid., 118.

34. James, *Meaning of Truth,* xii.

35. Ibid., xiii.

36. James, *Pluralistic Universe*, 112.

37. Ibid., 113.

38. Nancy Frankenberry, *Religion and Radical Empiricism,* SUNY Series in Religious Studies (Albany: State University of New York Press, 1987), 84.

39. Ibid., 88.

40. James, *Pluralistic Universe,* 114.

41. Bernstein, "Introduction," xxiii.

42. Ibid., xxvii.

43. William James, *The Will to Believe and Other Essays in Popular Philosophy* (New York: Dover Publications, 1956), x.

44. Ibid., xi–xii.

45. Ibid., xiii

46. James, *Pragmatism,* 105.

47. Ibid., 114.

48. Ibid.

49. James, *Pluralistic Universe,* 60.

50. Ibid., 139.

51. James, *Meaning of Truth*, 125.

52. See William James, *The Varieties of Religious Experience* (Cambridge: Harvard University Press, 1985).

53. Wayne Proudfoot, "Religion and Inquiry in William James," in *Pragmatism, Neo-Pragmatism, and Religion: Conversations with Richard Rorty*, eds. Charley D. Hardwick and Donald A. Crosby (New York: Peter Lang, 1997), 71.

54. See Grace H. Jantzen, *Power, Gender and Christian Mysticism*, Cambridge Studies in Ideology and Religion (Cambridge: Cambridge University Press, 1995).

55. Leigh Eric Schmidt, "The Making of Modern 'Mysticism,'" in *Journal of the American Academy of Religion* 71, no. 2 (June 2004): 294.

56. Several works offer helpful descriptions of the context of America in relation to Dewey's thought. See Cornel West, *The American Evasion of Philosophy: A Genealogy of Pragmatism*, Wisconsin Project on American Writers (Madison: University of Wisconsin Press, 1989), esp. chap. 3; Louis Menand, *The Metaphysical Club: A Story of Ideas in America* (New York: Farrar, Straus and Giroux, 2001); and Richard J. Bernstein, *The New Constellation: The Ethical-Political Horizons of Modernity/Postmodernity* (Cambridge: MIT Press, 1992), esp. 230–32. See also Ronald Takaki, *Strangers from a Distant Shore: A History of Asian Americans* (New York: Little, Brown, 1983), for the story of Asian American immigrants to the United States.

57. West, *American Evasion of Philosophy*, 80.

58. Bernstein, *New Constellation*, 230.

59. See John Dewey, *Reconstruction in Philosophy* (Boston: Beacon Press, 1957).

60. Ibid., xii.

61. Ibid., xii–xiii.

62. Ibid., xiii.

63. Ibid., xv.

64. Ibid., xxxii.

65. Ibid., esp. the introduction and chap. 1.

66. Ibid., v, xxxvi.

67. John Dewey, *The Quest for Certainty: A Study of the Relation of Knowledge and Action* (New York: Minton, Balch and Co., 1929), 45.

68. West, *American Evasion of Philosophy*, 70.

69. Dewey, *Reconstruction in Philosophy*, viii–ix; Dewey, *The Quest for Certainty*, 85; John Dewey, *Public and Its Problems* (New York: Henry Holt, 1927), 202.

70. Dewey, *Quest for Certainty*, 311–13.

71. Dewey, *Public and Its Problems*, 116.

72. Ibid., 126–27.

73. Ibid., 147.

74. Ibid., 148.

75. Ibid., 149

76. John Dewey, *A Common Faith*, The Terry Lectures Series (New Haven: Yale University Press, 1968).

77. Ibid., 7.

78. Ibid., 1.

79. Ibid., 65.

80. Ibid.

81. Ibid., 2.

82. Ibid., 26–27.

83. Ibid., esp. chap. 1.

84. Ibid., 33.

85. Ibid., 14.

86. Ibid., 14, 15.

87. Ibid., 71.

88. Ibid., 27–28.

89. Ibid., 49–50.

90. Ibid., 42.

91. Shailer Mathews, *The Atonement and the Social Process* (New York: Macmillan, 1930), 10.

92. Ibid.

93. Ibid., 12.

94. Ibid., 11.

95. Ibid.

96. Ibid.

97. Ibid.

98. Ibid., 16.

99. Shailer Mathews, *The Growth of the Idea of God* (New York: Macmillan, 1931).

100. Shailer Mathews, *Is God Emeritus?* (New York: Macmillan, 1940), esp. chap. 3.

101. Ibid., chap. 3, esp. sec. 5–6.

102. Gerald Birney Smith, *Social Idealism and the Changing Theology: A Study of the Ethical Aspects of Christian Doctrine* (New York: Macmillan, 1913), viii–ix, 167.

103. Ibid., esp. the preface.

104. Ibid., 167.

105. Ibid., 190.

106. Ibid., 170. See also Gerald Birney Smith, "Christianity and the Spirit of Democracy," in *The American Journal of Theology* 21, no. 3 (July 1917): 339–56.

107. Smith, *Social Idealism and the Changing Theology,* 170.

108. Ibid., 185.

109. Ibid., 186.

110. Ibid., 200.

111. Ibid., 187.

112. Smith, "Christianity and the Spirit of Democracy," 347.

113. Ibid., 348.

114. Gerald Birney Smith, "Task and Method of Systematic Theology," in *The American Journal of Theology* 14 (April 1910): 222.

115. Ibid., 225.

116. Ibid., 222.

117. Ibid.

118. Ibid., 226.

119. Ibid., 226ff.

120. Ibid., 226.

121. Ibid., 227.

122. Ibid., 229.

123. Ibid.

124. Ibid., 232.

125. Ibid., 232–33.

126. Smith, *Social Idealism and the Changing Theology*, 228.

127. Ibid., 228.

128. See Gerald Birney Smith, "The Modern Quest for God," in *Current Christian Thinking* (Chicago: University of Chicago Press, 1928), esp. chap. 9.

129. Smith, *Social Idealism and the Changing Theology*, 228.

130. See Gerald Birney Smith, *The Principles of Christian Living: A Handbook for Christian Ethics* (Chicago: University of Chicago Press, 1924), esp. chap. 17.

131. Shirley Jackson Case, "The Religious Meaning of the Past," in *Journal of Religion* 4 (1924): 576.

132. Ibid.

133. Ibid., 577.

134. Ibid., 578.

135. Ibid., 579.

136. Ibid.

137. Ibid., 582.

138. Ibid., 584.

139. Ibid., 585.

140. Ibid., 589.

141. Ibid., 586.

142. Ibid., 580.

143. Ibid., 586–87.

144. Ibid., 587.

145. Ibid., 590.

146. Ibid., 589–91.

147. See Shirley Jackson Case, *The Christian Philosophy of History* (Chicago: University of Chicago Press, 1943), esp. chap. 7.

148. Ibid.

149. Shirley Jackson Case, *Jesus—A New Biography* (Chicago: University of Chicago Press, 1927), vi.

150. Ibid., 58.

151. Ibid., 70.

152. Shirley Jackson Case, "The Religion of Jesus," excerpted in *The Chicago School of Theology—Pioneers in Religious Inquiry: The Early Chicago School, 1906–1959,* vol. 1, eds. W. Creighton Peden and Jerome A. Stone (Lewiston, N.Y.: Edwin Mellen, 1996), 249.

153. Ibid., 256.

154. Shirley Jackson Case, "Whither Historicism in Theology," excerpted in ibid., 280.

155. Mordecai M. Kaplan, *Judaism without Supernaturalism: The Only Alternative to Orthodoxy and Secularism* (New York: Reconstructionist Press, 1967), 21.

156. Ibid., 23.

157. Ibid., 23–24.

158. Ibid., 24.

159. Ibid.

160. Ibid.

161. Ibid.

162. See Mordecai M. Kaplan, *Judaism as a Civilization: Toward a Reconstruction of American-Jewish Life* (New York: The Jewish Publication Society of America and the Reconstructionist Press, 1981).

163. Kaplan, *Judaism without Supernaturalism*, 28.

164. Ibid., 29.

165. Ibid., 21.

166. Ibid., 10.

167. Ibid.

168. Ibid., 52.

169. Ibid.

170. Ibid., 16.

171. Ibid., 39–40.

172. See West, *The American Evasion of Philosophy,* esp. chap. 4; and Giles Gunn, *Thinking across the American Grain: Ideology, Intellect, and the New Pragmatism* (Chicago: University of Chicago Press, 1992), 2–3; and Giles Gunn, *Beyond Solidarity: Pragmatism and Difference in a Globalized World* (Chicago: University of Chicago Press, 2001).

173. W. E. B. Du Bois, *The Souls of Black Folk* (New York: The New American Library, 1969), 221–22.

174. W. E. B. Du Bois, *Dust of Dawn: An Essay Toward an Autobiography of a Race Concept* (New York: Schocken Books, 1971), 164.

175. Ibid.

176. Du Bois, *Souls of Black Folk,* esp. chap. 10.

177. W. E. B. Du Bois, "The Negro Church," in *Du Bois on Religion,* ed. Phil Zuckerman (Walnut Creek, Calif.: AltaMira Press, 2000), 46.

178. See esp. Du Bois, *Souls of Black Folk.*

179. Ibid., esp. chap. 10.

180. Du Bois, *Dusk of Dawn,* 171.

4. Toward a Contemporary Historicism

1. See Richard J. Bernstein, "The Pragmatic Century," in *The Pragmatic Century: Conversations with Richard J. Bernstein,* ed. Sheila Greeve Davaney and Warren Frisina (Albany: State University of New York Press, 2006).

2. H. Richard Niebuhr, *The Social Sources of Denominationalism* (New York: Holt, 1929).

3. F. P. Miller, H. Richard Niebuhr, and Wilhelm Pauck, *The Church against the World* (Chicago: Willett, Clark, and Co., 1935).

4. H. Richard Niebuhr, *The Kingdom of God in America* (New York: Harper & Brothers, 1937).

5. H. Richard Niebuhr, *The Responsible Self: An Essay in Christian Moral Philosophy* (New York: Harper & Row, 1963).

6. Ibid., 95–96.

7. H. Richard Niebuhr, *The Meaning of Revelation* (New York: Macmillan, 1941), 10.

8. See H. Richard Niebuhr, *Radical Monotheism and Western Culture* (New York: Harper & Row, 1960).

9. Ibid., 118.

10. Niebuhr, *Meaning of Revelation,* ix.

11. Ibid., x.

12. Ibid., esp. 29–30, 114.

13. Ibid., 25–28.

14. Ibid., 58–60, 71.

15. Ibid., 26.

16. Ibid., 122.

17. Ibid., 31–37, 122.

18. Ibid., 122.

19. Ibid., 32.

20. Ibid., 126.

21. See, e.g., Thomas J. J. Altizer, *The Gospel of Christian Atheism* (Philadelphia: Westminster Press, 1966); Thomas J. J. Altizer and William Hamilton, *Radical Theology and the Death of God* (Indianapolis: Bobbs-Merrill, 1966); and Richard L. Rubenstein, *After Auschwitz: Radical Theology and Contemporary Judaism* (Indianapolis: Bobbs-Merrill, 1966).

22. See, e.g., Gustavo Gutiérrez, *A Theology of Liberation: History, Politics, and Salvation* (Maryknoll, N.Y.: Orbis Books, 1973); James H. Cone, *God of the Oppressed* (New York: Seabury Press, 1975); Mary Daly, *Beyond God the Father: Toward a Philosophy of Women's Liberation* (Boston: Beacon Press, 1973); see also Rosemary R. Ruether, *Sexism and God-Talk: Toward a Feminist Theology* (Boston: Beacon Press, 1983).

23. Lonnie D. Kliever, *The Shattered Spectrum: A Survey of Contemporary Theology* (Louisville: John Knox Press, 1981).

24. For recent examples, see J. Michael Clark, *Defying the Darkness: Gay Theology in the Shadows* (Cleveland: Pilgrim Press, 1993); Gustavo Gutiérrez, *The Density of the Present: Selected Writings* (Maryknoll, N.Y.: Orbis Books, 1999); Emmanuel Katongolle, ed., *African Theology Today* (Scranton, Pa.: University of Scranton Press, 2002); Mercy Amba Oduyoye, *Introducing African Women's Theology,* Introductions in Feminist Theology (Cleveland: Pilgrim Press, 2001); Aloysius Pieris, *An Asian Theology of Liberation,* Faith Meets Faith (Maryknoll, N.Y.: Orbis Books, 1988); Kwok Pui-Lan, *Introducing Asian Feminist Theology,* Introductions in Feminist Theology (Sheffield: Sheffield Academic Press, 2000).

25. Peter Novick, *That Noble Dream: The "Objectivity Question" and the American Historical Profession* (Cambridge: Cambridge University Press, 1988), 471.

26. Simon S. Maimela, "Black Theology and the Quest for a God of Liberation," in *Theology at the End of Modernity: Essays in Honor of Gordon D. Kaufman,* ed. Sheila Greeve Davaney (Philadelphia: Trinity Press International, 1991), 152.

27. The attacks on feminist thought as engaging in a false universalizing were widespread and cross-disciplinary. For such criticisms in theology, see esp. Jacquelyn Grant, *White Women's Christ and Black Women's Jesus: Feminist Christology and Womanist Response* (Atlanta: Scholars Press, 1989).

28. Edward Farley, *Ecclesial Reflection: An Anatomy of Theological Method* (Philadelphia: Fortress Press, 1982); Gordon D. Kaufman, *An Essay in Theological Method* (Missoula, Mont.: Scholars Press, 1979); Sallie McFague, *Metaphorical Theology: Models of God in Religious Language* (Philadelphia: Fortress Press, 1982); David Tracy, *Blessed Rage for Order: The New Pluralism in Theology* (Minneapolis: Winston-Seabury Press, 1975).

29. See David Harvey, *The Condition of Postmodernity: An Enquiry into the Origins of Cultural Change* (Oxford: Blackwell, 1990); Fredric Jameson, *Postmodernism, or the Logic of Late Capitalism* (Durham, N.C.: Duke University Press, 1984); and Linda J. Nicholson, ed., *Feminism/Postmodernism,* Thinking Gender (New York: Routledge, 1990). For a discussion of postmodernism and theology, see Paul Lakeland, *Postmodernity: Christian Identity in a Fragmented Age,* Guides to Theological Inquiry (Minneapolis: Fortress Press, 1997).

30. See Robert Cummings Neville, *The Highroad around Modernism* (Albany: State University of New York Press, 1992), for an attempt to offer nuanced distinctions between the early modern period and the various historical trajectories that followed. Neville is particularly incensed at many postmodernists' ignorance of the American tradition of pragmatism.

31. The "New Historicism" that has emerged in literary studies demonstrates the fluid relationship between a diffused postmodernism and new forms of historicism. See H. Aram Veeser, ed., *The New Historicism* (New York: Routledge, 1989), and Claire Colebrook, *New Literary Histories: New Historicism and Contemporary Criticism* (Manchester: Manchester University Press, 1997).

32. Mark C. Taylor, *Erring: A Postmodern A/Theology* (Chicago: University of Chicago Press, 1984). By "Book," Taylor refers not only to *the* Book of the Western tradition but uses the term as a metaphor for a coherent system, a plot with a beginning and end.

33. Ibid., 99.

34. Tracy, *Blessed Rage for Order.*

35. Ibid., 34.

36. See esp. George A. Lindbeck, *The Nature of Doctrine: Religion and Theology in a Postliberal Age* (Philadelphia: Westminster Press, 1984), in which Tracy is identified with the experiential-expressionist model of theology.

37. David Tracy, *The Analogical Imagination: Christian Theology and the Culture of Pluralism* (New York: Crossroad, 1981).

38. Ibid., 108, 110, 102.

39. Ibid., chap. 4.

40. David Tracy, *Plurality and Ambiguity: Hermeneutics, Religion, Hope* (New York: Harper & Row, 1987), 71.

41. Ibid., 79.

42. Ibid., 68.

43. Ibid., 27, 81.

44. Ibid.

45. David Tracy, "Lindbeck and the New Program for Theology: A Reflection," *The Thomist* 49 (1985): 470.

46. David Tracy, *Dialogue with the Other: The Inter-Religious Dialogue,* Louvain Theological and Pastoral Monographs 1 (Grand Rapids: Eerdmans, 1990).

47. Lindbeck, *Nature of Doctrine.*

48. Ibid., 34.

49. Ibid., 49.

50. Ibid., 33.

51. Ibid.

52. Ibid., 35.

53. Ibid.

54. Ibid., 48.

55. Ibid., 37.

56. Ibid., 38.

57. Ibid., 80.

58. Lindbeck developed this view of the correct hermeneutical key for understanding the biblical narratives more fully in his essay "Scripture, Consensus, and Community," in *Biblical Interpretation in Crisis: The Ratzinger Conference on Bible and Church,* Encounter Series, ed. Richard John Neuhaus (Grand Rapids: Eerdmans, 1989).

59. Lindbeck, *Nature of Doctrine,* 81.

60. Ibid., 113.

61. Ibid., 118.

62. See William Werpekowski, "Ad Hoc Apologetics," *Journal of Religion* 66 (1986): 282–301, for a postliberal articulation of how participants of different traditions might interact.

63. See Carl E. Braaten and Robert W. Jenson, eds., *Reclaiming the Bible for the Church* (Grand Rapids: Eerdmans, 1995).

64. James Clifford, *The Predicament of Culture: Twentieth-Century Ethnography, Literature, and Art* (Cambridge: Harvard University Press, 1988), 23.

65. Kathryn Tanner, *Theories of Culture: A New Agenda for Theology,* Guides to Theological Inquiry (Minneapolis: Fortress Press, 1997), 41.

66. For a fuller articulation of theology in this mode, see Sheila Greeve Davaney, *Pragmatic Historicism: A Theology for the Twenty-First Century* (Albany: State University of New York Press, 2000).

67. Importantly, for contemporary historicists, power is interpreted not only as coercive but also as productive and hegemonies are increasingly seen as never complete but as always entailing counter-discourses and practices. See especially Michel Foucault, *Power/Knowledge: Selected Interviews and Other Writings, 1972–1977,* ed. Colin Gordon (London: Harvester Press, 1980); and Raymond Williams, *Marxism and Literature,* Marxist Introductions (Oxford: Oxford University Press, 1977).

68. It is not only theologians such as Lindbeck who seem to stress a self-referential, inward-looking interpretation of historicism but also historicist philosophers such as Richard Rorty who celebrate new forms of ethnocentrism. See Richard Rorty, *Objectivity, Relativism, and Truth,* Philosophical Papers, vol. 1 (Cambridge: Cambridge University Press, 1991), esp. pt. 3.

69. See esp. Gordon D. Kaufman, *In Face of Mystery: A Constructive Theology* (Cambridge: Harvard University Press, 1993). Despite this turn to nature Kaufman remains significantly focused on a linguistically oriented historicism.

70. Sallie McFague, "Cosmology and Christianity: Implications of the Common Creation Story for Theology," in Davaney, ed., *Theology at the End of Modernity,* 31.

71. See William Dean, "Humanistic Historicism and Naturalistic Historicism," in Davaney, ed., *Theology at the End of Modernity,* 41–59.

72. Across a number of disciplines there has been a flourishing of critical reflection on the significance of space and now what is being called place to emphasize the importance of specific locales. See David Harvey, *Spaces of Capital: Towards a Critical Geography* (New York: Routledge, 2001).

73. Aloysius Pieris, *Fire and Water: Basic Issues in Asian Buddhism and Christianity,* Faith Meets Faith (Maryknoll, N.Y.: Orbis Books, 1996), 161.

74. Clifford, *Predicament of Culture,* 4.

75. See George E. Rupp, *Christologies and Cultures: Toward a Typology of Religious Worldviews,* Religion and Reason 10 (Berlin: Mouton, 1974), for an example of how resonance *between* segments of traditions may well be greater than agreement *within* traditions.

76. Jonathan Z. Smith, "Fences and Neighbors: Some Contours of Early Judaism," in *Imagining Religion: From Babylon to Jonestown,* Chicago Studies in the History of Judaism (Chicago: University of Chicago Press, 1982).

77. Ibid., 2.

78. Ibid., 4.

79. Ibid.

80. Ibid.

81. Clifford Geertz, *Available Light: Anthropological Reflections on Philosophical Topics* (Princeton, N. J.: Princeton University Press, 2000), 224.

82. Ibid., 225.

83. Clifford, *Predicament of Culture,* 11.

84. Clifford Geertz, *Available Light,* chap. 11.

85. Ibid.

86. Richard Rorty, *Consequences of Pragmatism: Essays 1972–1980* (Minneapolis: University of Minnesota Press, 1982), xli.

87. See Maimela, "Black Theology and the Quest for a God of Liberation," 154, for a sustained attack on the use of the past, especially the Bible as a "final court of appeal."

88. See Don Cupitt, *Life, Life* (Santa Rosa, Calif.: Polebridge Press, 2003).

89. See e.g., J. Samuel Preus, *Explaining Religion: Criticism and Theory from Bodin to Freud* (Oxford: Oxford University Press, 1996); Wayne Proudfoot, *Religious Experience* (Berkeley: University of California Press, 1985); and Russell T. McCutcheon, *Manufacturing Religion: The Discourse on Sui Generis Religion and the Politics of Nostalgia* (Oxford: Oxford University Press, 1997).

90. Lindbeck, *Nature of Doctrine,* esp. chaps. 1, 2; and Gordon D. Kaufman, *The Theological Imagination*: *Constructing the Concept of God* (Philadelphia: Westminster Press, 1981).

91. See Lawrence E. Sullivan, "'Seeking an End to the Primary Text' or 'Putting an End to the Text as Primary'" in *Beyond the Classics? Essays in Religious Studies and Liberal Education,* ed. Frank E. Reynolds and Sheryl Burkhalter (Atlanta: Scholars Press, 1990), and Kathryn Tanner, "Theology and Popular Culture," in *Changing Conversations: Religious Reflection and Cultural Analysis,* ed. Dwight N. Hopkins and Sheila Greeve Davaney (New York: Routledge, 1996).

92. Clifford, *Predicament of Culture,* 14.

93. Tanner, *Theories of Culture,* 70.

94. Gordon D. Kaufman, *God—Mystery—Diversity: Christian Theology in a Pluralistic World* (Minneapolis: Fortress Press, 1996), esp. chap. 12.

95. Linell E. Cady, *Religion, Theology, and Public Life* (Albany: State University of New York Press, 1988).

96. See Kaufman, *Theological Imagination,* esp. chap. 7; and *God—Mystery—Diversity,* esp. pts. 1, 4.

97. See esp. Cornel West's version of prophetic pragmatism in *The American Evasion of Philosophy: A Genealogy of Pragmatism,* Wisconsin Project on American Writers (Madison: The University of Wisconsin Press, 1989), chap. 6; and Rebecca Chopp, "Feminism's Theological Pragmatics: A Social Naturalism of Women's Experience," *The Journal of Religion* 67 (April 1987): 239–56; and "Theology and the Poetics of Testimony," in *Converging on Culture: Theologians in Dialogue with Cultural Analysis and Criticism,* ed. Delwin Brown, Sheila Greeve Davaney, and Kathryn Tanner (Oxford: Oxford University Press, 2001); and Davaney, *Pragmatic Historicism*, esp. chap. 6.

98. Chopp, "Theology and the Poetics of Testimony," 68.

99. Dean, "Humanistic Historicism and Naturalistic Historicism"; and Sallie McFague, *The Body of God: An Ecological Theology* (Minneapolis: Fortress Press, 1994); "An Earthly Theological Agenda," *Christian Century* 108 (January 2–9, 1991): 12–15; and *Super, Natural Christians: How We Should Love Nature* (Minneapolis: Fortress Press, 1997).

100. Proudfoot, *Religious Experience,* 199.

Glossary

Absolute: Philosophical and theological notion of a transcendent unconditioned reality that is juxtaposed to all finite, changing realities.

Aesthetic historicism: A type of historicism identified by Hayden White and opposed to naturalistic and metaphysical historicisms. This type of historicism focused on the historian, not the past.

A/theology: An anti-theology articulated by postmodernist Mark C. Taylor.

Birmingham School: Twentieth-century school of social thought identified with revised forms of Marxism, at Birmingham University. Central figure, Raymond Williams.

British-style empiricism: Modern form of empiricism that claims all knowledge comes from experience, especially sense experience.

Correlation: A theological and philosophical method that correlates present day concerns with answers/positions from the past.

Deconstructionism: A trajectory within twentieth-century postmodernism.

Deism: A movement commencing in the eighteenth century that sought a religion based on reason and that argued for a God who did not intervene in historical or physical reality.

Empathy (*Einfühlung*): Sympathetic understanding by which an interpreter can enter into the world she or he interprets.

Evolutionary apologetic: A trajectory identified by Ernst Troeltsch that argued that religions represented different stages of human evolution.

Experiential-expressivist theology: A term used by postliberal theologian George Lindbeck to designate the liberal form of theology associated with Schleiermacher.

Frankfurt Institute: A school of philosophical and political thought established in Germany in 1923, moved to Geneva and then to New York. Associated with Marxist thought. Central figures included Max Horkheimer, Theodor Adorno, Herbert Marcuse, and Erich Fromm.

Geist: Spirit or God, a term used by Hegel.

Henotheism: Belief in and commitment to one center of value but one center among many competing values. Term associated with H. Richard Niebuhr.

Historical method: Theory and method for studying historical realities, associated with historicism and the modern discipline of history.

Historical primordium (Jonathan Z. Smith): Originating historical event.

Historical relativism: The claim that all human thought and experience are relative to and conditioned by their place and time.

Historical School: The German School of historians who shaped the emerging discipline of history in the nineteenth century. Central figures included Wilhelm von Humboldt, Leopold von Ranke, Johann Gustav Droysen, and Friedrich Meinecke.

Historicism: Modern movement in theology, philosophy, and literary theory focused on history and associated with the claim that human existence is thoroughly embedded in time and place.

Historicist modernity: The second phase of the modern period commencing in the late eighteenth century and flourishing in the nineteenth century.

Historiography: Theory and method related to historical studies.

History of Religions School: School of thought that developed in the nineteenth century in Germany. It focused on nontheological analysis of religions with a strong interest in the study of religions other than Christianity.

Idealism: Philosophical approach especially associated with modern philosophy stemming from the Enlightenment and emphasizing reason.

Intratextual theology: Theology that is oriented toward the beliefs and practices within a tradition. It is often associated with postliberalism.

Materialism: School of thought that asserts the priority of the material and material conditions in explaining reality.

Metaphysics of history: Philosophical interpretations of history and the relation of history to the rest of reality. Hegel was the most significant philosopher in the nineteenth century developing such a metaphysics of history in which historical processes played a central role in the development of reality.

The More: The term used by William James to designate a transcendent, divine reality that was not supernatural.

Multitraditionedness: Idea recognizing that human identity is shaped by plural traditions.

Multiverse: Term of William James that indicated the universe was composed of multiple realities.

Natural religion: Modern notion of religion as an innate characteristic of human existence and not tied to historical religions.

Neoorthodoxy: Theological perspective that developed in aftermath of the First World War, opposed to liberalism and most closely associated with Karl Barth.

Philosophy of life: Term used by Wilhelm Dilthey to refer to all human activity as the object of human inquiry.

Pietism: Religious movement, emerging in late seventeenth century, associated with Lutherans and some Calvinists, focused on religious feeling and practice rather than belief.

Polytheism: Belief in and devotion to multiple deities or sacred realities.

Polythetic approach: Theoretical method, associated with biological sciences, for classifying groups. This method of classification details the plurality of features that make up any group or class of objects.

Postliberalism: Theological movement emergent in late twentieth century, opposed to liberalism and oriented toward tradition. A movement closely associated with George Lindbeck.

Postmodernism: Philosophical and cultural movement emergent in late twentieth century in opposition to especially Enlightenment modernity. Proponents often reject foundationalisms of any kind, notions of sure knowledge, progress and human autonomy.

Pragmatic historicism: Theological and philosophical movement that stresses the historicity of all human claims, experience, and practice and that argues that human claims and practices should be evaluated pragmatically in terms of their consequences.

Pragmatism: Philosophical movement emerging first in the late nineteenth century in America and flourishing in the early twentieth century. The movement is associated most fully with Charles Sanders Pierce, William James, and John Dewey.

Prussian School of History: One strand of the German Historical School associated most clearly with Johann Gustav Droysen.

Quest of/for the historical Jesus: The search for accurate historical information about Jesus whose first phase is often dated from Reimarus to Albert Schweitzer.

Radical empiricism: Notion, most often associated with William James, that humans engage reality beyond their five senses and that relations between realities are as real as the realities themselves.

Radical monotheism: Theological notion associated with H. Richard Niebuhr that emphasized the reality of God beyond all finite realities that simultaneously called all existence into question and endowed it with meaning.

Rationalism: Philosophical perspective often associated with the Enlightenment that emphasized reason rather than sense experience as the source of human knowledge.

Revisionist theology: Theological trajectory in late twentieth century associated with David Tracy.

Romanticism: Movement of the nineteenth century associated in theology with Friedrich Schleiermacher.

Self-activity: The activity through which the human self develops.

Taxonomic approaches: Classification, especially in biology, of groups according to shared or common features.

Telos: Goal or end that is assumed to draw reality toward it.

Theism Belief in a transcendent God.

Transnaturalist: Term associated with Mordecai Kaplan that named a form of religious naturalism.

Verstehen: Understanding.

Weltanschauungen: Philosophies of life or worldviews.

Index